GEOMETRY 3/4

Walker Maths Essentials: Geometry 3/4
1st Edition
Charlotte Walker
Victoria Walker

Cover design: Cheryl Smith, Macarn Design
Text designer: Cheryl Smith, Macarn Design
Production controller: Siew Han Ong

Any URLs contained in this publication were checked for currency during the production process. Note, however, that the publisher cannot vouch for the ongoing currency of URLs.

Acknowledgements
Cover photo courtesy of Shutterstock.

We wish to thank the Boards of Trustees of Darfield and Riccarton High Schools for allowing us to use materials and ideas developed while teaching. Our thanks also go to all past and present colleagues, especially Kath Wilson, who have generously shared their experience and ideas.

For product information and technology assistance,
in Australia call **1300 790 853**;
in New Zealand call **0800 449 725**

For permission to use material from this text or product, please email **aust.permissions@cengage.com**

National Library of New Zealand Cataloguing-in-Publication Data
A catalogue record for this book is available from the National Library of New Zealand

978 0 17 045197 0

Cengage Learning Australia
Level 7, 80 Dorcas Street
South Melbourne, Victoria Australia 3205

Cengage Learning New Zealand
Unit 4B Rosedale Office Park
331 Rosedale Road, Albany, North Shore 0632, NZ

For learning solutions, visit **cengage.co.nz**

Printed in China by 1010 Printing International Limited.
1 2 3 4 5 6 7 26 25 24 23 22

CONTENTS

Glossary

Make your own glossary of key terms:

Term	Definition	Picture/Example
Degrees		
Equilateral triangle		
Isosceles triangle		
Scalene triangle		
Quadrilateral		
Acute angle		
Right angle		
Obtuse angle		
Straight angle		
Reflex angle		

ISBN: 9780170451970

Term	Definition	Picture/Example
Polygon		
Regular		
Irregular		
Symmetrical		
Two-dimensional (2D)		
Three-dimensional (3D)		
Translation		
Reflection		
Rotation		
Enlargement		

ISBN: 9780170451970

Shapes

Polygons

A polygon is a shape that:
- is two-dimensional, or 2D (flat)
- has three or more straight sides, and
- is closed (has no gaps).

Examples:

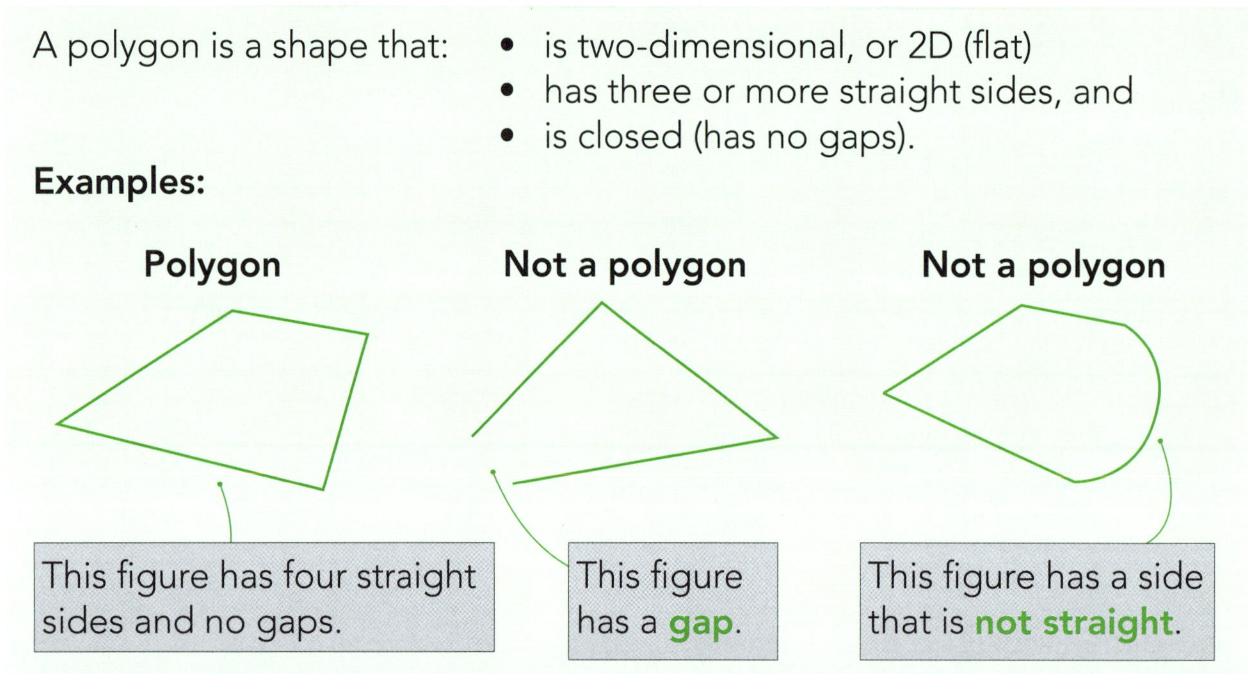

Circle the correct statement for each of these shapes.

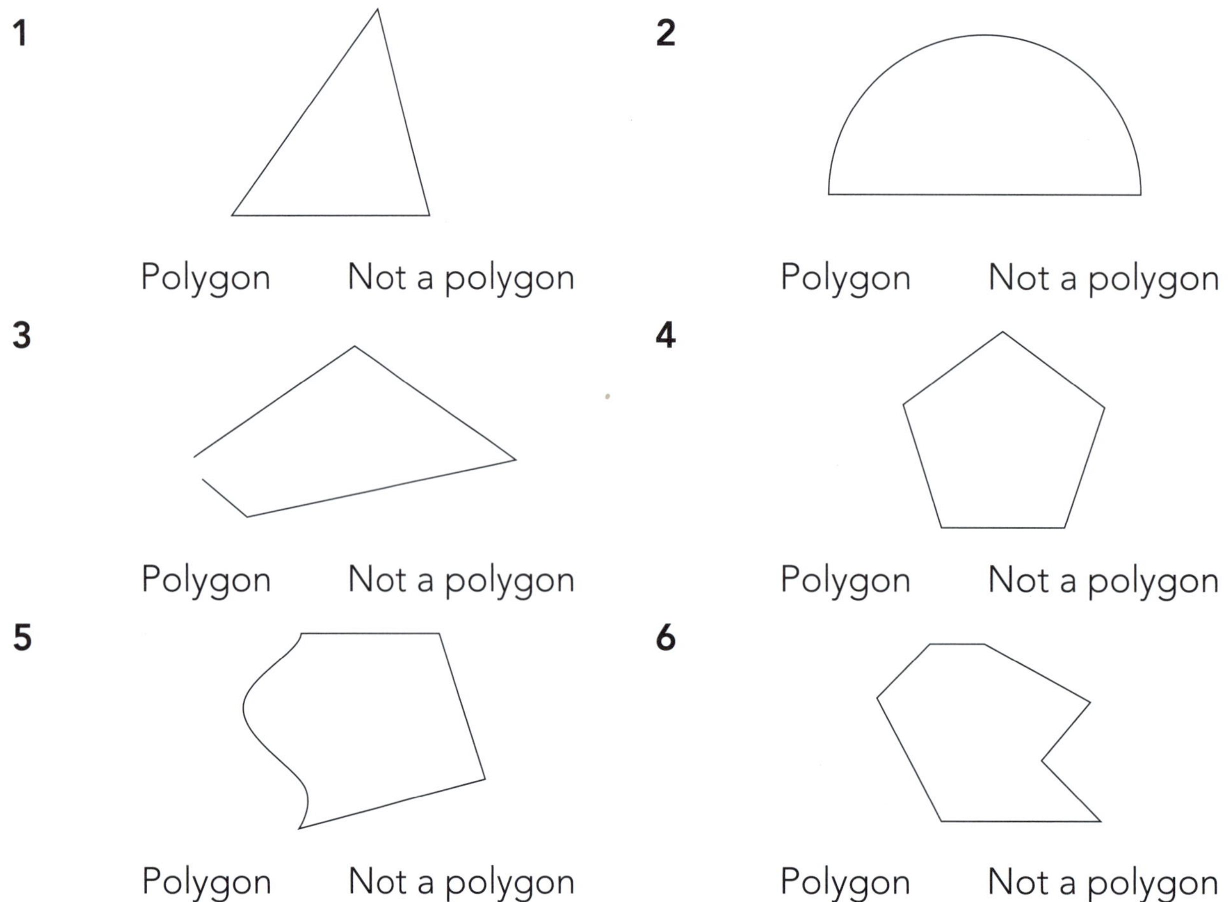

ISBN: 9780170451970

Shape language

There are a number of other terms we use to describe or categorise shapes.

Term	Meaning	Example
Triangle	A closed shape with exactly three straight sides.	
Quadrilateral	A closed shape with exactly four straight sides.	
Regular	A shape with all sides and angles equal.	
Irregular	A shape with two or more unequal sides or angles.	
Isosceles	A triangle or trapezium with two equal sides.	
Symmetrical (reflective)	A shape which can have a fold line that cuts the shape into two equal halves.	

Within a figure, sides or angles with the same number of **sticks** have equal **lengths**.

ISBN: 9780170451970

Term	Meaning	Example
Parallel	Lines that are always the same distance apart and will never meet. Within a figure, sides with the same number of **arrows** are **parallel**.	
Right angle	An angle of exactly 90°.	

Example:

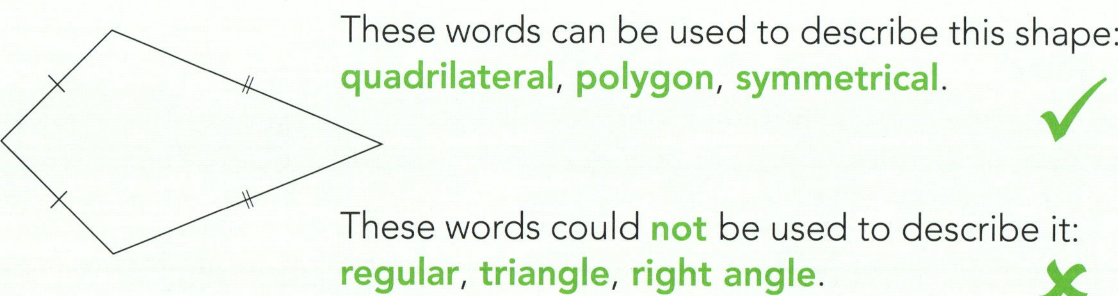

These words can be used to describe this shape: **quadrilateral**, **polygon**, **symmetrical**. ✓

These words could **not** be used to describe it: **regular**, **triangle**, **right angle**. ✗

Highlight the word(s) that can be used to describe these shapes.

1

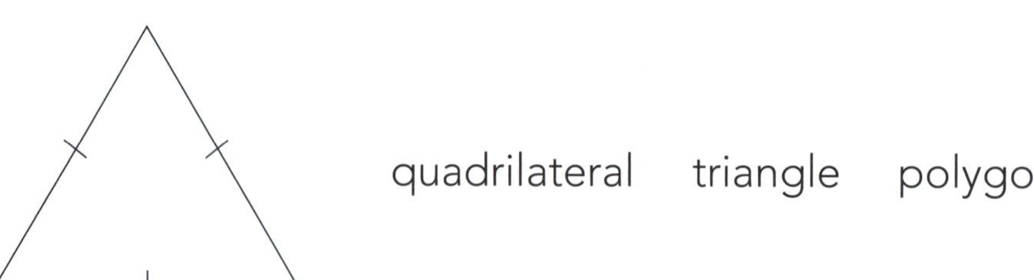

quadrilateral triangle polygon regular

2

triangle polygon quadrilateral irregular

ISBN: 9780170451970

3 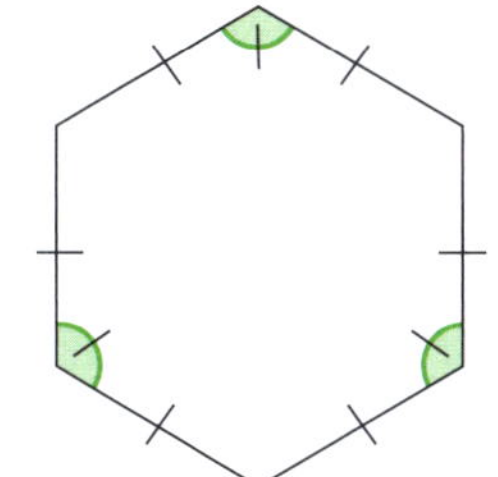

symmetrical regular right angle polygon

4 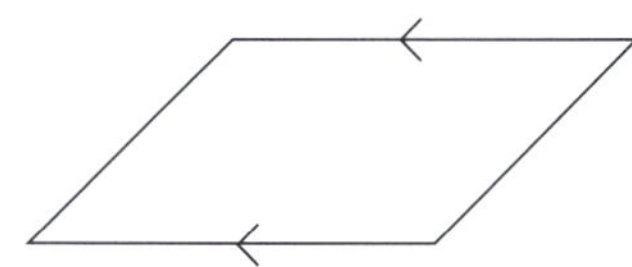

irregular regular quadrilateral polygon

5 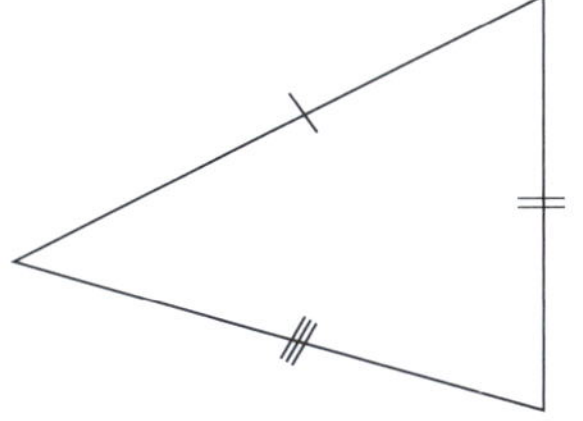

irregular regular isosceles triangle

6 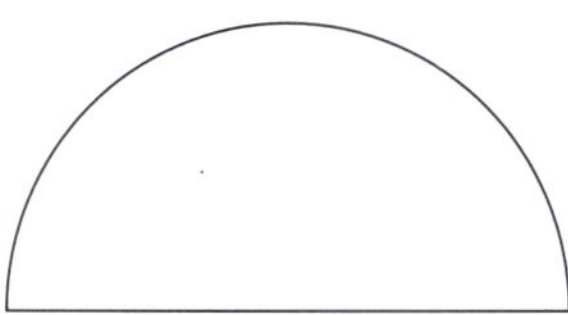

polygon symmetrical

7 Sketch a shape that is a quadrilateral.

8 Sketch a shape that is isosceles.

9 Sketch a triangle that has a right angle.

ISBN: 9780170451970

Naming triangles

- A **triangle** is any shape with exactly **three straight sides**.
- There are four words that are often used to describe triangles.
- Two of these words can sometimes be used to describe a single triangle, e.g. a triangle can be both scalene and right angled.

Equilateral triangle: all three sides are the same length.

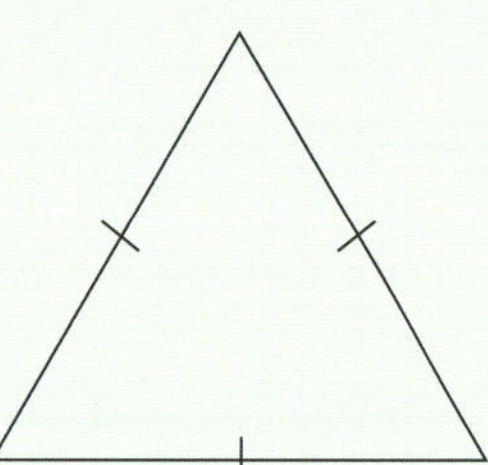

Isosceles triangle: exactly two sides are the same length.

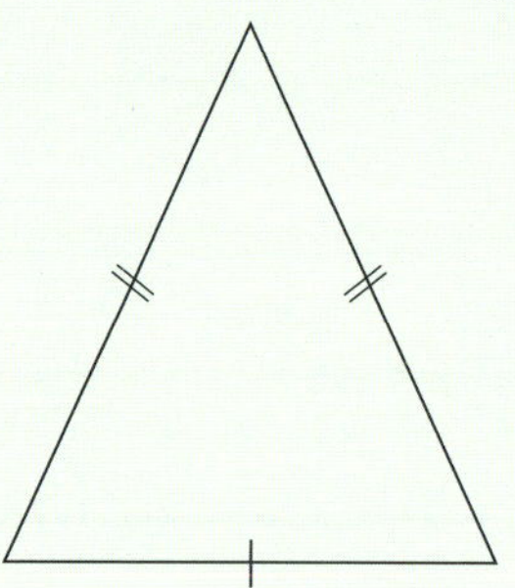

Scalene triangle: all sides have different lengths.

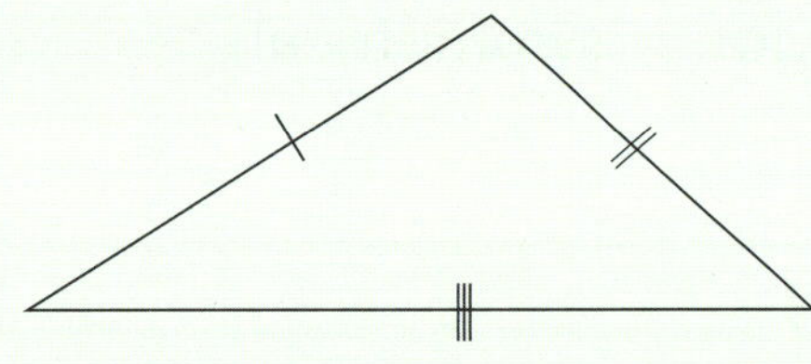

Right-angled triangle: one angle is 90°.

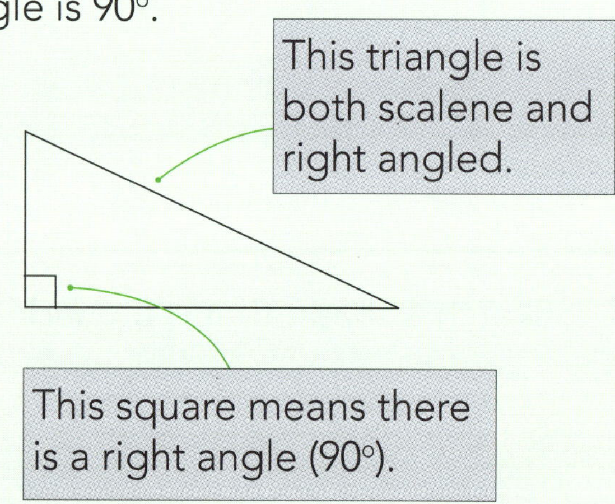

Use one or more of the words to describe these triangles.

1

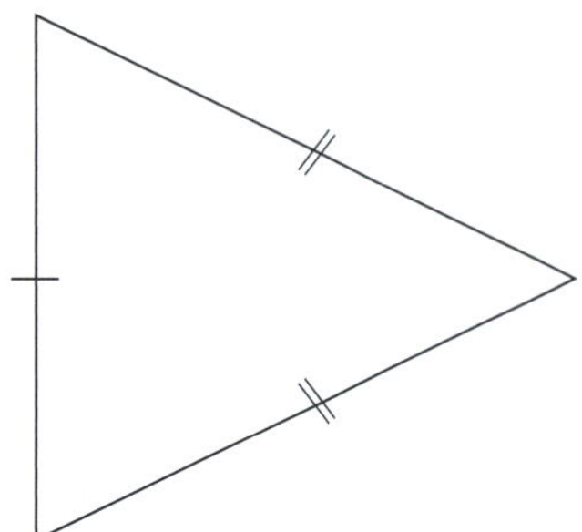

____

2

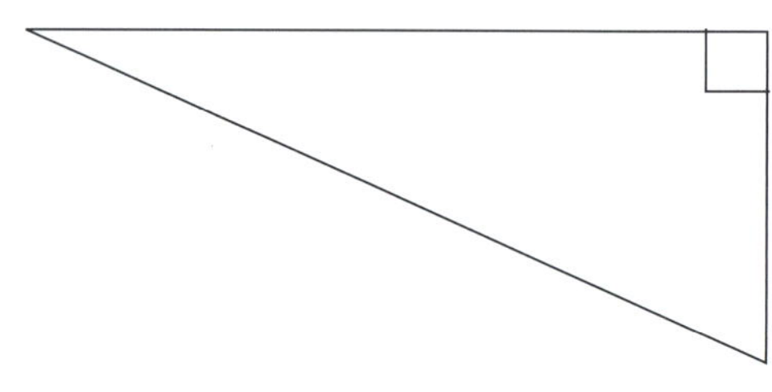

____

 ISBN: 9780170451970

3

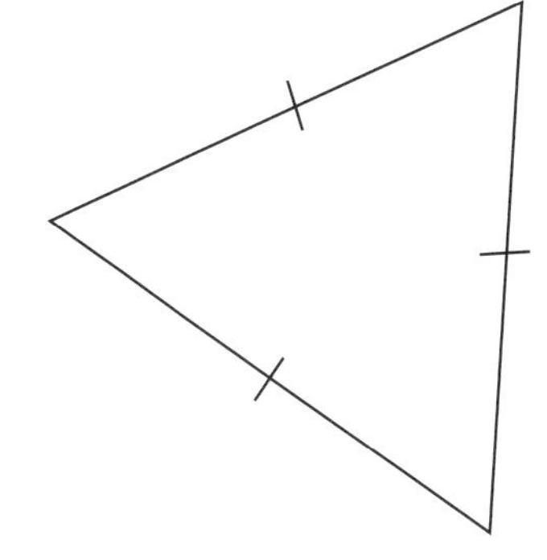

4

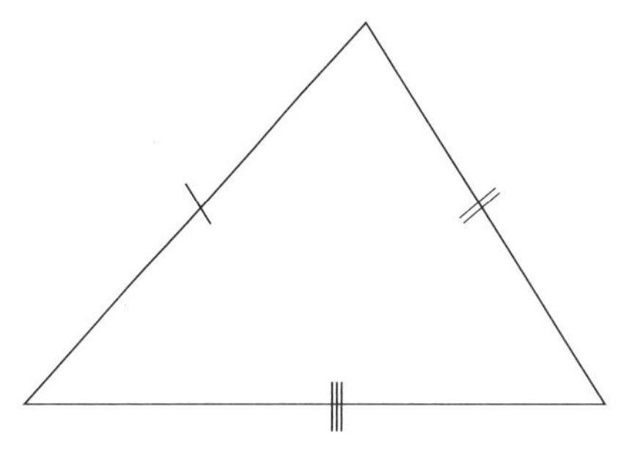

5

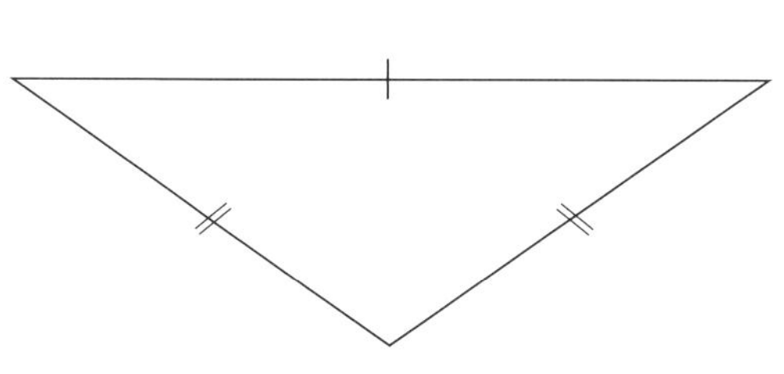

6

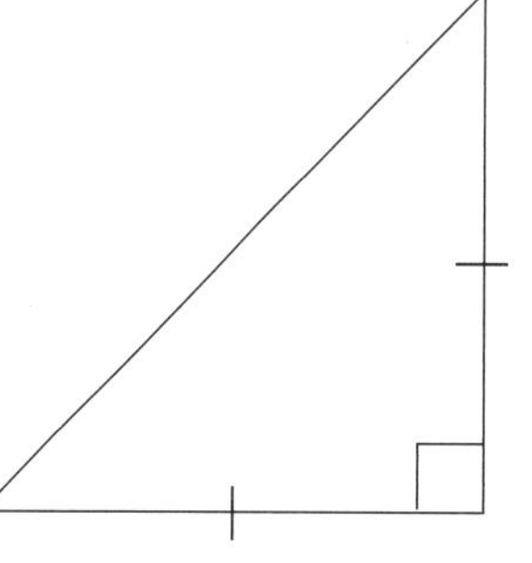

7

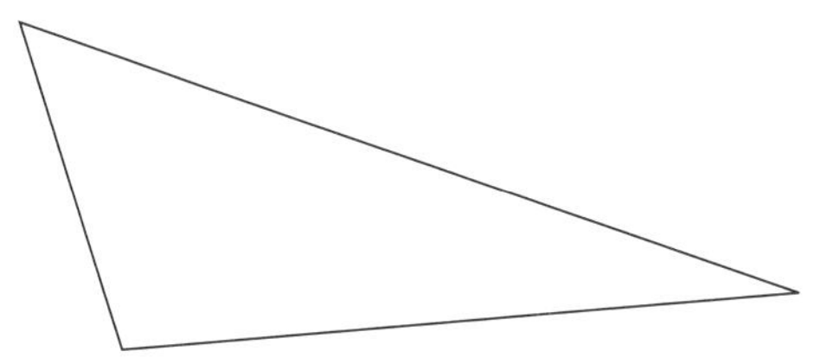

8

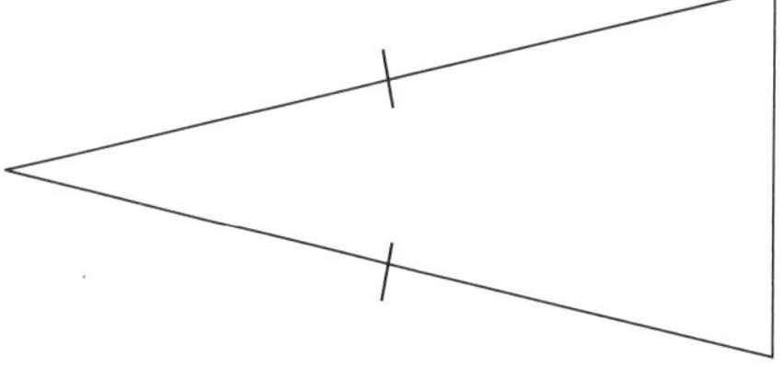

9 How many triangles are in this shape?

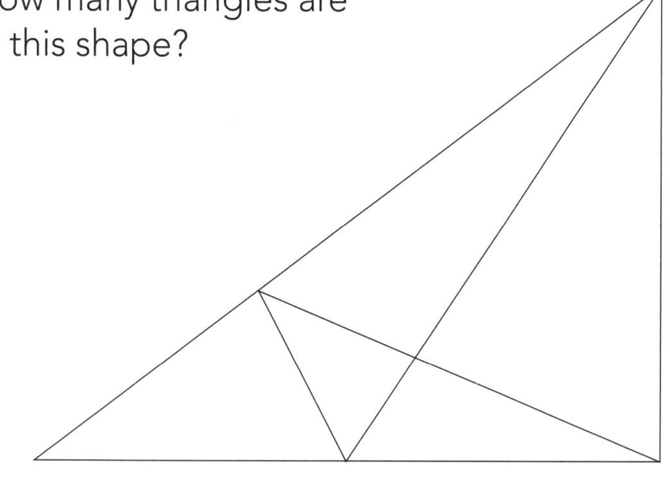

ISBN: 9780170451970

Naming quadrilaterals

- A **quadrilateral** is any closed (no gaps) shape with **exactly four straight sides**.
- There are eight special sorts of quadrilateral.

Match each shape with its name.

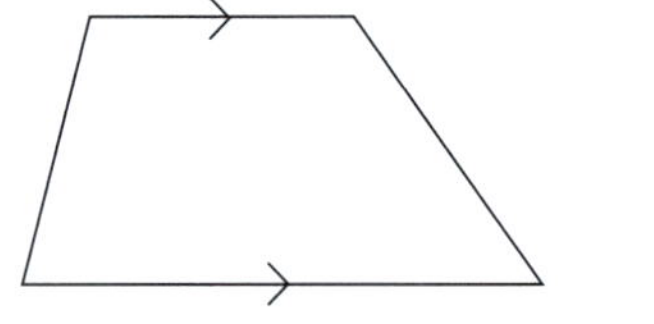	•	• Square
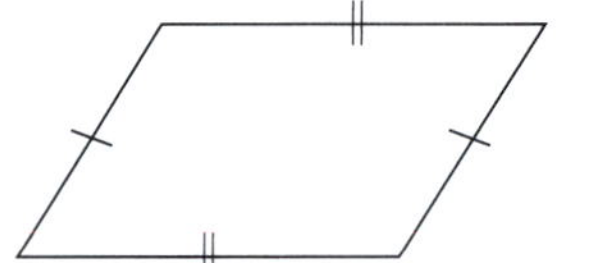	•	• Rectangle
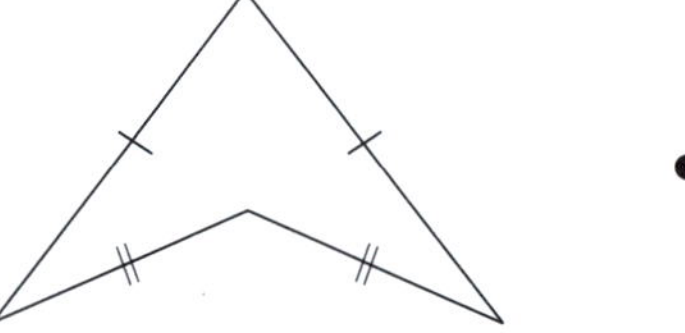	•	• Rhombus
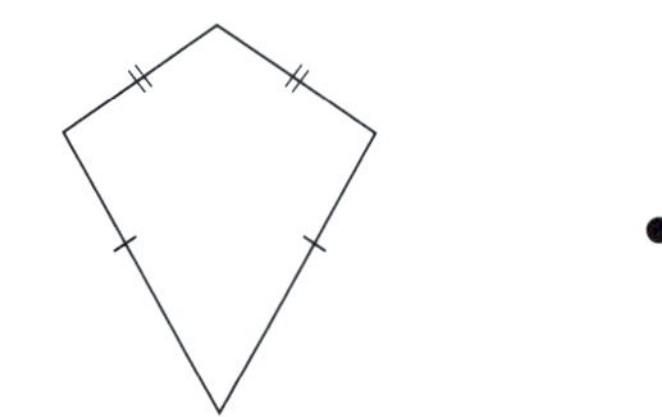	•	• Parallelogram
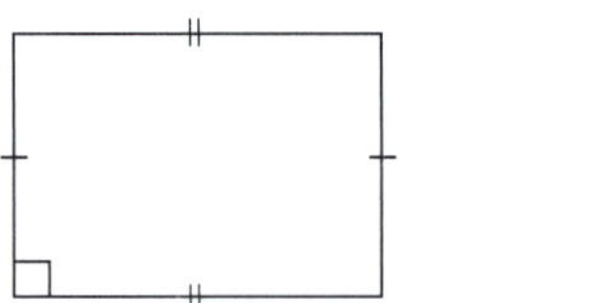	•	• Trapezium
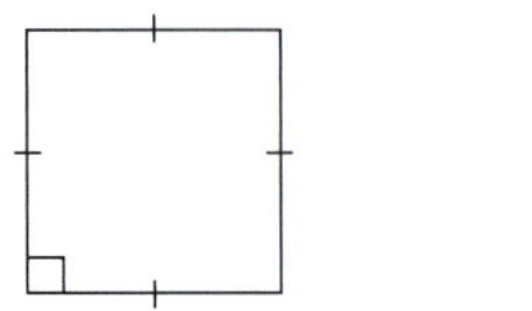	•	• Isosceles trapezium
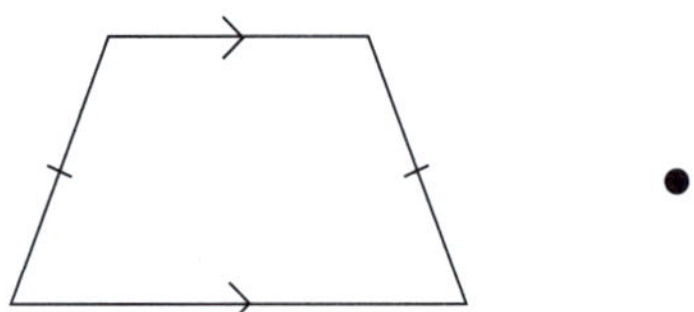	•	• Kite
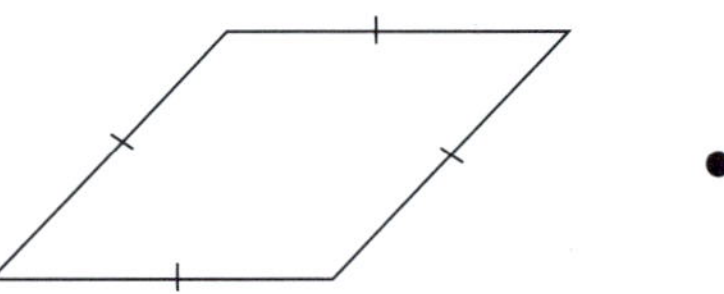	•	• Arrowhead

ISBN: 9780170451970

Naming other 2D shapes

- Here are some other shapes with names that you need to know.

hexagon	circle	nonagon	heptagon
decagon	octagon	semicircle	pentagon

Match the names above with the shapes below.

1

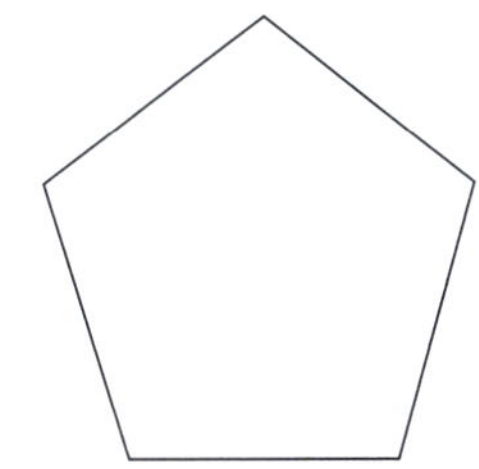

2

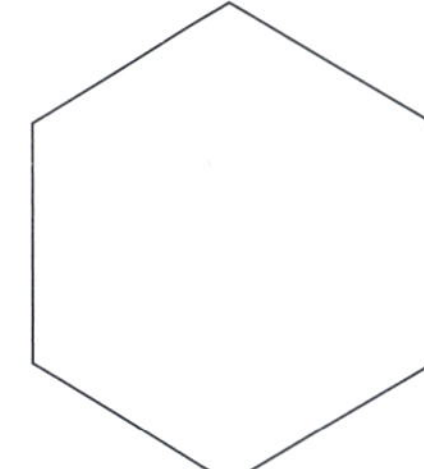

3

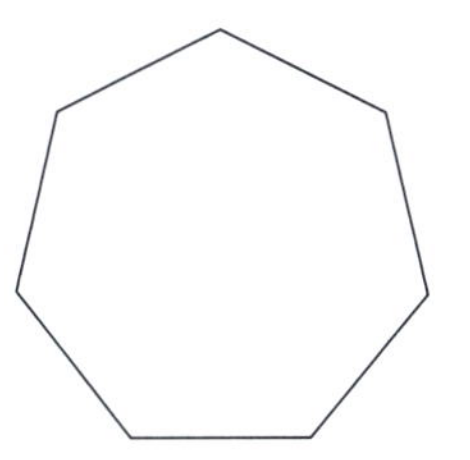

4

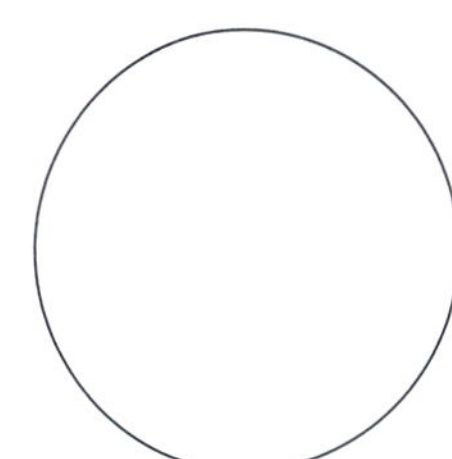

5

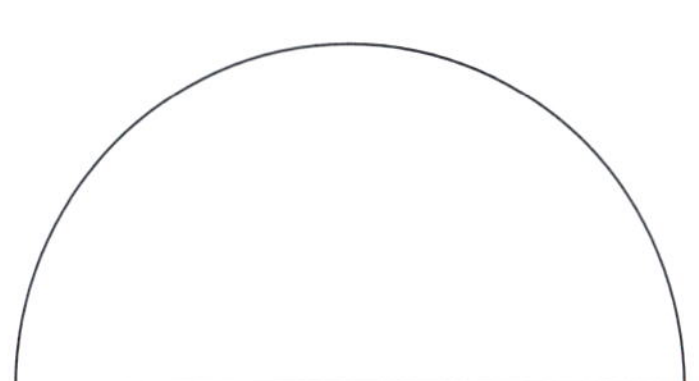

6

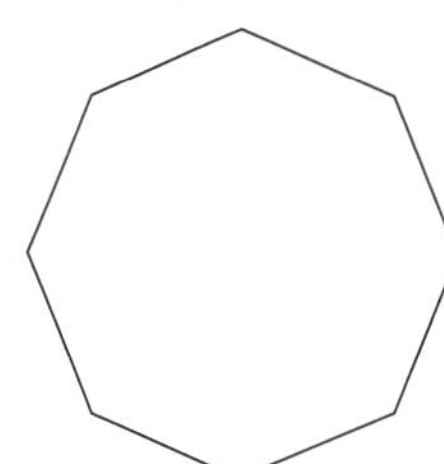

7

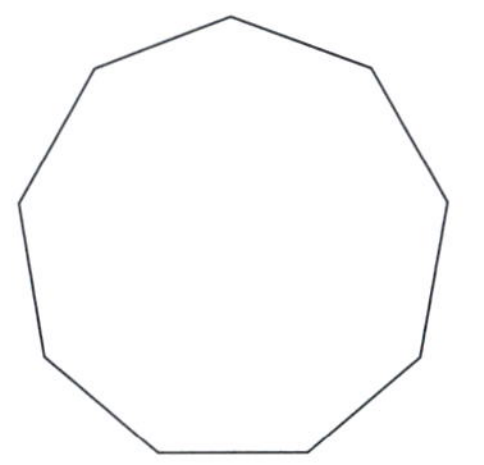

8

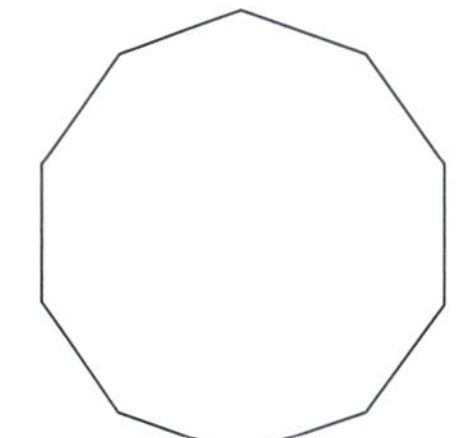

Challenge 1

How many rectangles are in this picture?

Number of rectangles: ____________________

How many quadrilaterals are in this picture?

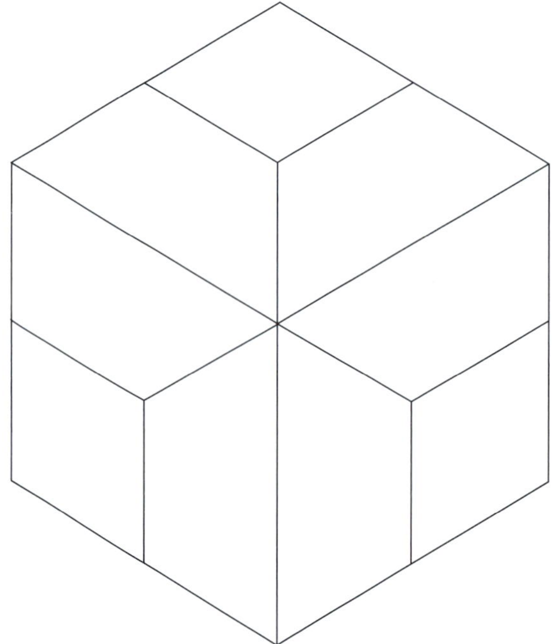

Number of quadrilaterals: ____________________

 ISBN: 9780170451970

Angles

What is an angle?

- An angle is formed where two lines meet at a point.
- An angle measures the rotation of one line onto another line.

- An angle is measured in **degrees**.
- Degrees are indicated by a small ° after a number, e.g. 90°.
- 1° (one degree) is very small.

Here are some good angles to be familiar with.

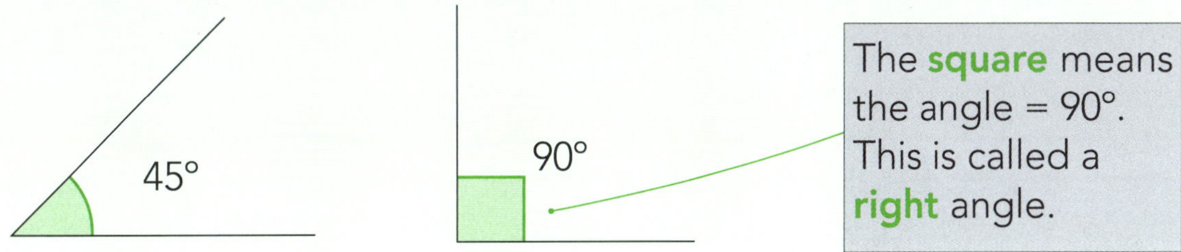

Two 90° angles make 180°.

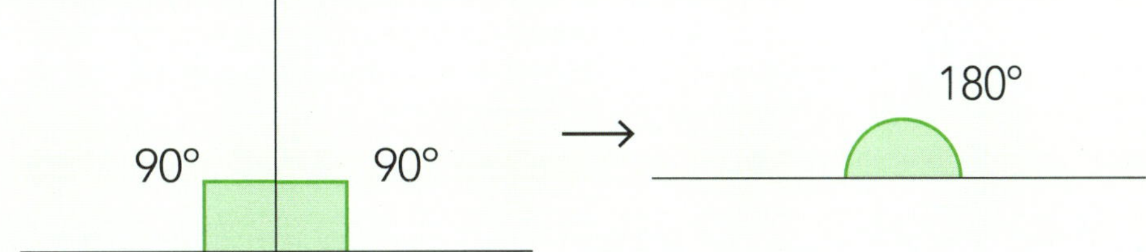

Four 90° angles make 360°, or a full rotation.

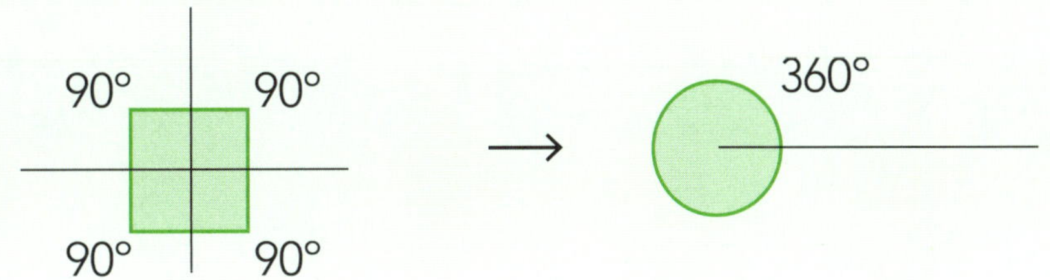

ISBN: 9780170451970

Matching angles

Match each angle with its picture.

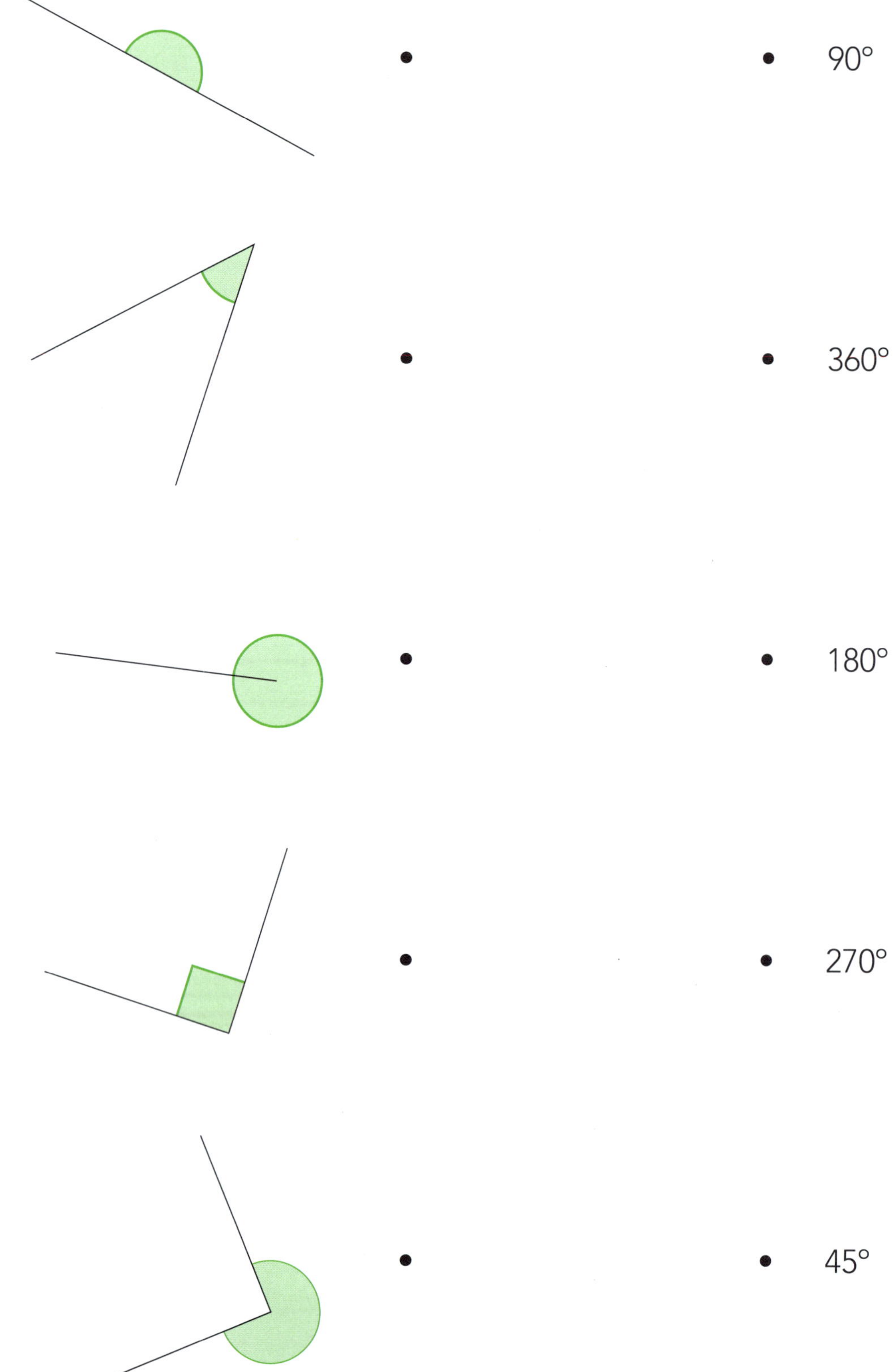

 ISBN: 9780170451970

Estimating angles

- You can estimate the size of an angle if you know these common ones.

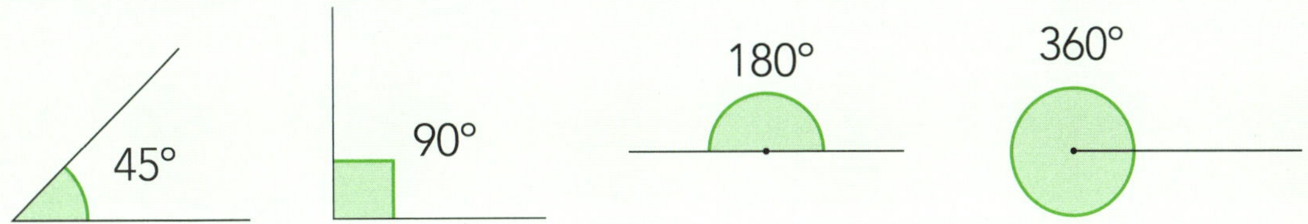

Examples: Estimate the sizes of these angles.

1

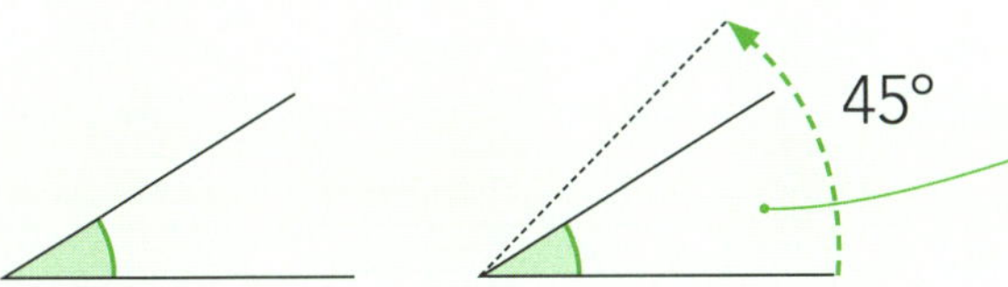

This angle looks less than 45°. So anything between 30° and 40° would be a good estimation.

So we can estimate that this angle is 30°.

2

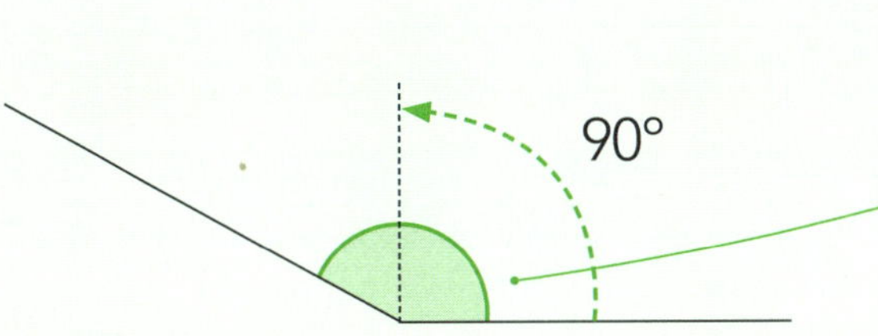

This angle is more than halfway between 90° and 180°. So anything between 140° and 160° would be a good estimation.

So we might estimate that this angle is 150°.

3

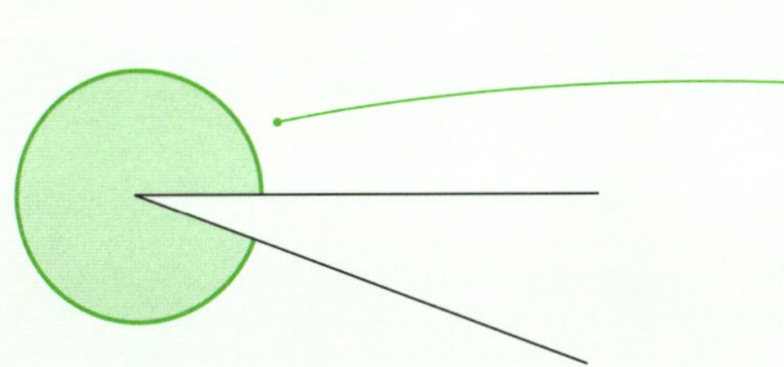

This angle is a bit less than 360°. So anything between 330° and 350° would be a good estimation.

So we might estimate that this angle is 340°.

ISBN: 9780170451970

Match the angles in the box to the images below.

320°	200°	20°	40°
250°	120°	80°	170°

1

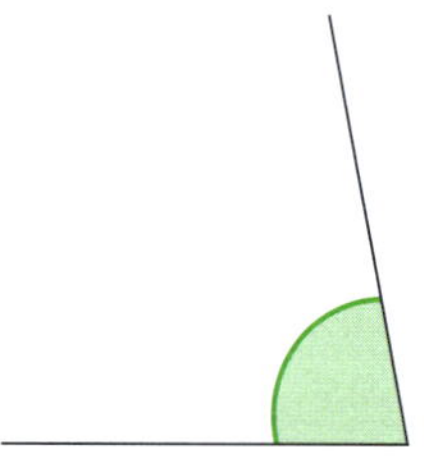

2

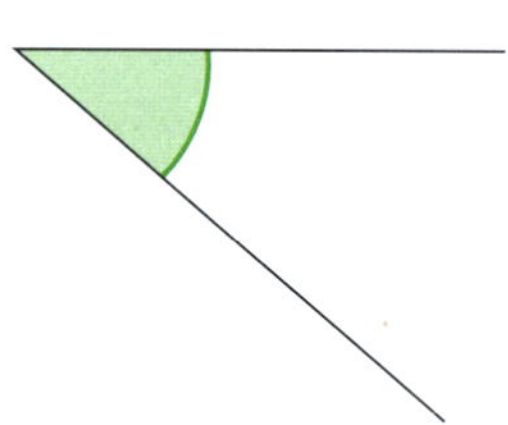

3

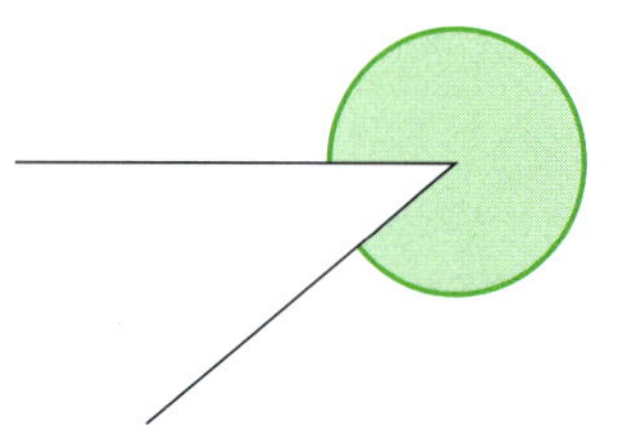

4

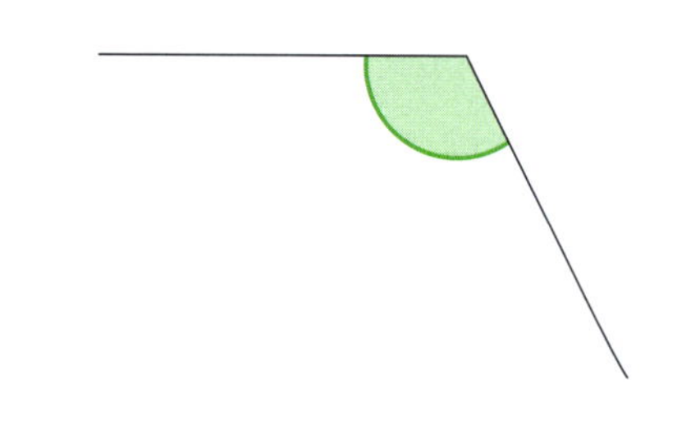

5

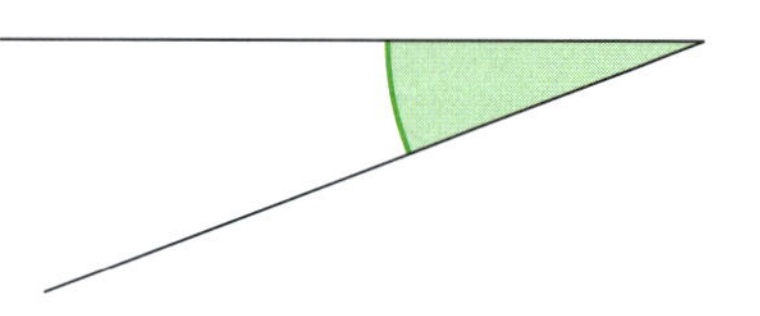

6

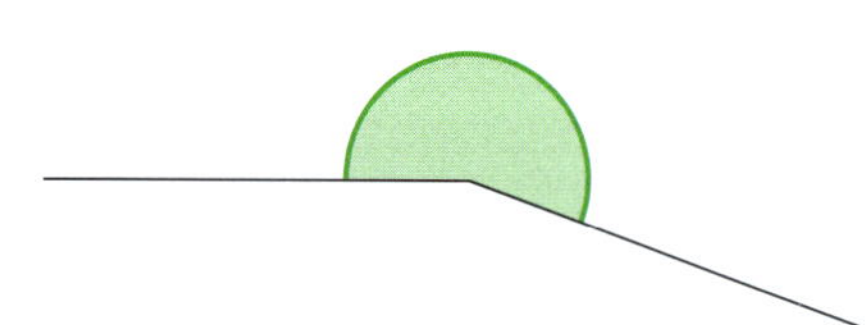

7

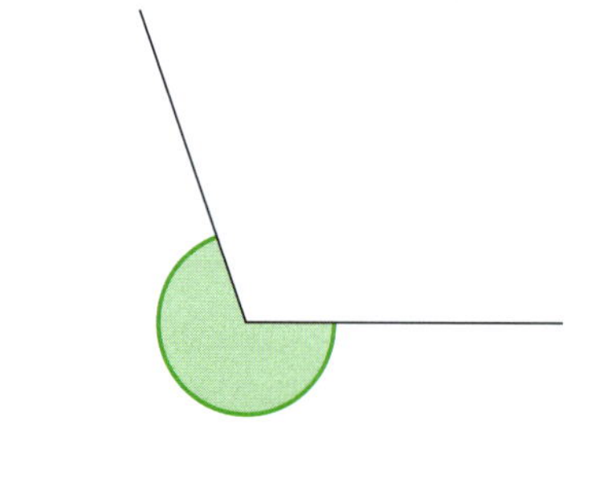

8

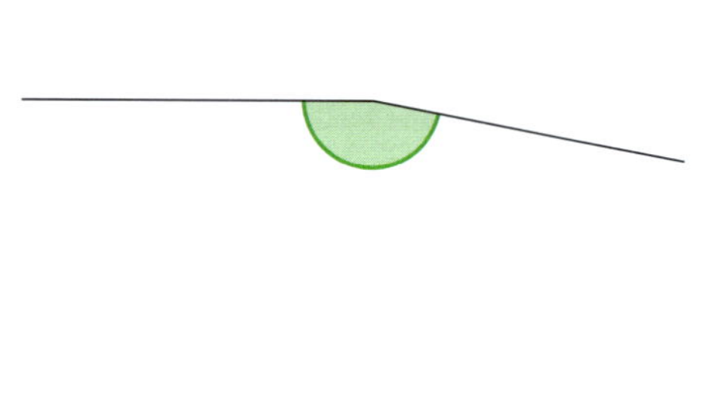

 ISBN: 9780170451970

Types of angles

Name	Picture	Description
Acute angle	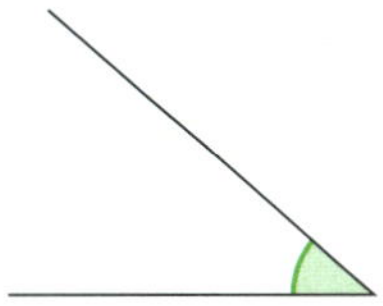	An angle between 0° and 90°.
Right angle	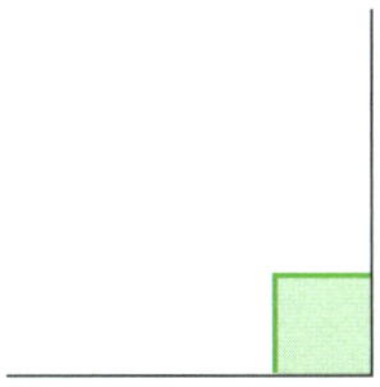	An angle that is 90°.
Obtuse angle	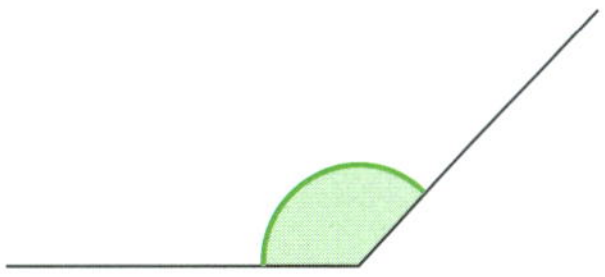	An angle between 90° and 180°.
Straight angle	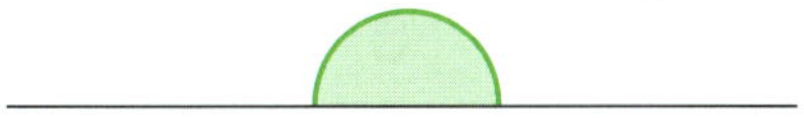	An angle that is 180°.
Reflex angle	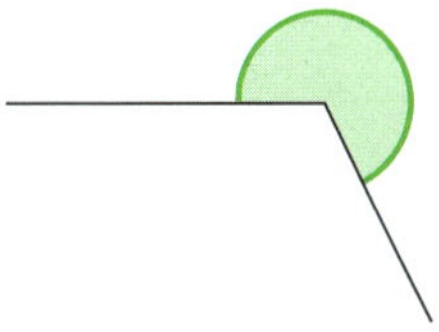	An angle between 180° and 360°.

Write down the name of each type of angle.

1

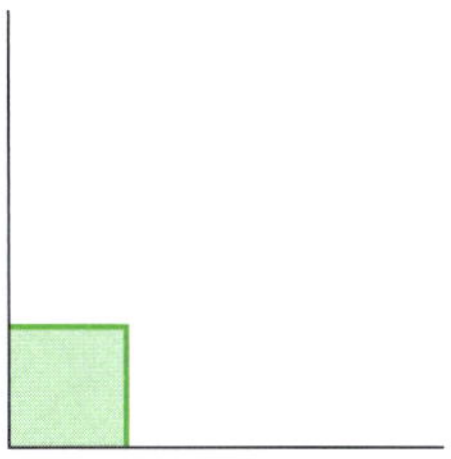

____

2

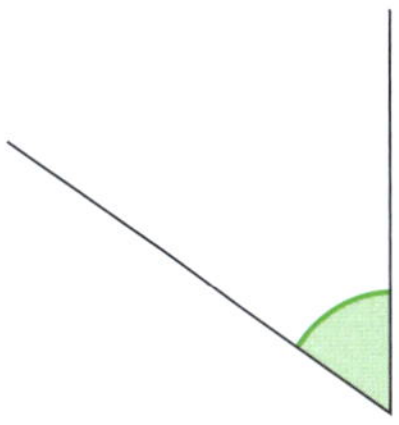

____

ISBN: 9780170451970

3

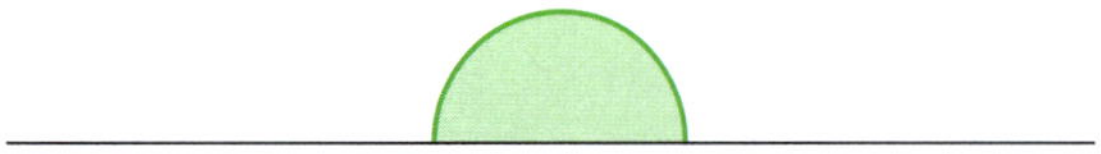

4

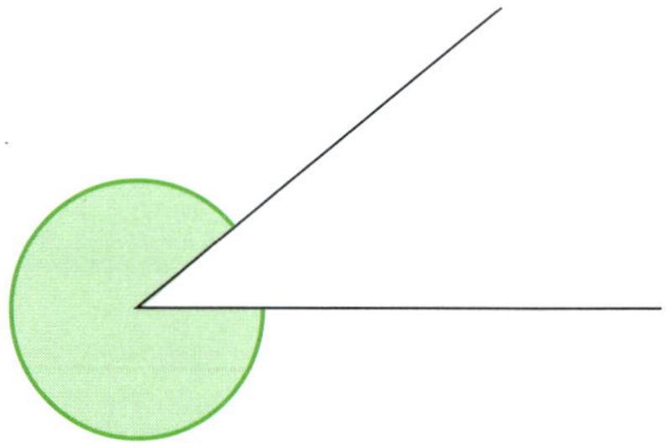

5

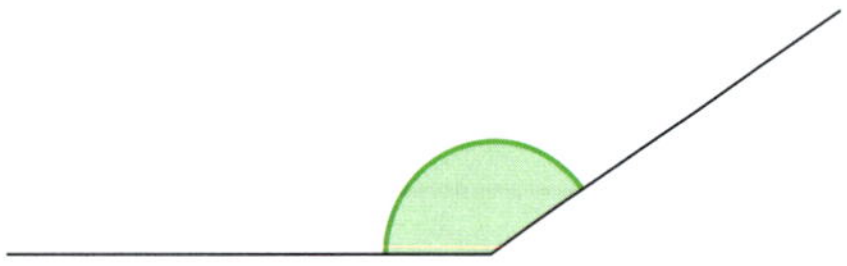

6

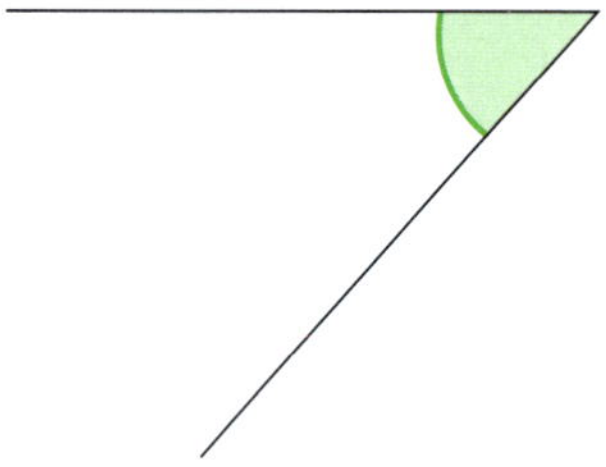

7

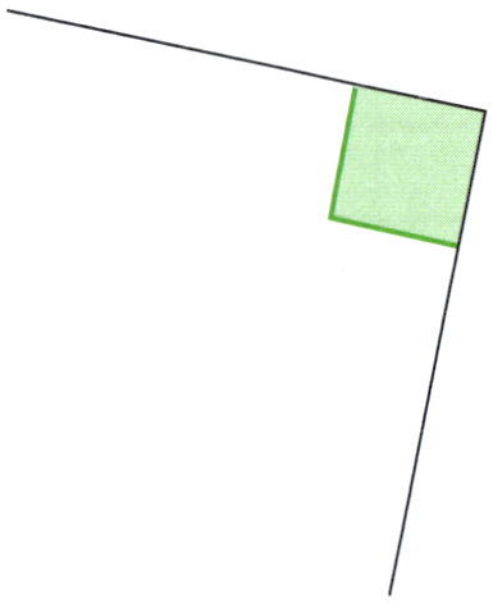

8

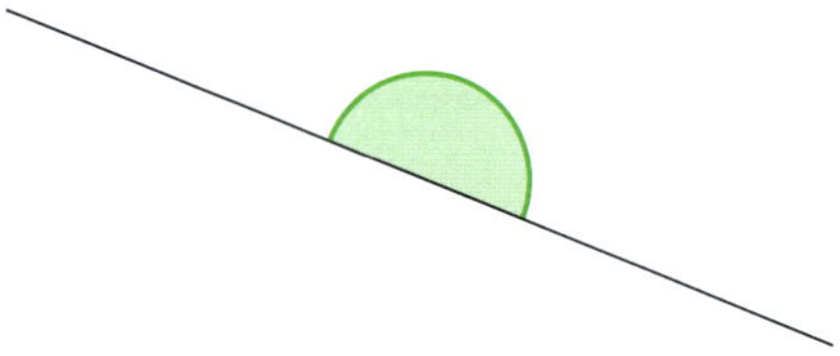

9

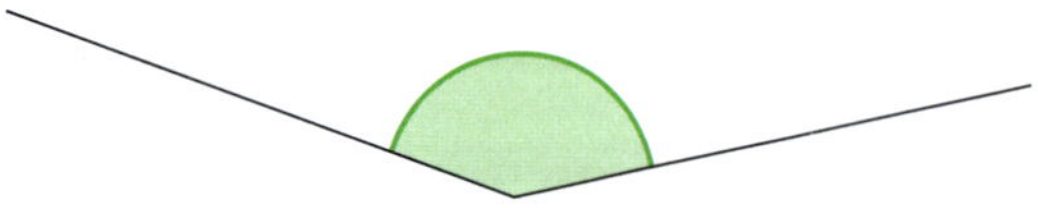

10

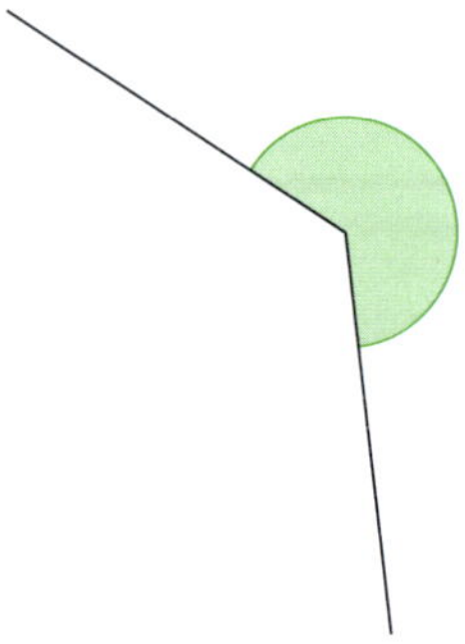

 ISBN: 9780170451970

Naming angles

- Angles can be named in two ways.

1 Using the **three** letters **outside** each vertex.

This angle is ∠DEF or ∠FED.

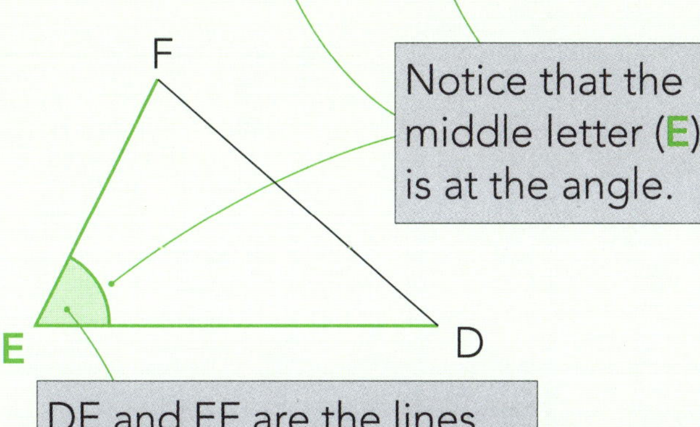

2 Using the **one** letter **inside** the angle.

This angle is ∠*y*.

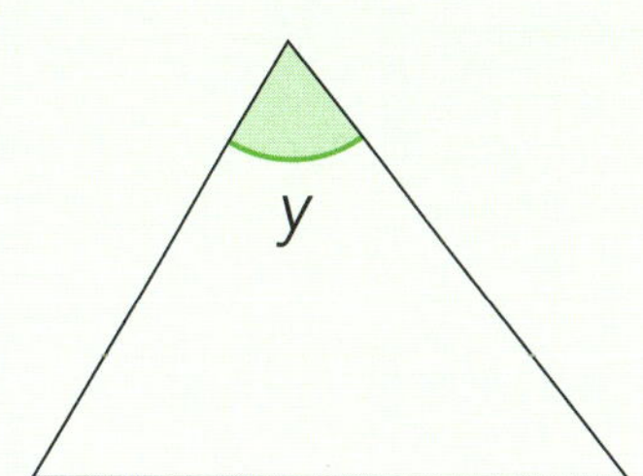

Match the angle names to the angles in the diagrams.

∠CBA	∠b	∠a
∠d	∠BAD	∠ABD

1

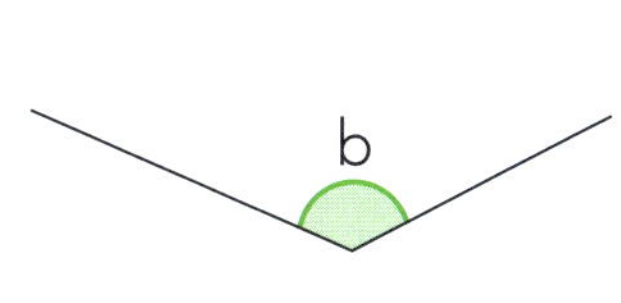

____

2

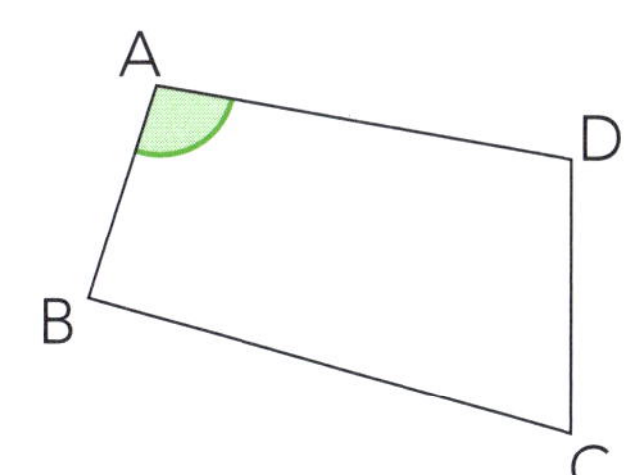

____

3

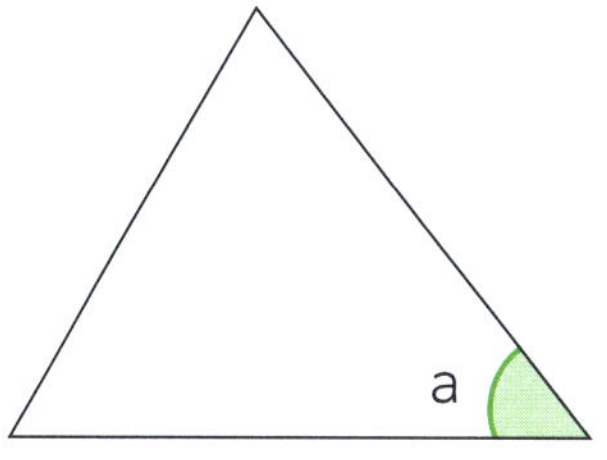

____

4

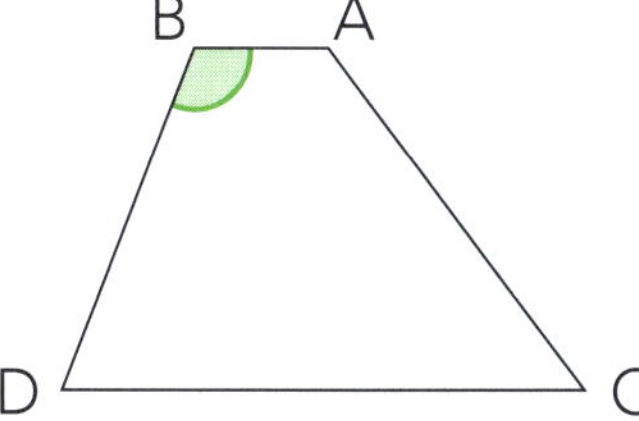

____

5

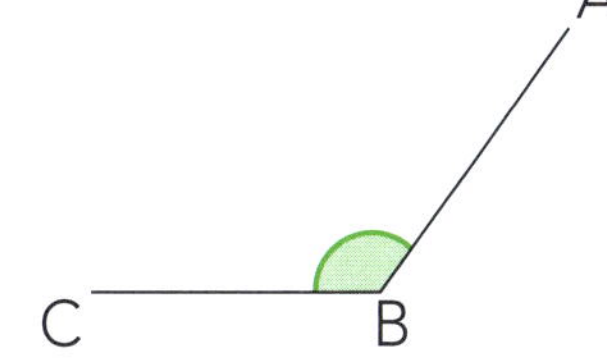

____

6

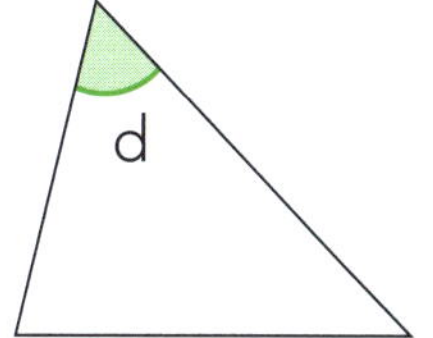

____

ISBN: 9780170451970

Highlight or shade the named angles on these diagrams and name the shaded angle.

7

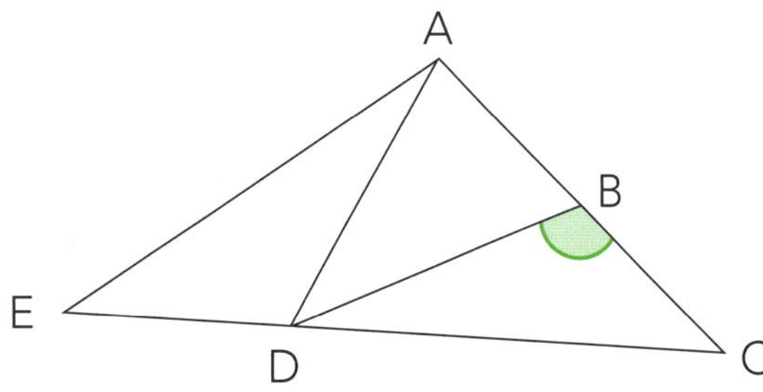

Shaded angle: ______________

8 ∠FHA

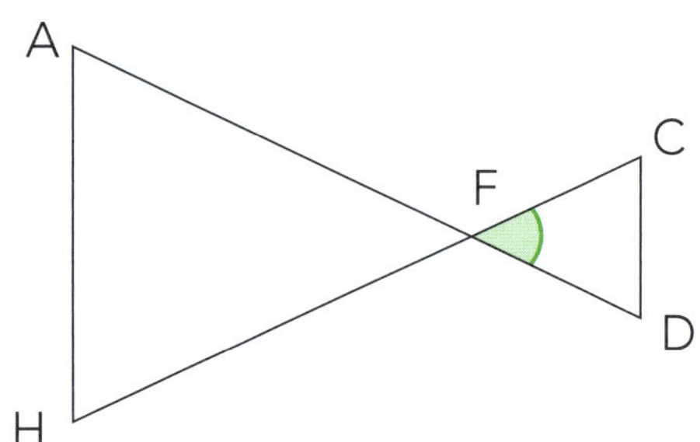

Shaded angle: ______________

9 ∠DFP

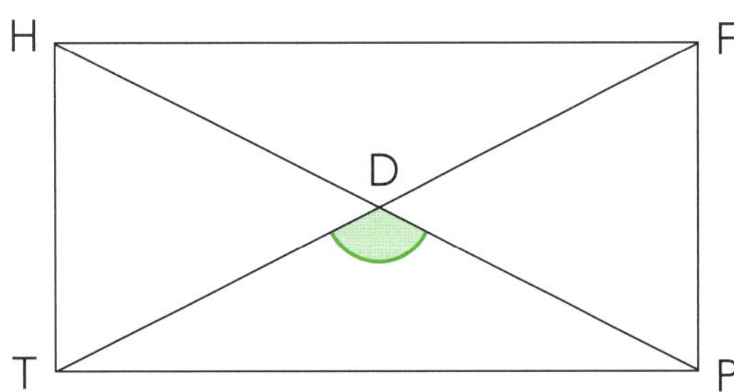

Shaded angle: ______________

10 ∠HFT

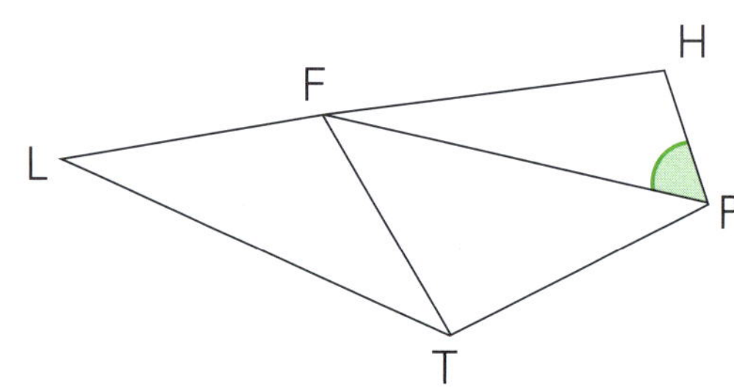

Shaded angle: ______________

11 ∠ZHP

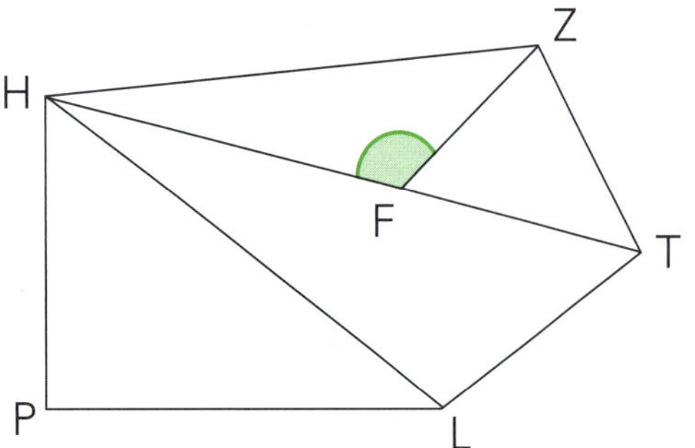

Shaded angle: ______________

12 ∠ZLT

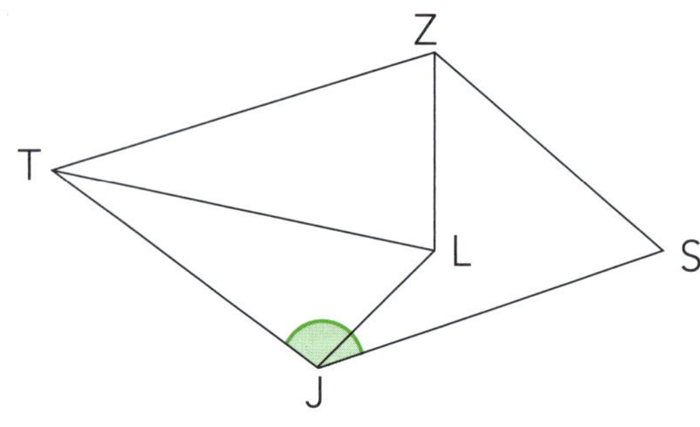

Shaded angle: ______________

  ISBN: 9780170451970

Angles in a right angle

- Angles in a right angle **add to 90°**, and are known as **complementary angles**.

Notice that this is an 'e'.
Something compl**i**mentary is free.

1 Find the value of y.

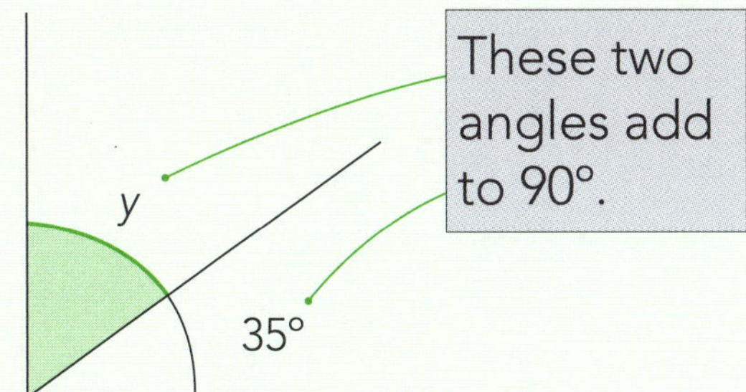

$y + 35° = 90°$

$y = 90° - 35°$

$y = 55°$

2 Find the value of x.

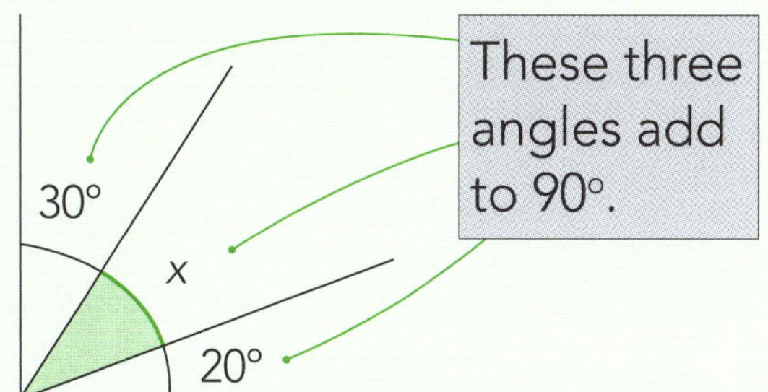

$30° + x + 20° = 90°$

$x = 90° - 30° - 20°$

$x = 40°$

Calculate the size of the marked angles.

1

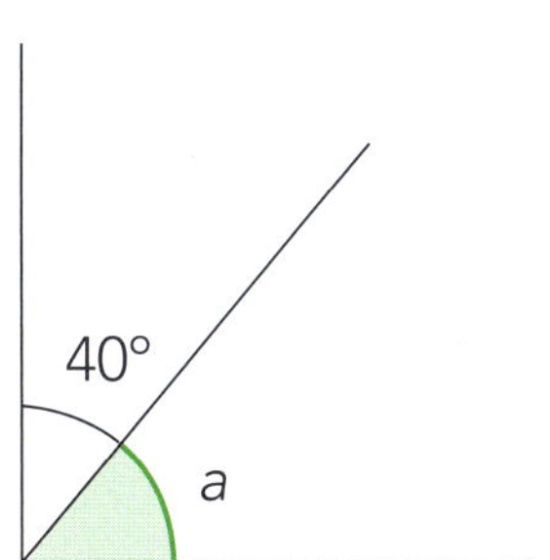

2

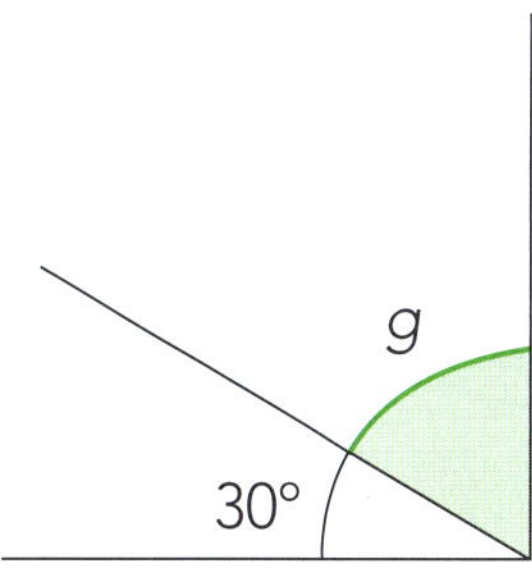

3

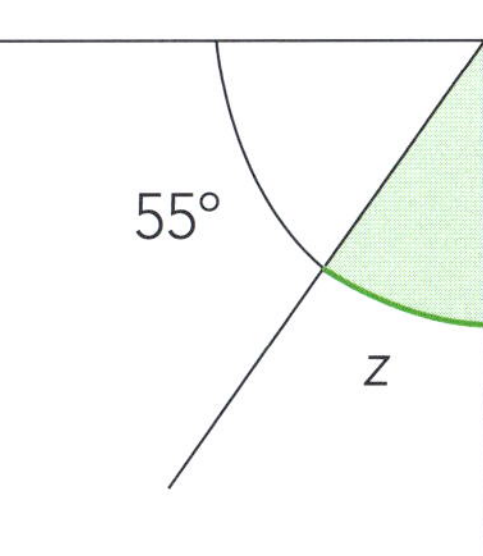

4

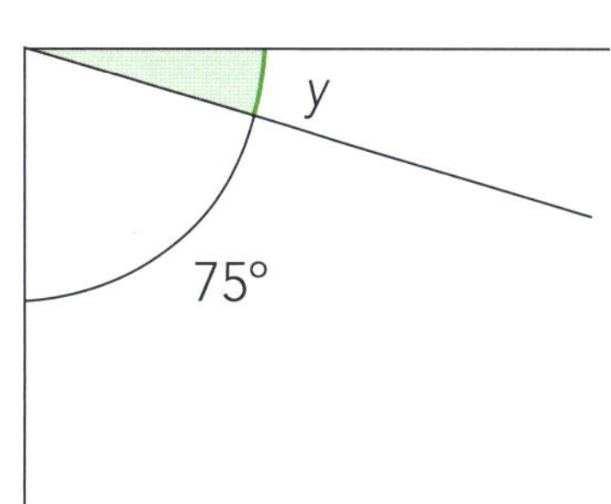

ISBN: 9780170451970

5

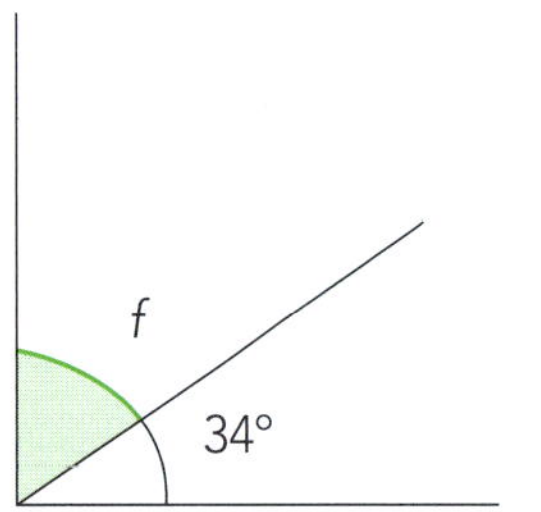

6

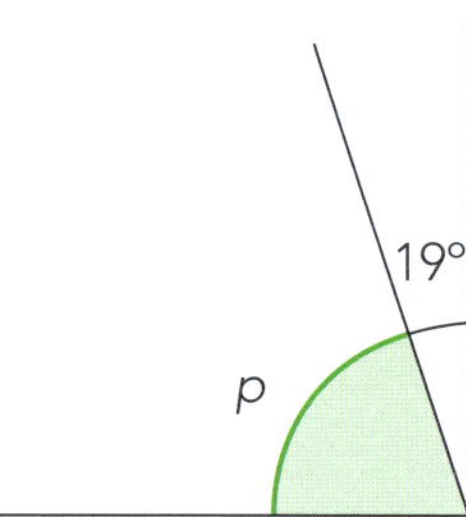

7

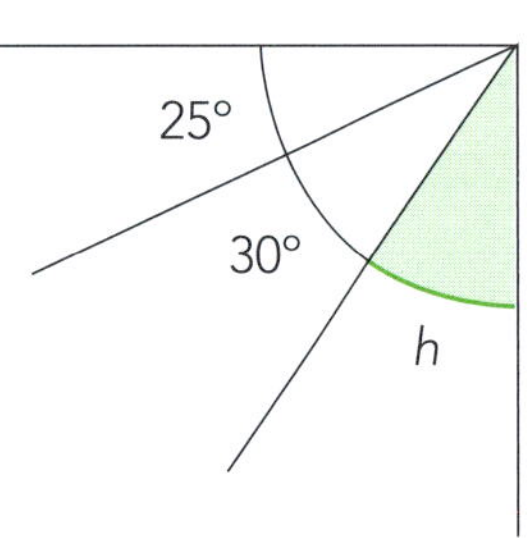

8

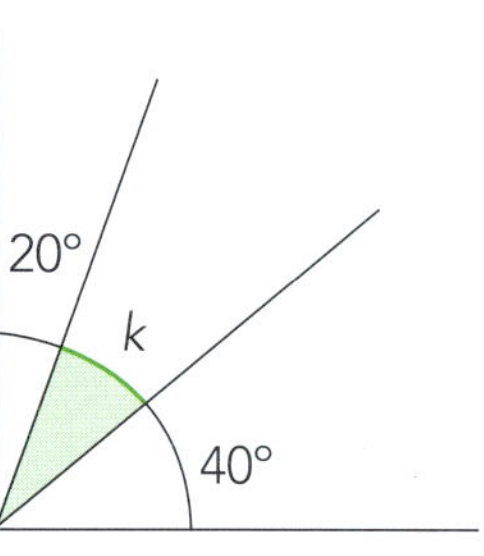

9

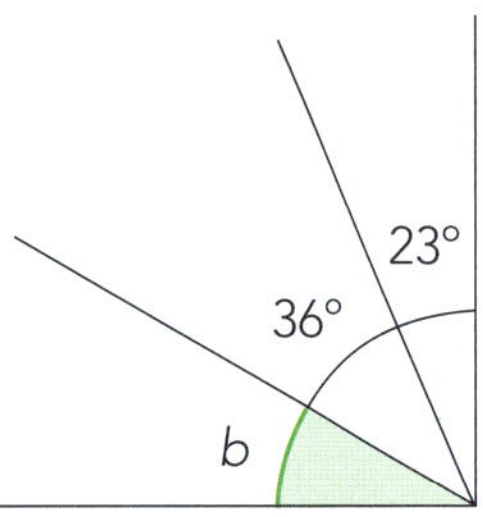

10

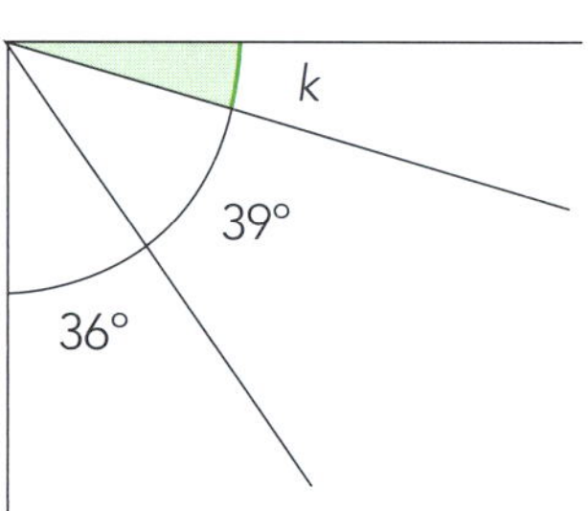

11 ∠AFE is a right angle. ∠AFB, ∠BFC and ∠CFD are all 26°.

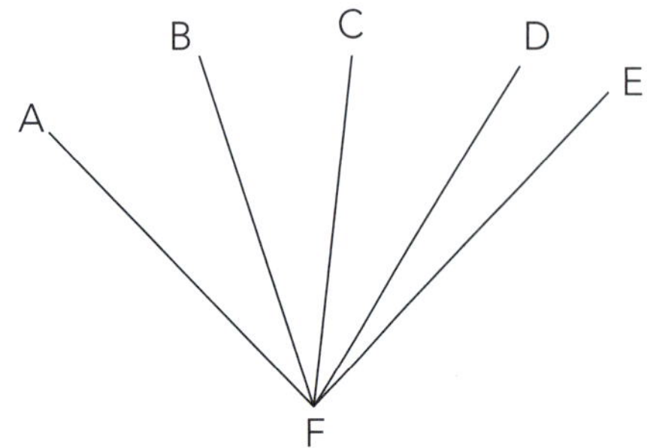

Calculate the size of ∠DFE.

12 ∠PUT is a right angle. ∠QUR = 20°, and ∠RUS and ∠SUT are both 27°.

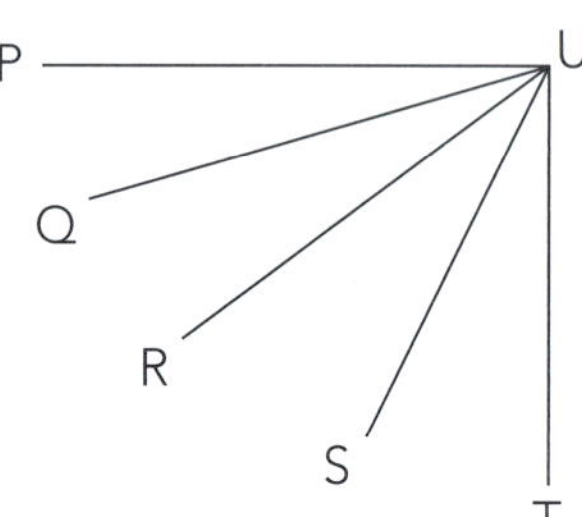

Calculate the size of ∠PUQ.

 ISBN: 9780170451970

Angles on a line

- Angles on a line **add to 180°** and are known as **supplementary** angles.

Examples:

1 Find the value of x.

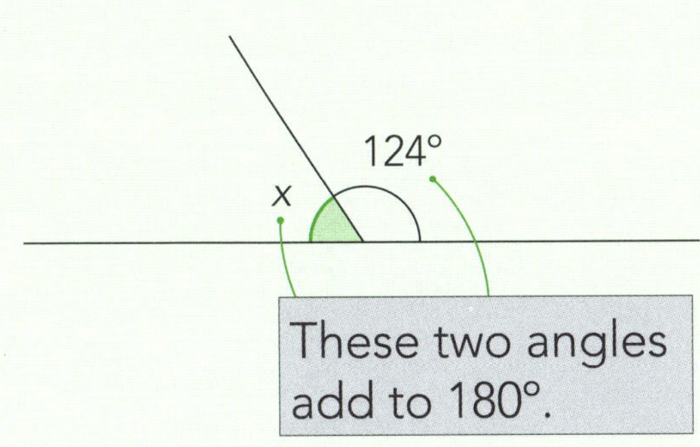

$x + 124° = 180°$

$x = 180° - 124°$

$x = 56°$

2 Find the value of y.

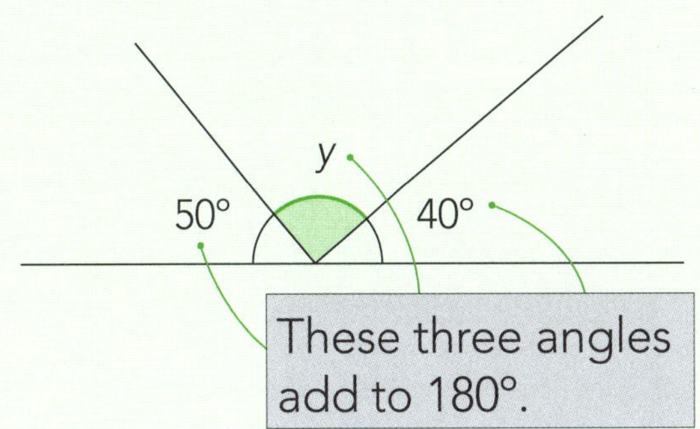

$50° + y + 40° = 180°$

$y = 180° - 50° - 40°$

$y = 90°$

Calculate the size of the marked angles.

1

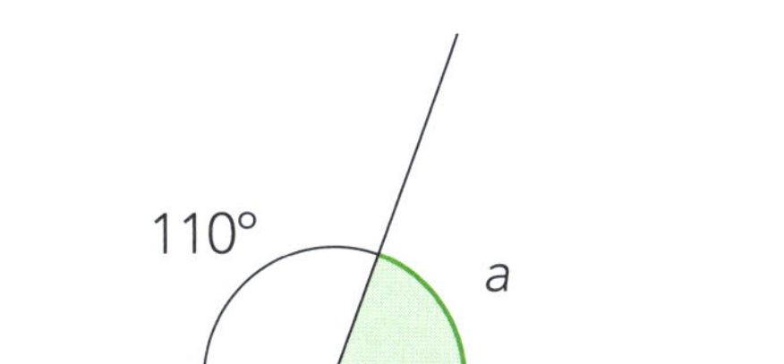

2

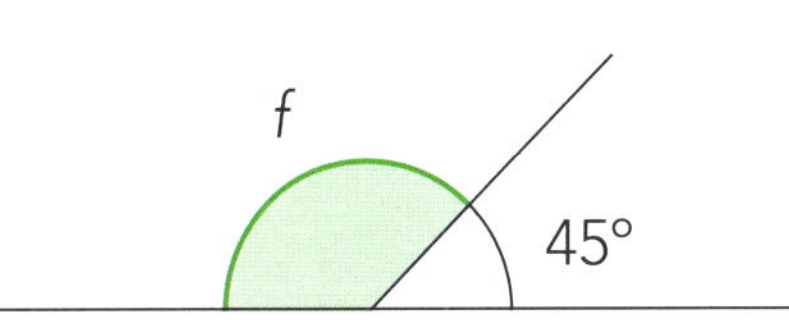

3

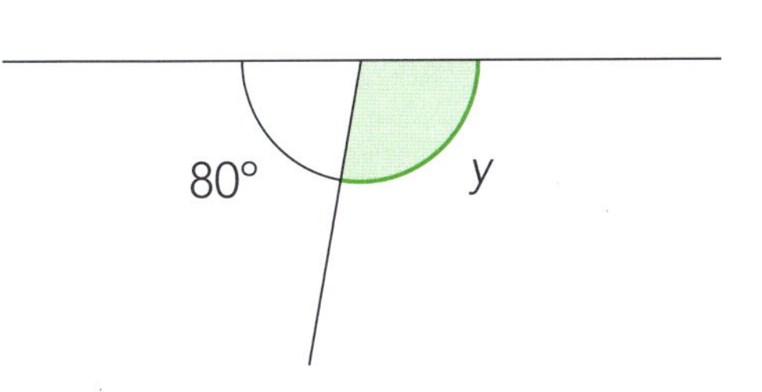

4

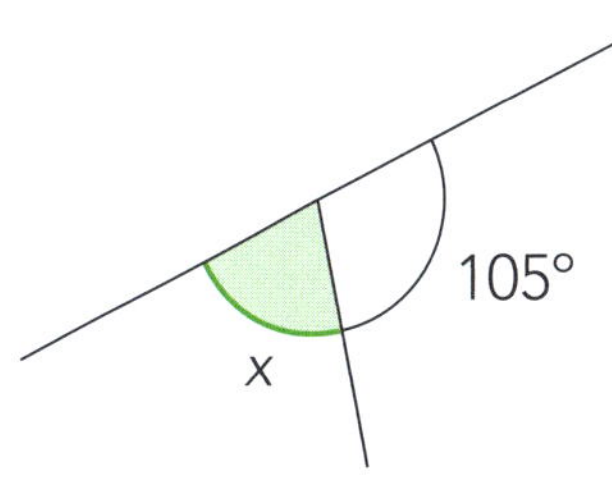

5

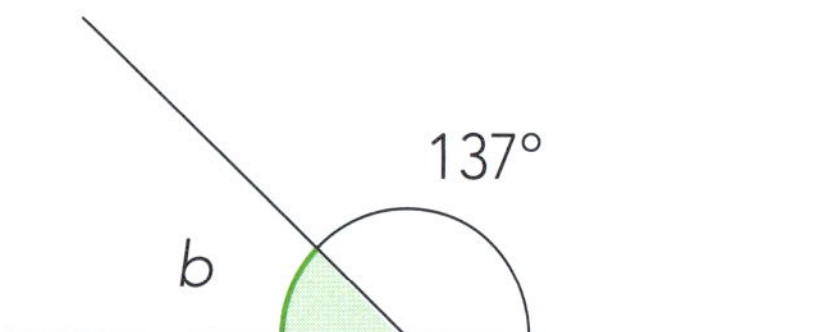

6

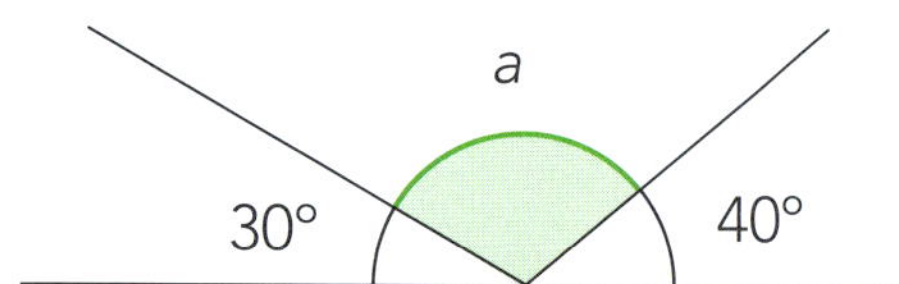

7

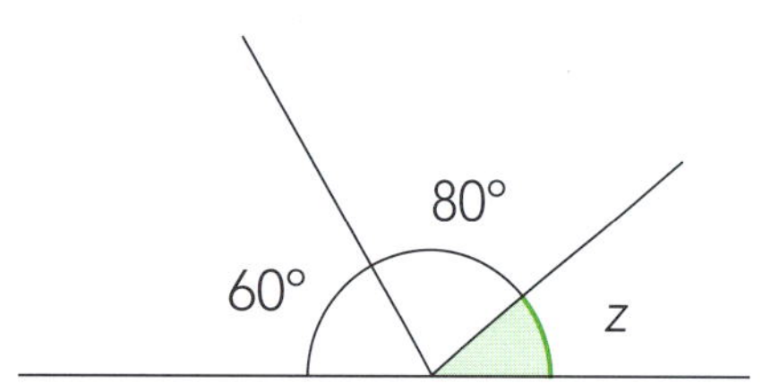

8

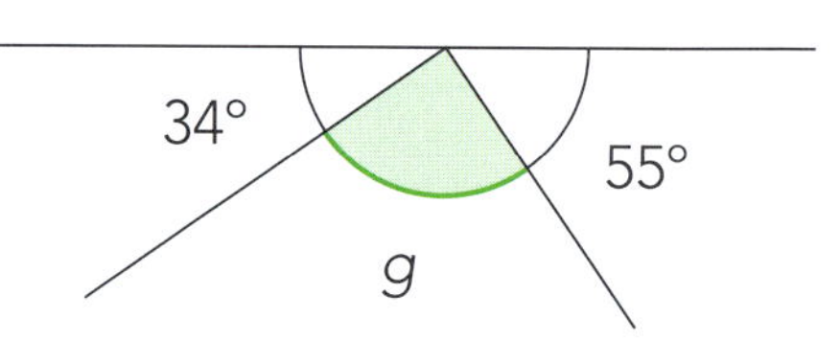

9

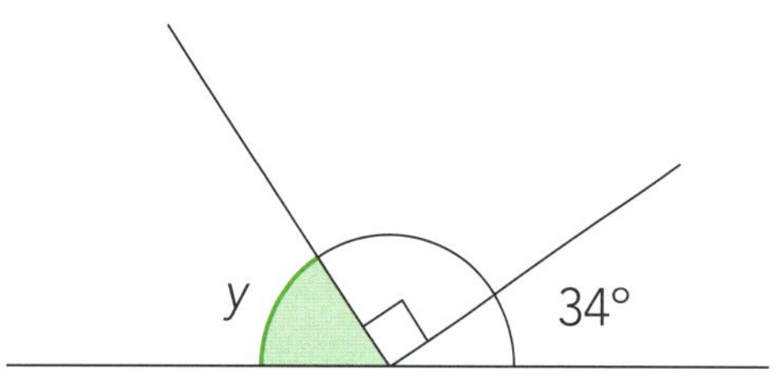

10

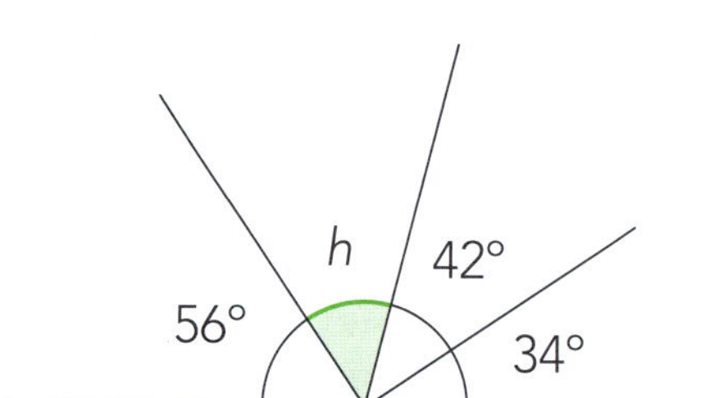

11 ∠DCE = 31° and ∠ICH = 99°.

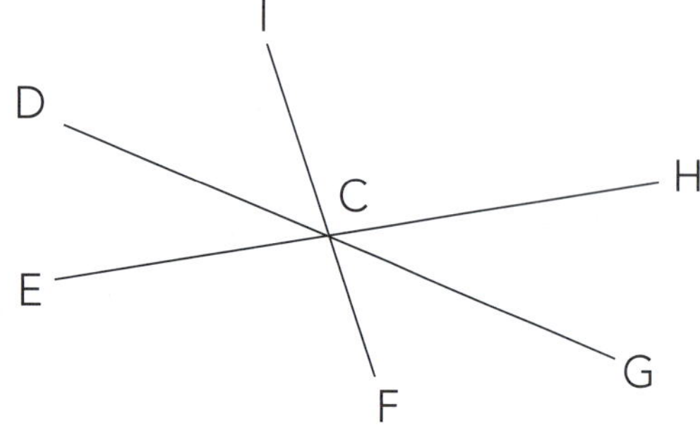

Calculate the size of ∠DCI.

12 ∠HMI = 63°, ∠IMJ = 52° and ∠KML = 31°.

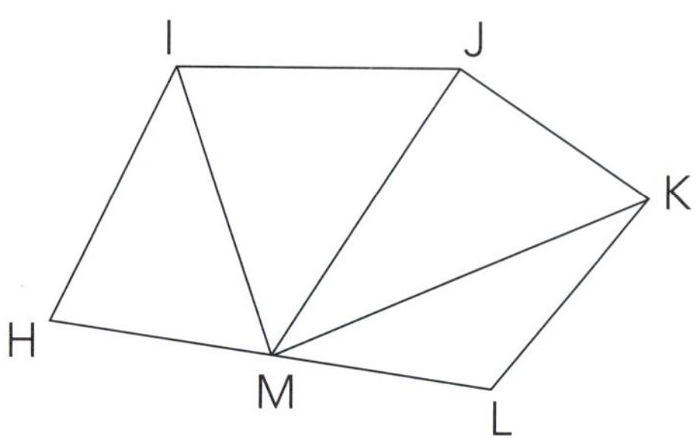

Calculate the size of ∠JMK.

 ISBN: 9780170451970

Angles at a point

- Angles at a point **add to 360°**.
- 360° is also called a **full rotation**.

Examples:

1 Find the value of y.

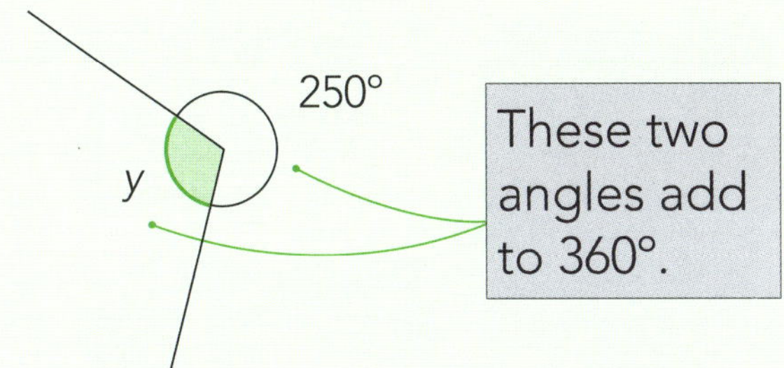

$y + 250° = 360°$
$y = 360° - 250°$
$y = 110°$

2 Find the value of x.

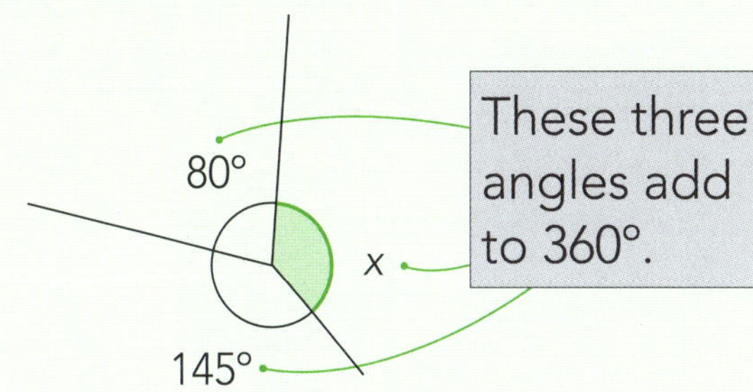

$80° + x + 145° = 360°$
$x = 360° - 80° - 145°$
$x = 135°$

Calculate the size of the marked angles.

1

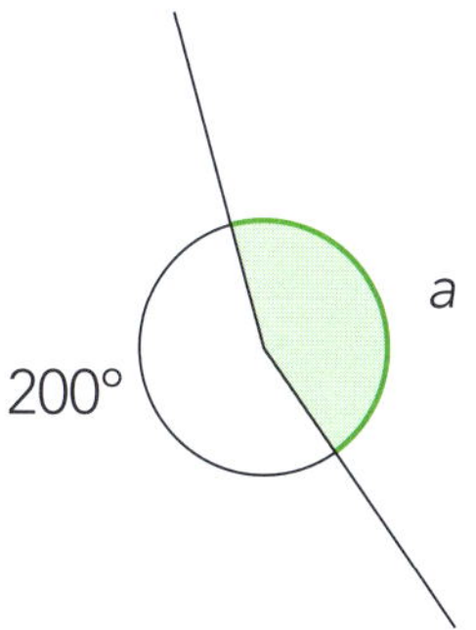

2

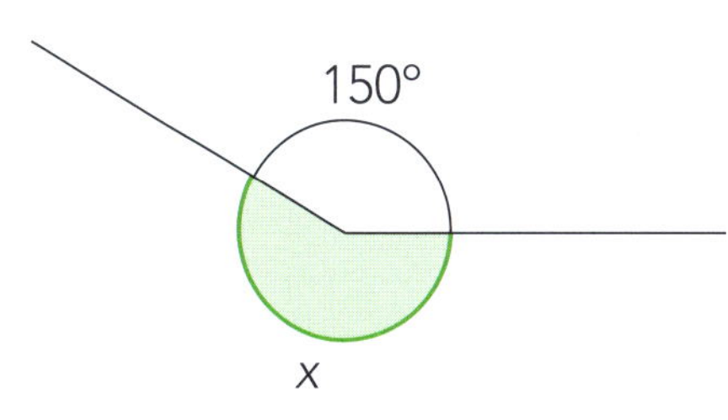

3

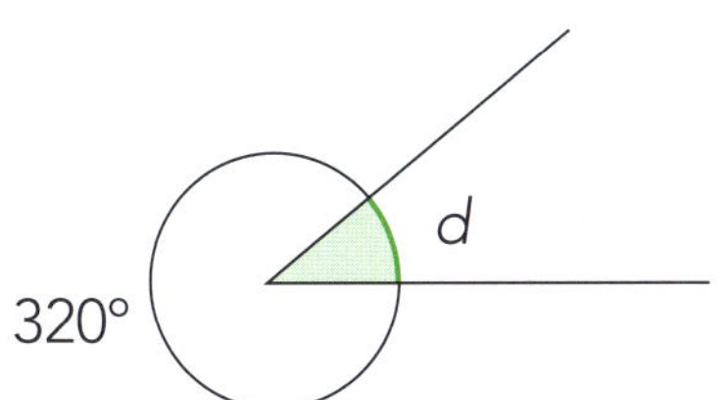

4

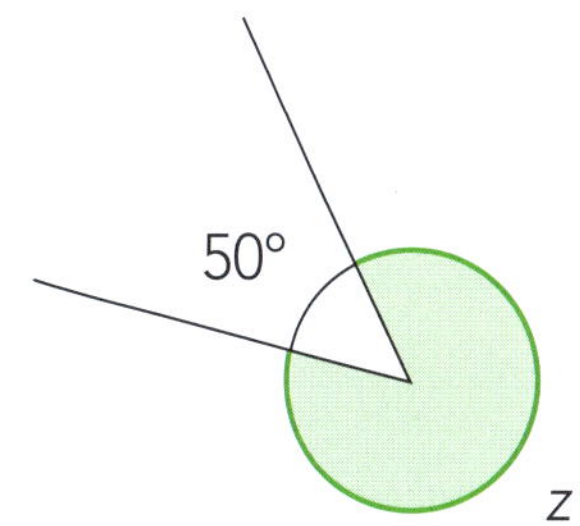

ISBN: 9780170451970

5

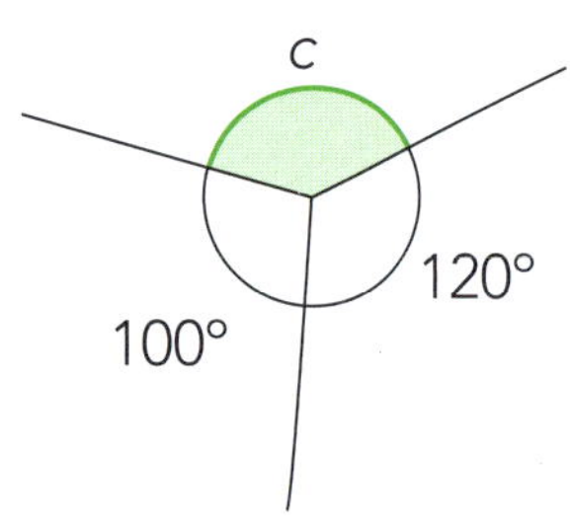

6

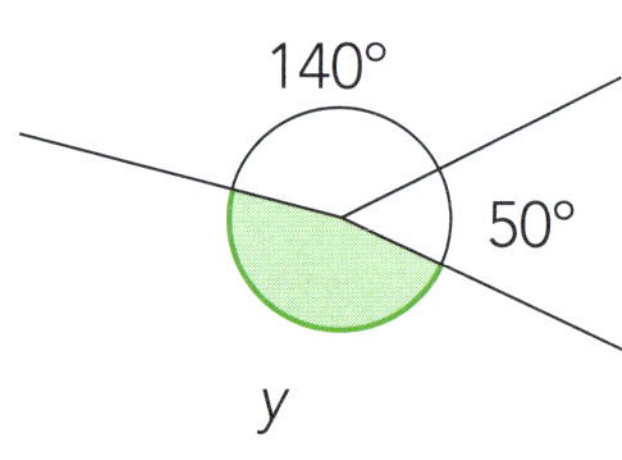

7

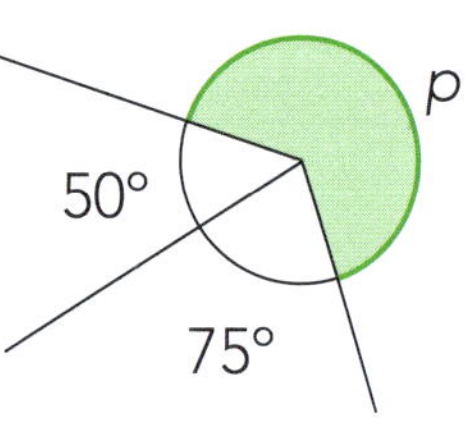

8

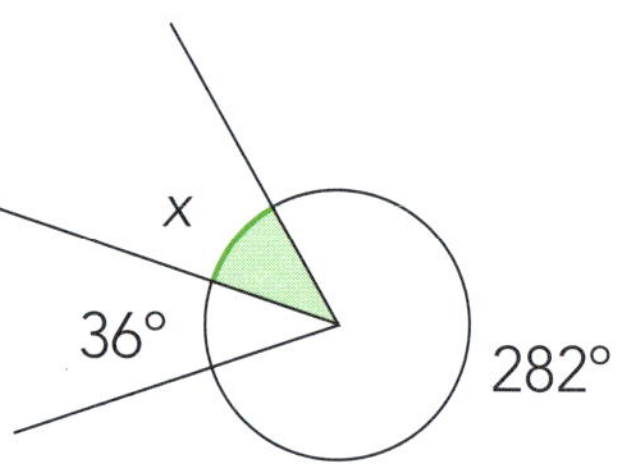

9

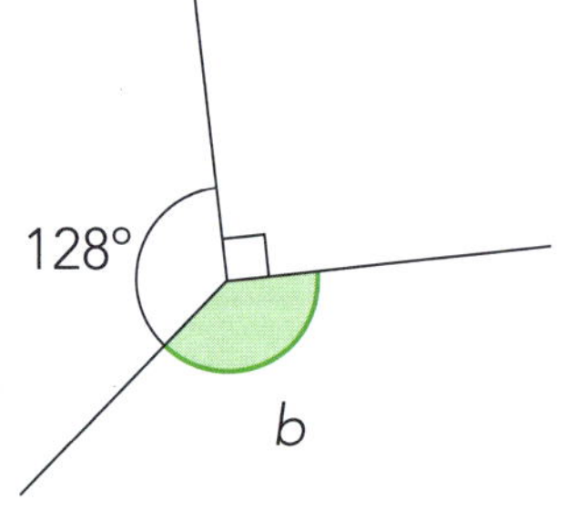

10

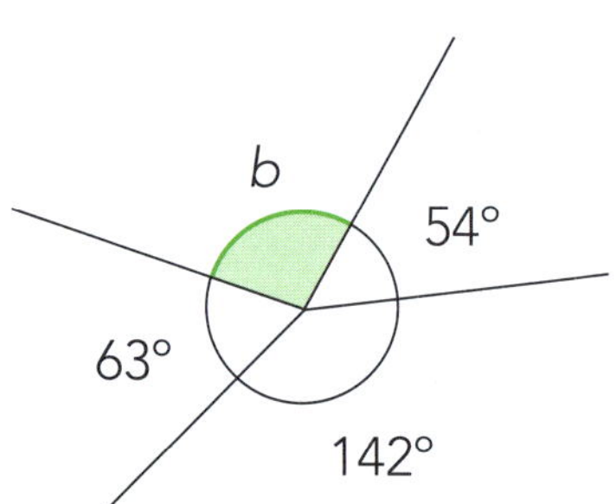

11 ∠CDA = 111° and ∠ADB = 135°.

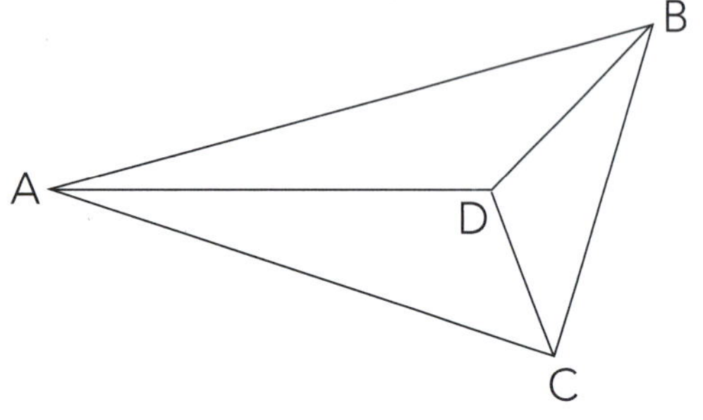

Calculate the size of ∠CDB.

12 ∠YZV = 34°, ∠WZX = 82° and ∠XZY = 131°.

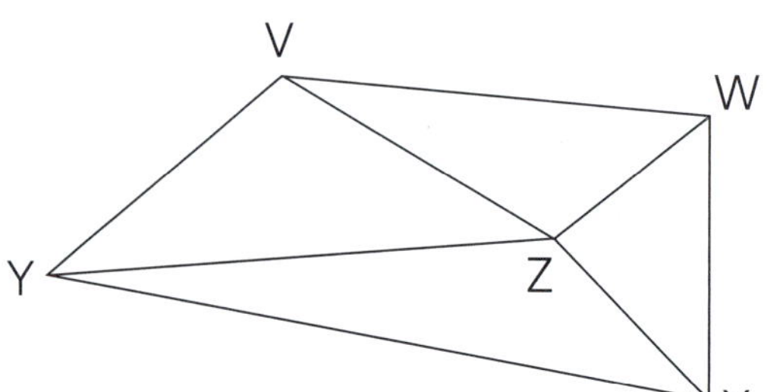

Calculate the size of ∠VZW.

ISBN: 9780170451970

Vertically opposite angles

- Vertically opposite angles are **equal**.
- Notice that these do **not** have to be vertical. They can be at any orientation.

Examples:

1 Find the value of x.

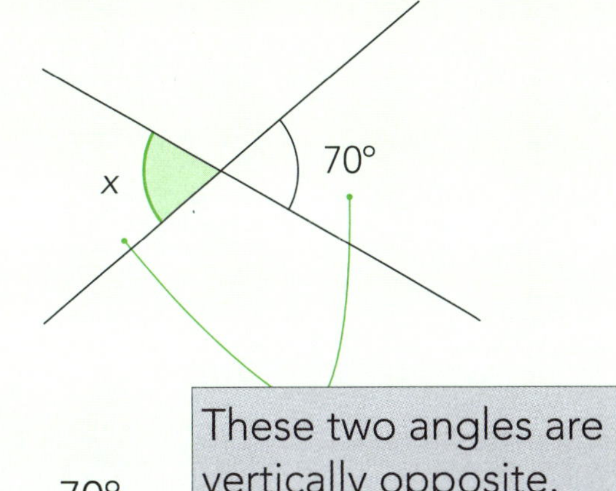

$x = 70°$

2 Find the value of z.

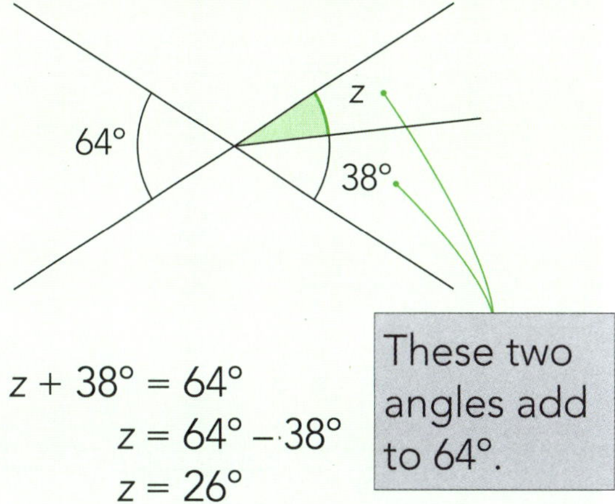

$z + 38° = 64°$
$z = 64° - 38°$
$z = 26°$

Calculate the size of the marked angles.

1

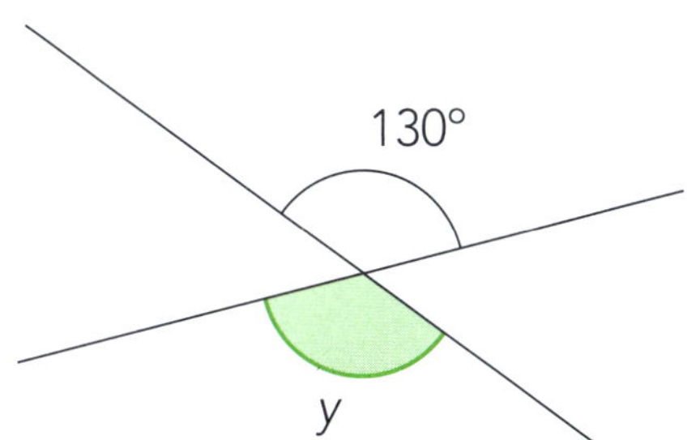

2

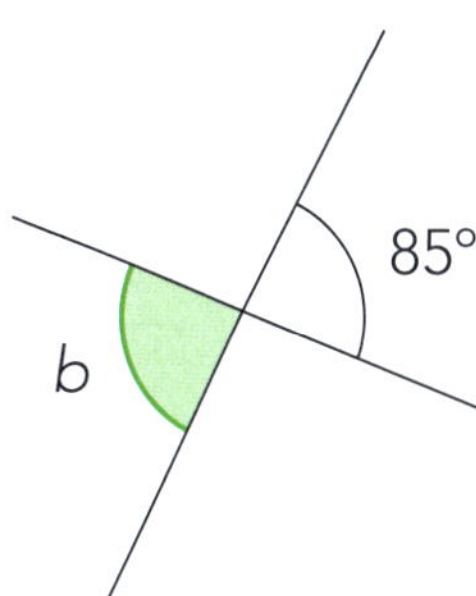

3

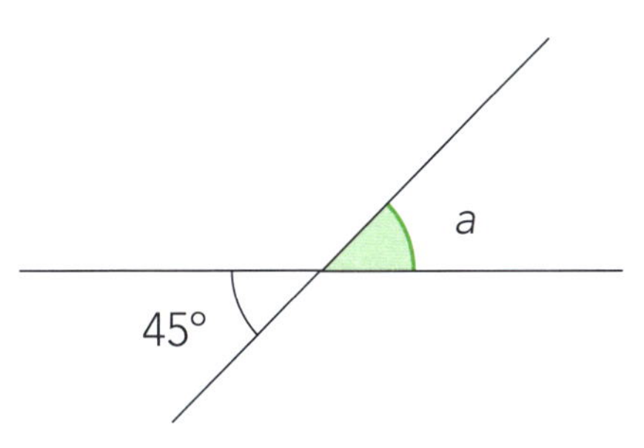

4

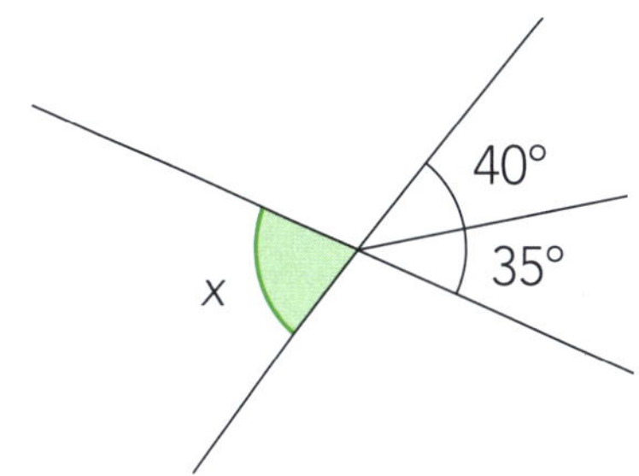

ISBN: 9780170451970

5

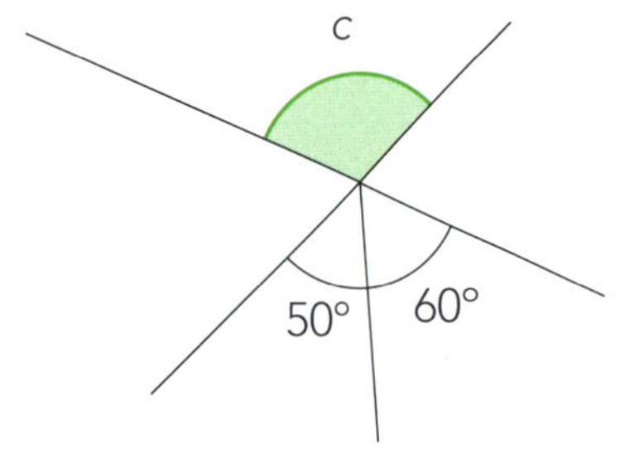

6

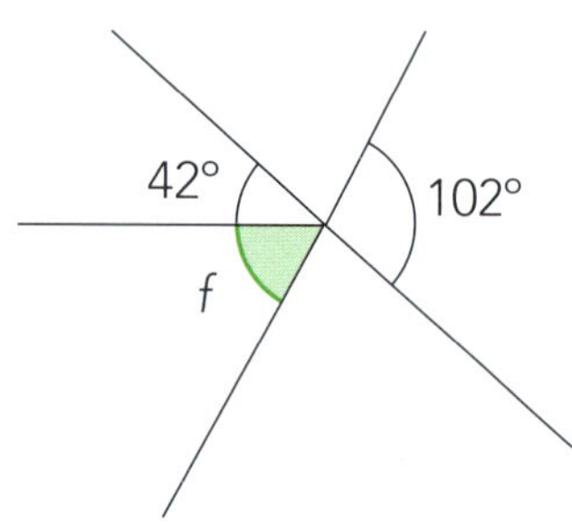

7

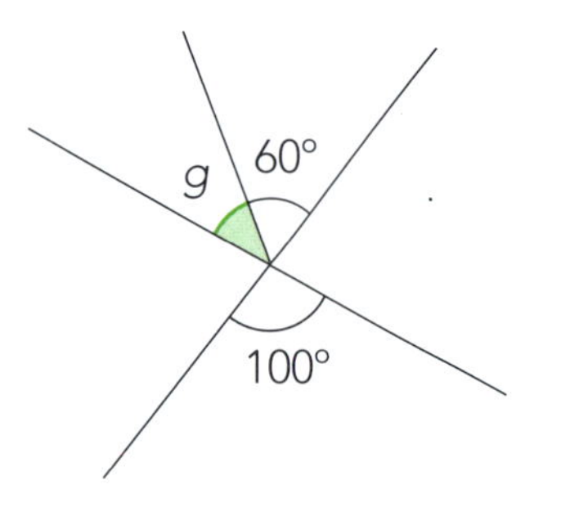

8

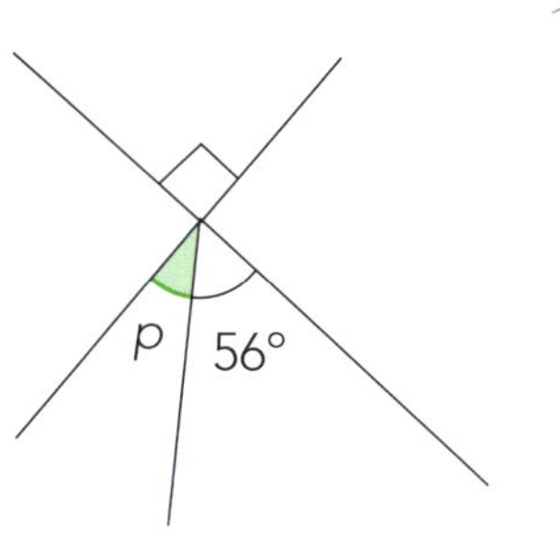

9

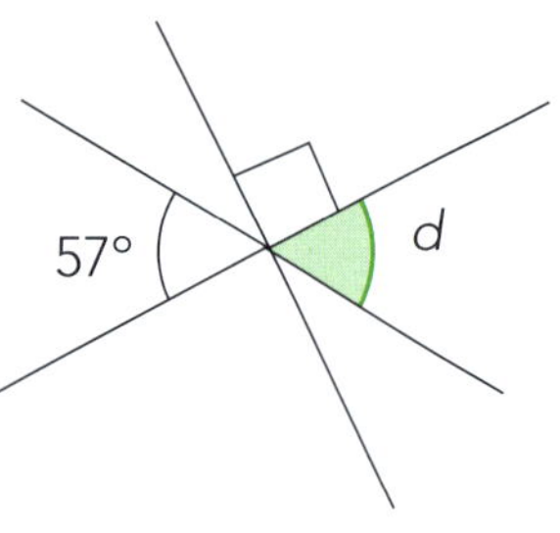

10

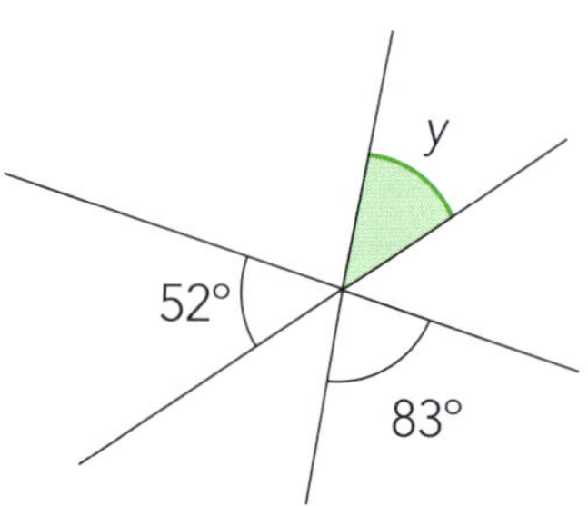

11 ∠LPM = 83° and ∠KPO = 128°.

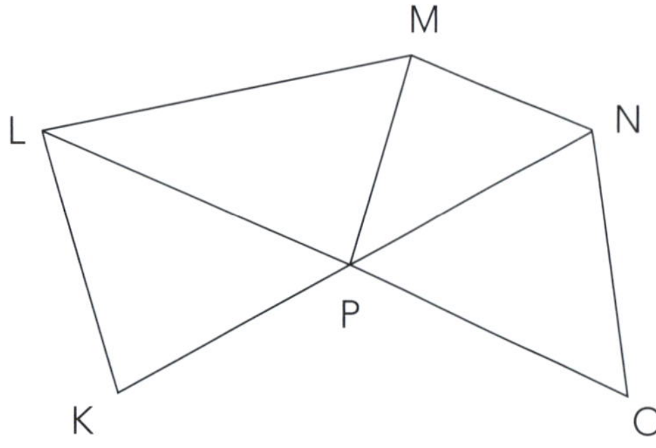

Calculate the size of ∠MPN.

12 ∠RXS = 33°, ∠SXT = 40° and ∠UXV = 52°.

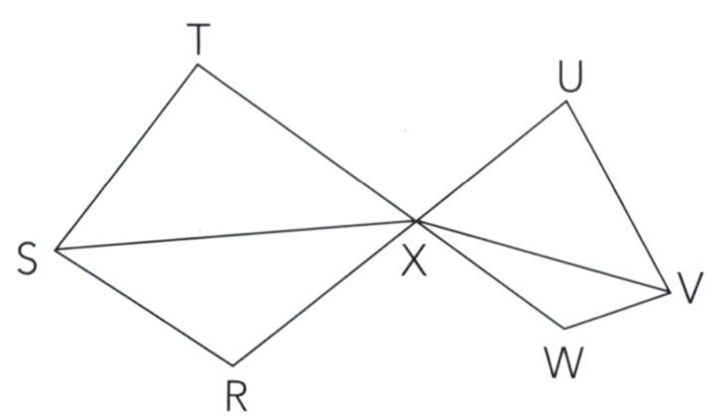

Calculate the size of ∠WXV.

 ISBN: 9780170451970

Angles in a triangle

- The angles in a triangle **add to 180°**.

Examples:

1 Find the value of y.

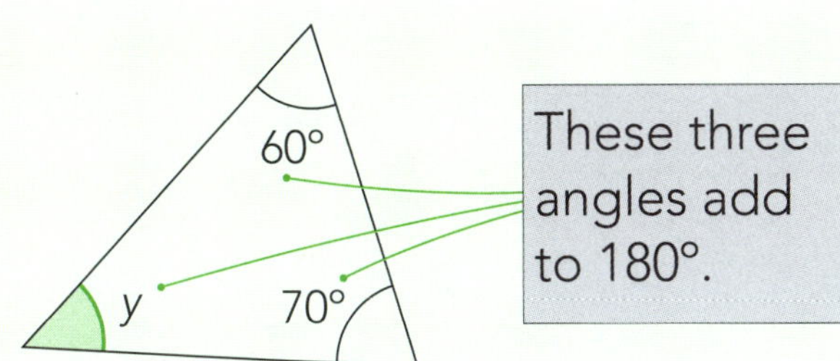

$y + 60° + 70° = 180°$

$y = 180° - 60° - 70°$

$y = 50°$

2 Find the value of x.

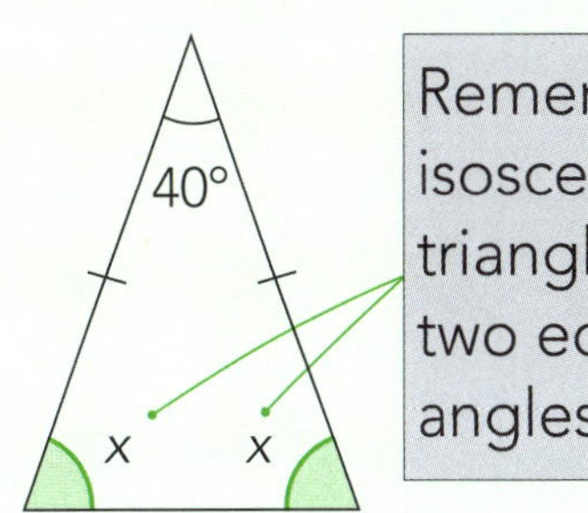

$x + x + 40° = 180°$

$2x = 180° - 40°$

$2x = 140°$

$x = 70°$

Calculate the size of the marked angles.

1

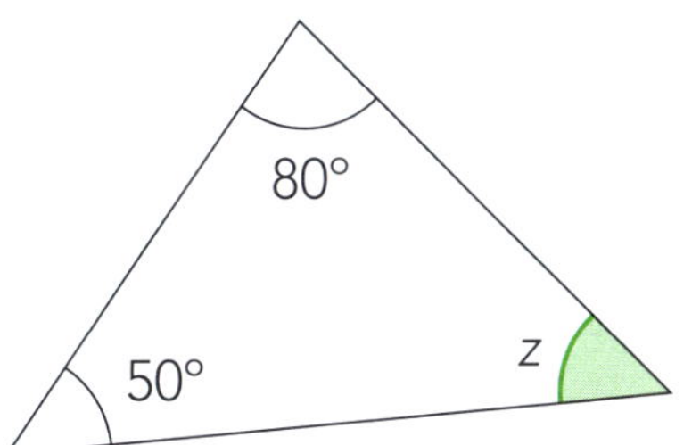

2

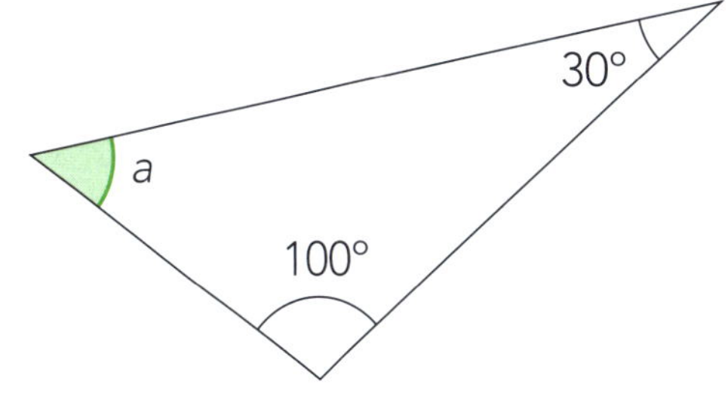

3

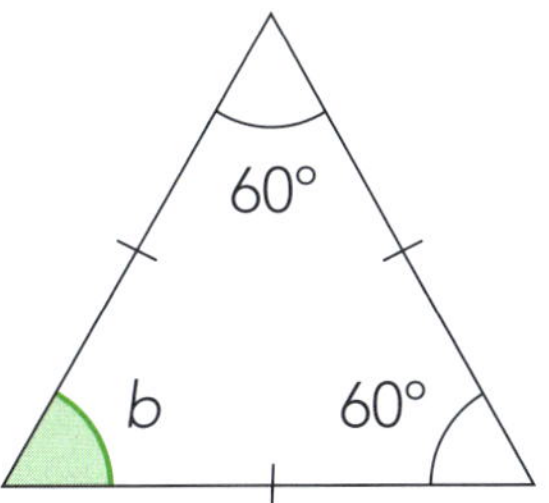

4

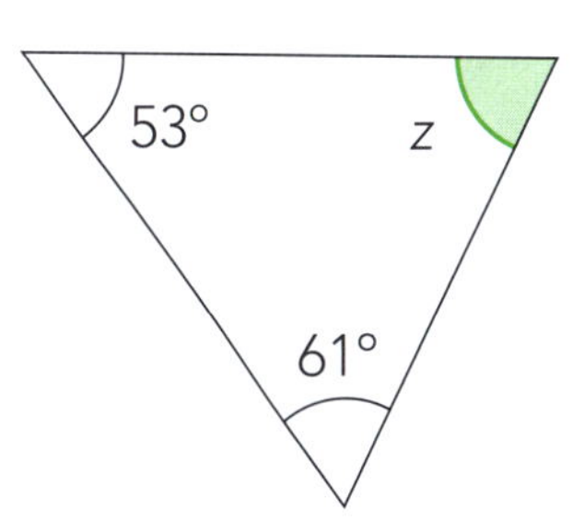

5

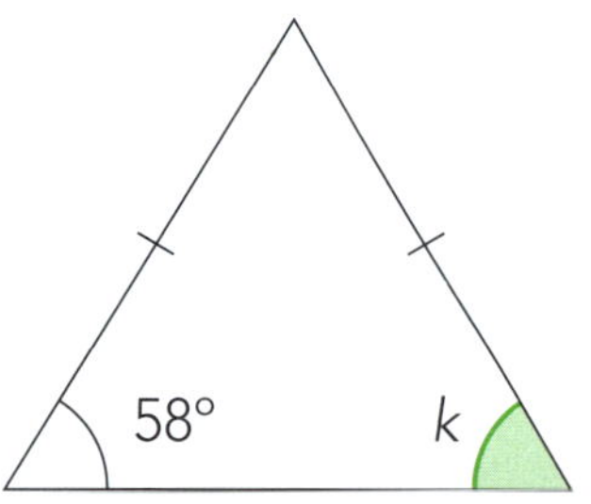

6

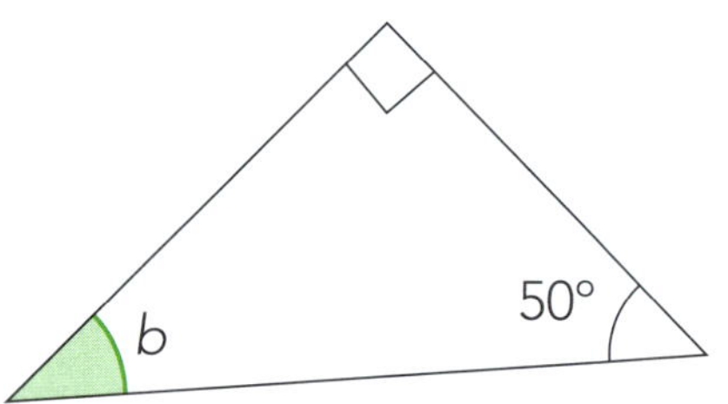

7

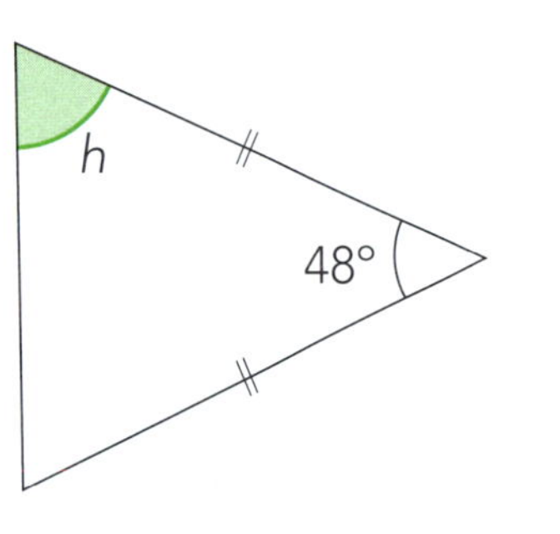

8

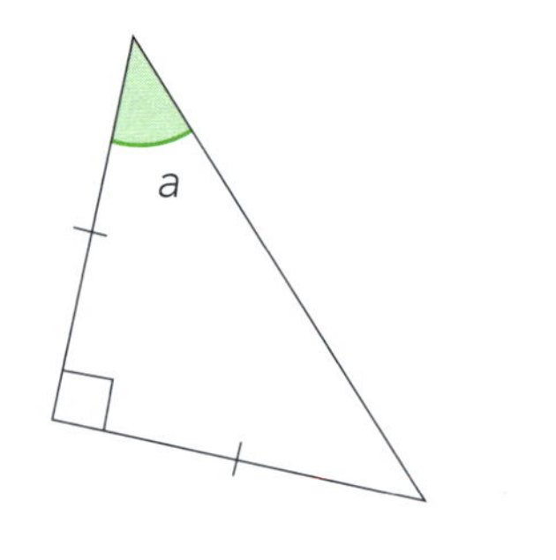

9

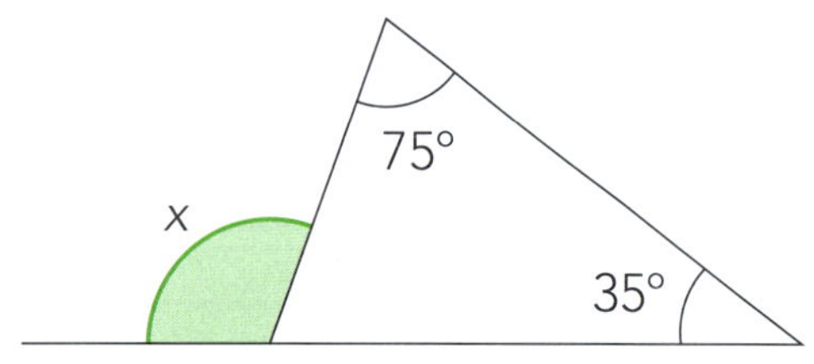

10

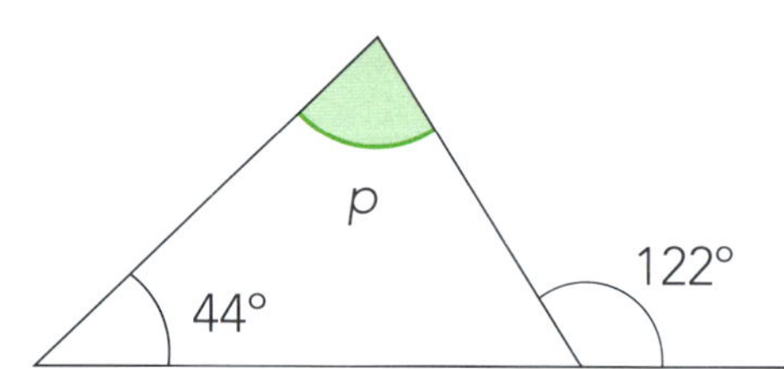

11 ∠HEF = 68°, ∠EFH = 26°, ∠HFG = 85° and ∠FGH = 60°.

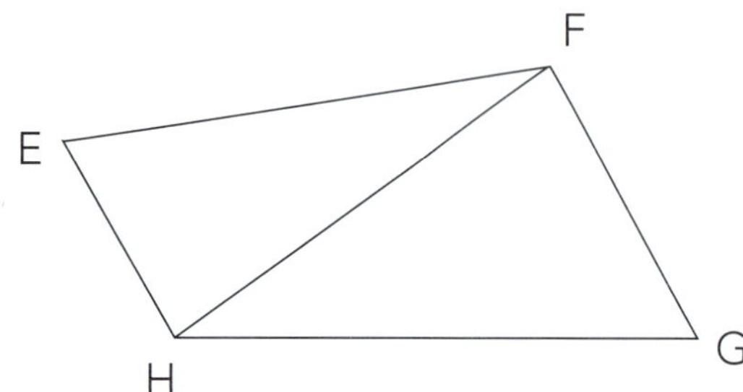

Calculate the size of ∠EHG.

12 ∠VST = 34°, ∠VTU = 58° and ∠VUT = 49°.

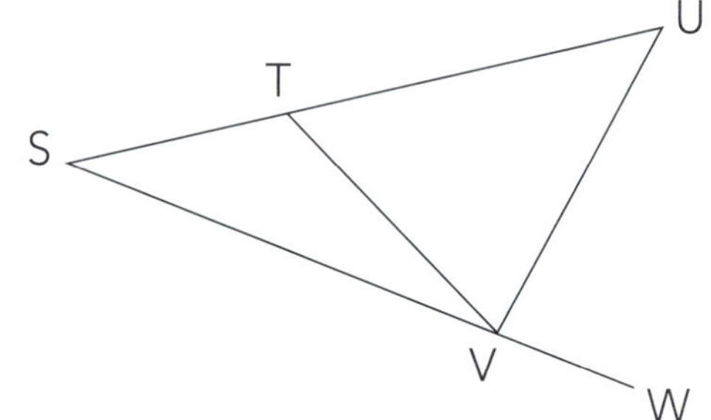

Calculate the size of ∠UVW.

 ISBN: 9780170451970

Angles in a quadrilateral

- A quadrilateral is any closed shape (no gaps) with exactly **four straight sides**.
- The four angles in a quadrilateral **add to 360°**.

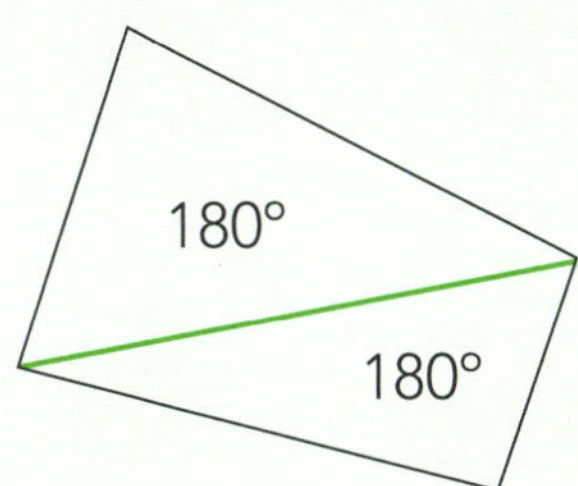

You could think of a quadrilateral as being made up of two triangles.

180° + 180° = 360°

Examples:

1 Find the value of x.

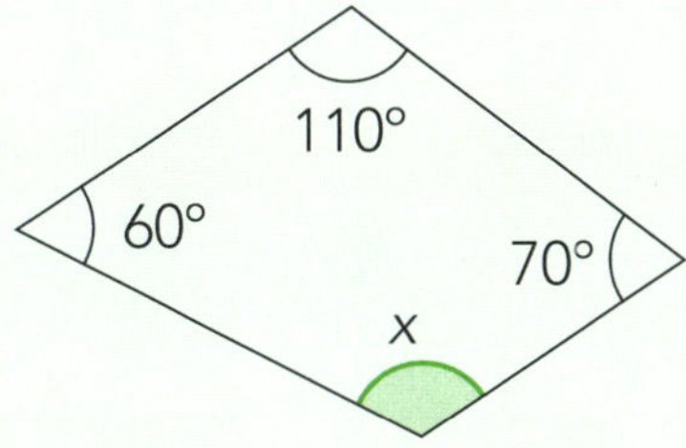

$x + 60° + 110° + 70° = 360°$
$x = 360° - 60° - 110° - 70°$
$x = 120°$

2 Find the value of y.

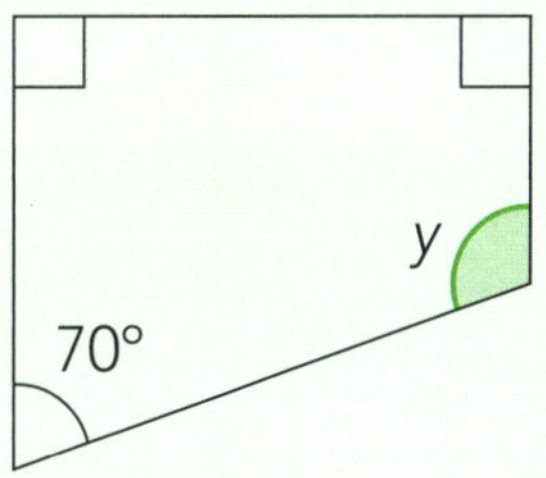

$y + 70° + 90° + 90° = 360°$
$y = 360° - 70° - 180°$
$y = 110°$

Calculate the size of the marked angles.

1

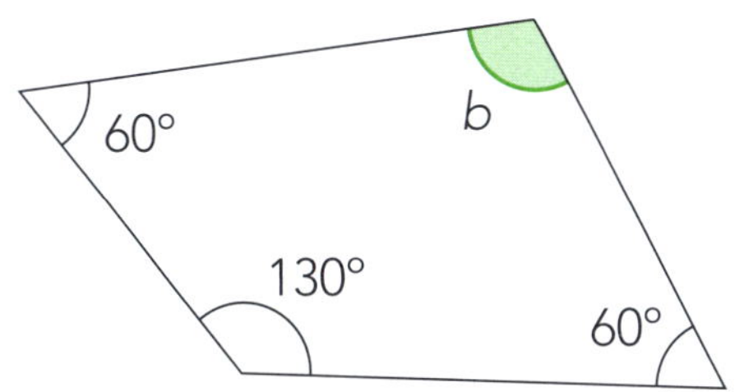

2

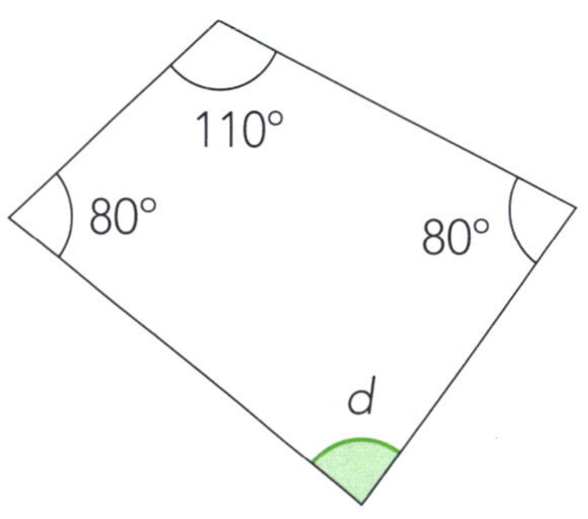

ISBN: 9780170451970

3

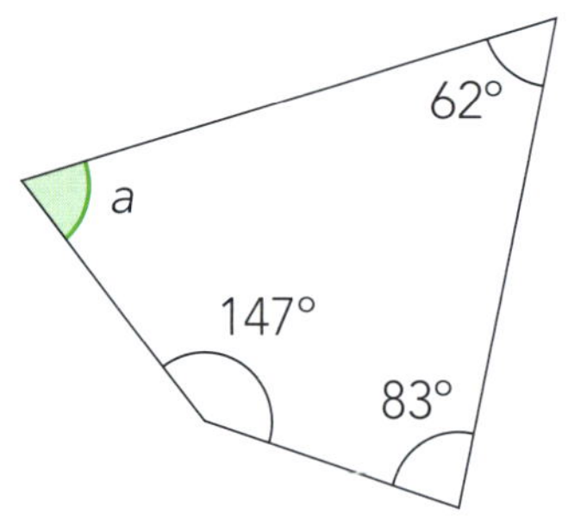

4

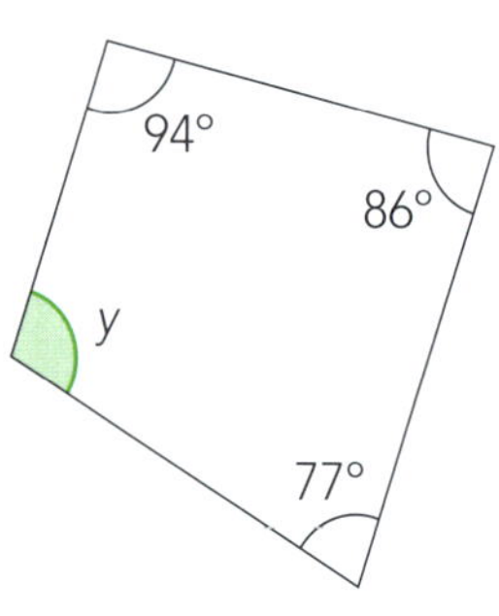

5

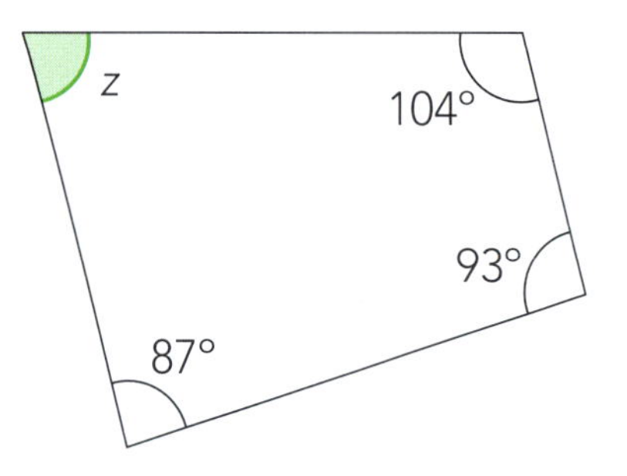

6

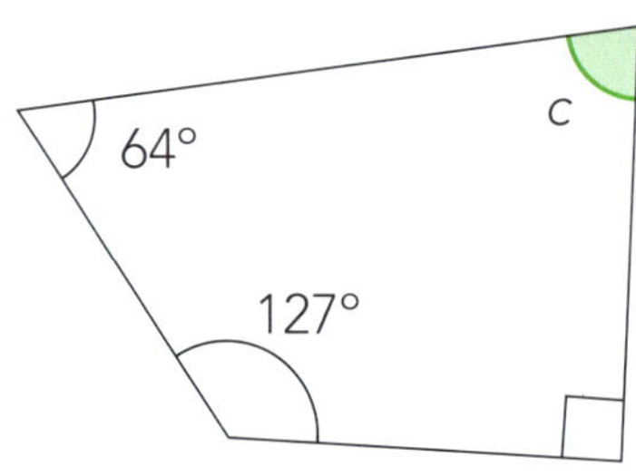

7

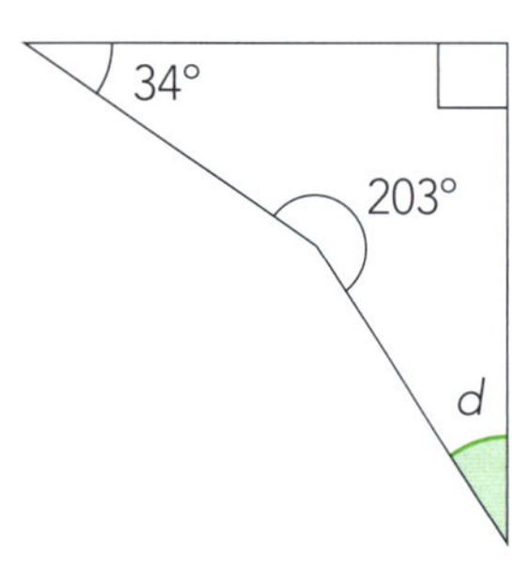

8

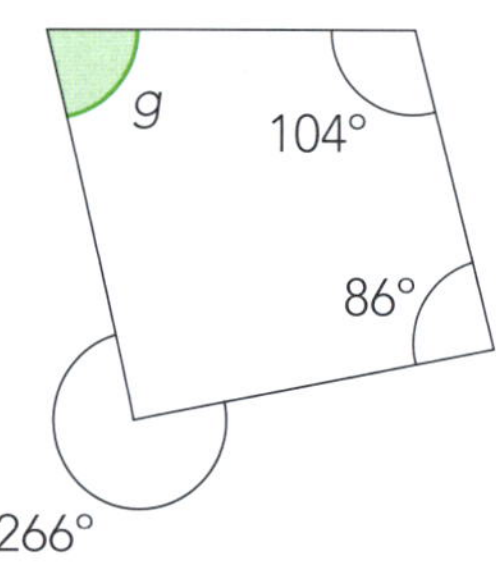

9 $\angle DEF = 70°$, reflex $\angle FGH = 231°$ and reflex $\angle GHE = 308°$.

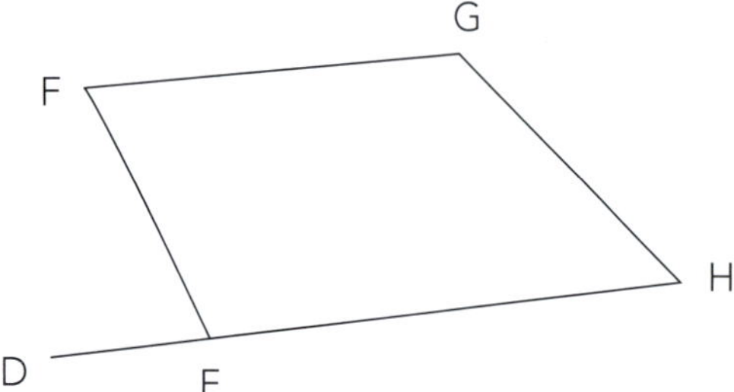

Calculate the size of $\angle EFG$.

10 Reflex $\angle JKL = 252°$, $\angle MLN = 60°$ and $\angle ONP = 72°$.

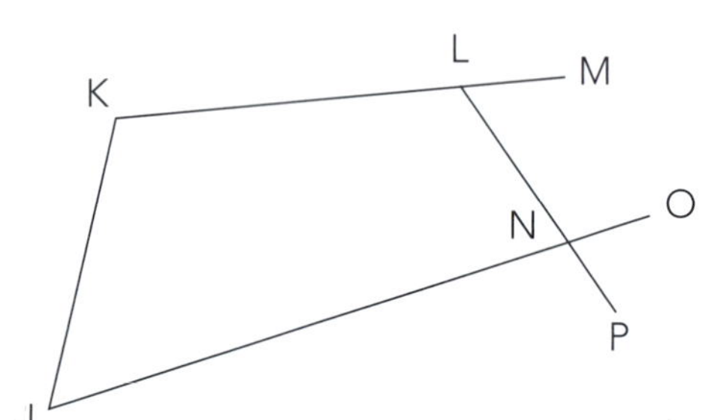

Calculate the size of $\angle KJN$.

 ISBN: 9780170451970

Mixing it up

Calculate the size of the missing angles.

1

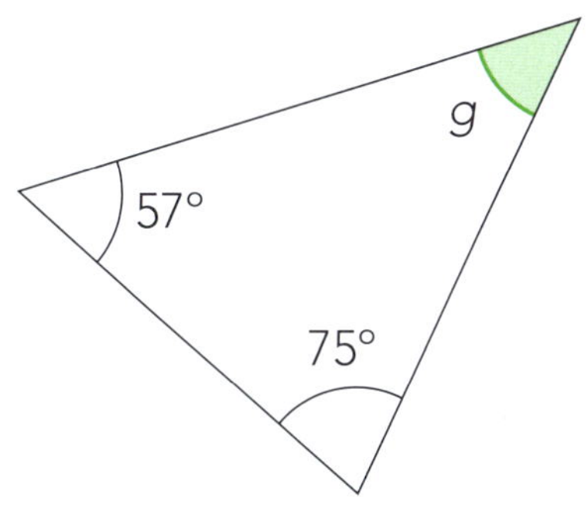

2

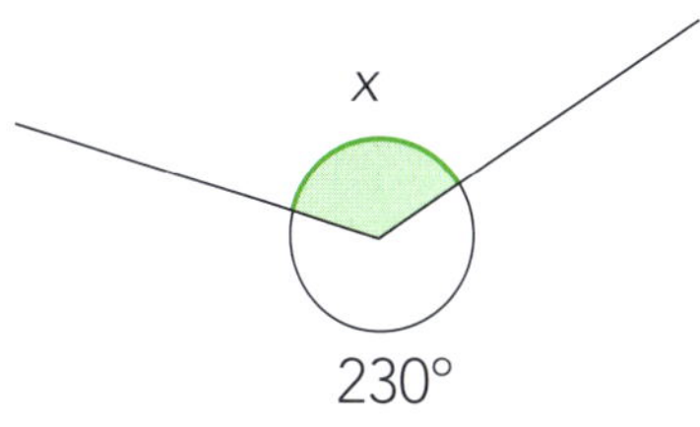

3

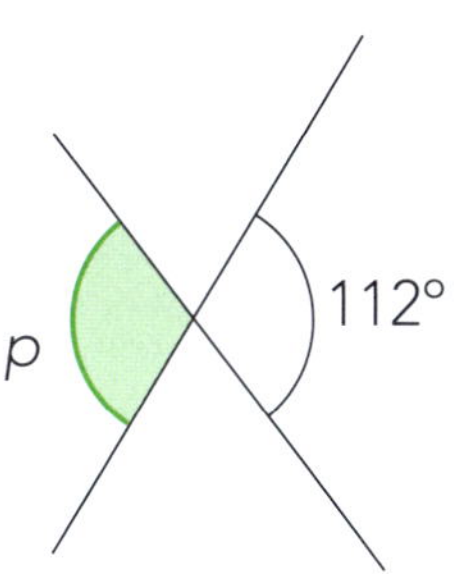

4

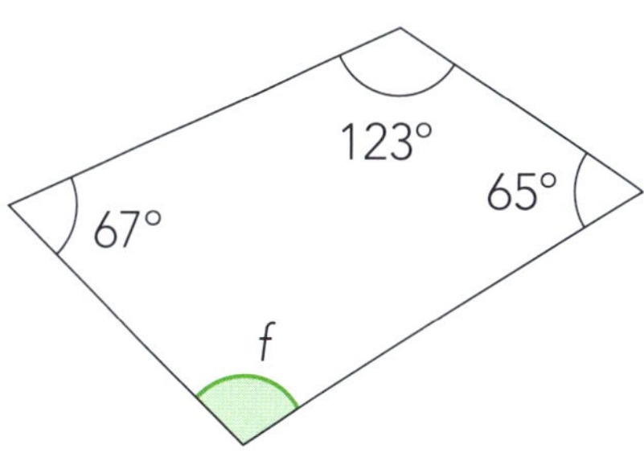

5

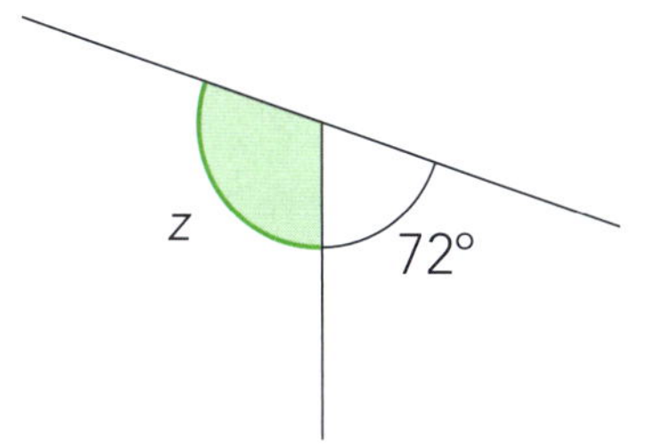

6

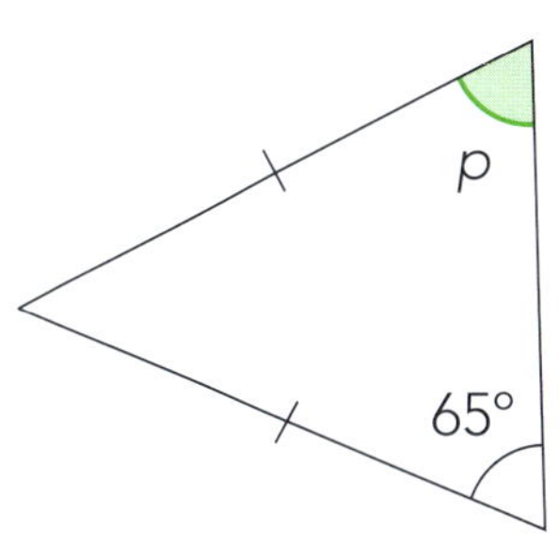

ISBN: 9780170451970

7

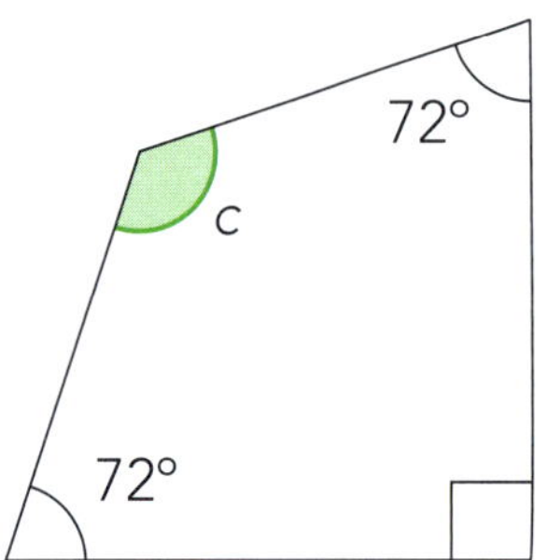

8

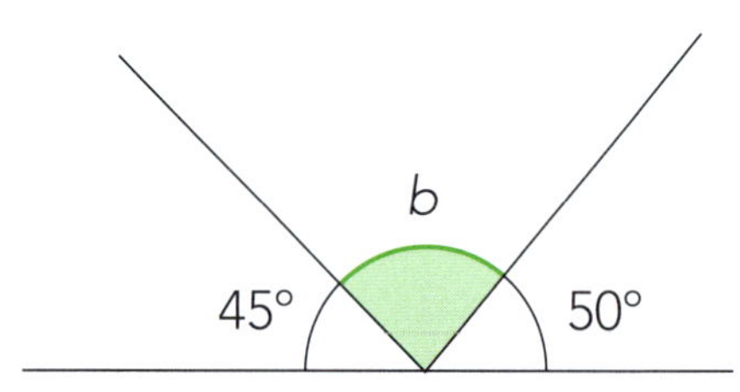

9

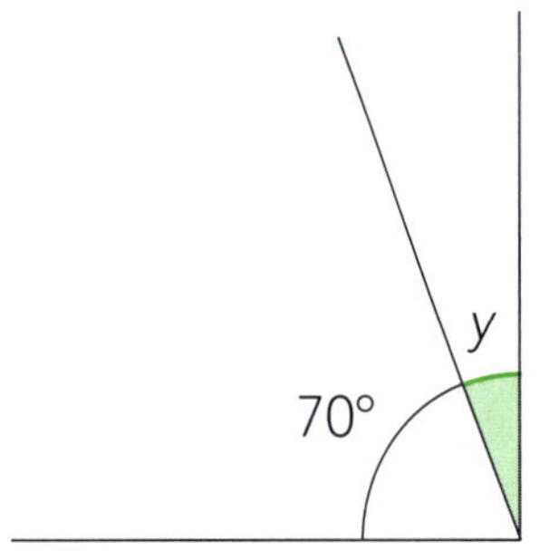

10

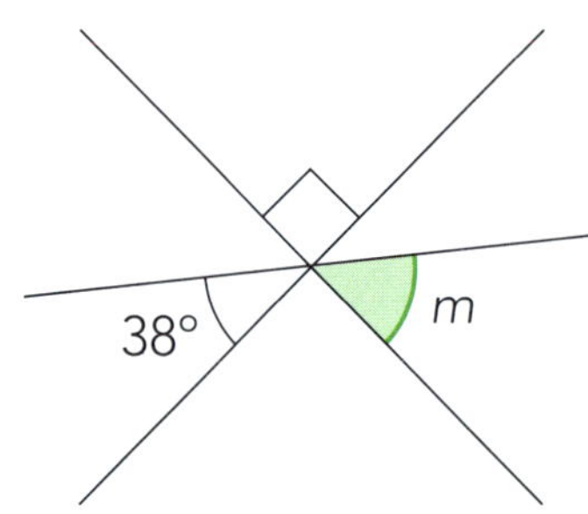

11

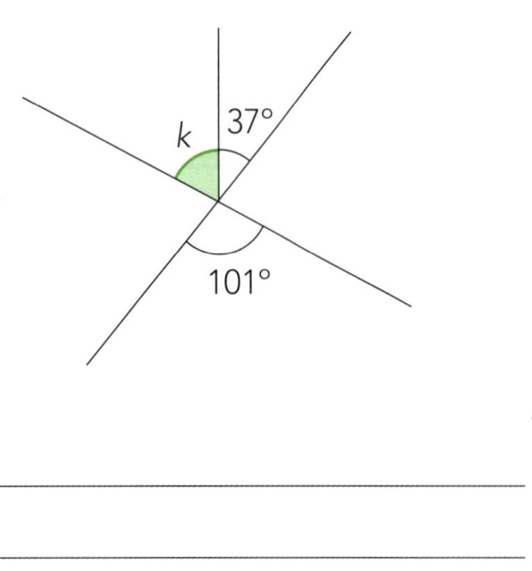

12

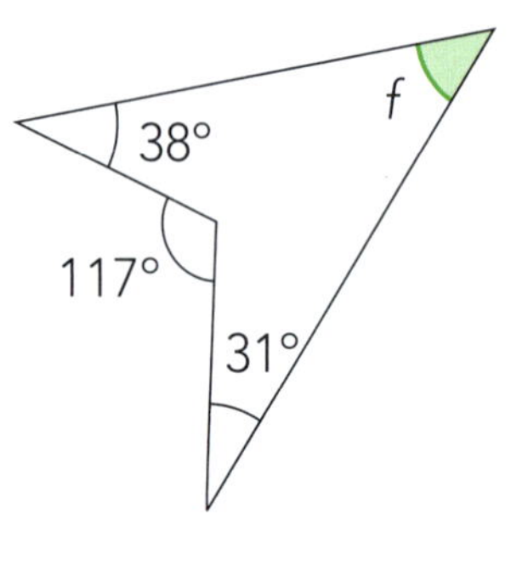

 ISBN: 9780170451970

Challenge 2

Calculate the missing angles in this rectangular figure.

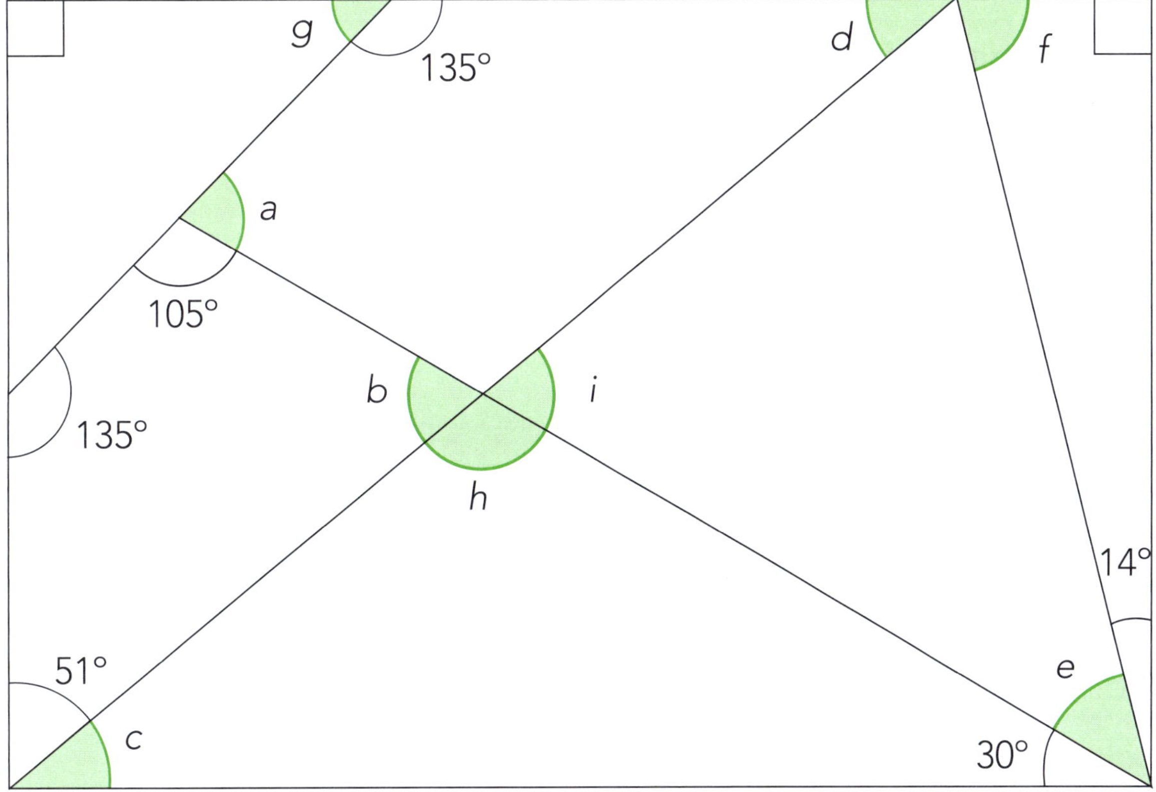

a = ______________
= ______________

b = ______________
= ______________

c = ______________
= ______________

d = ______________
= ______________

e = ______________
= ______________

f = ______________
= ______________

g = ______________
= ______________

h = ______________
= ______________

i = ______________
= ______________

ISBN: 9780170451970

2D and 3D shapes

2D and 3D language

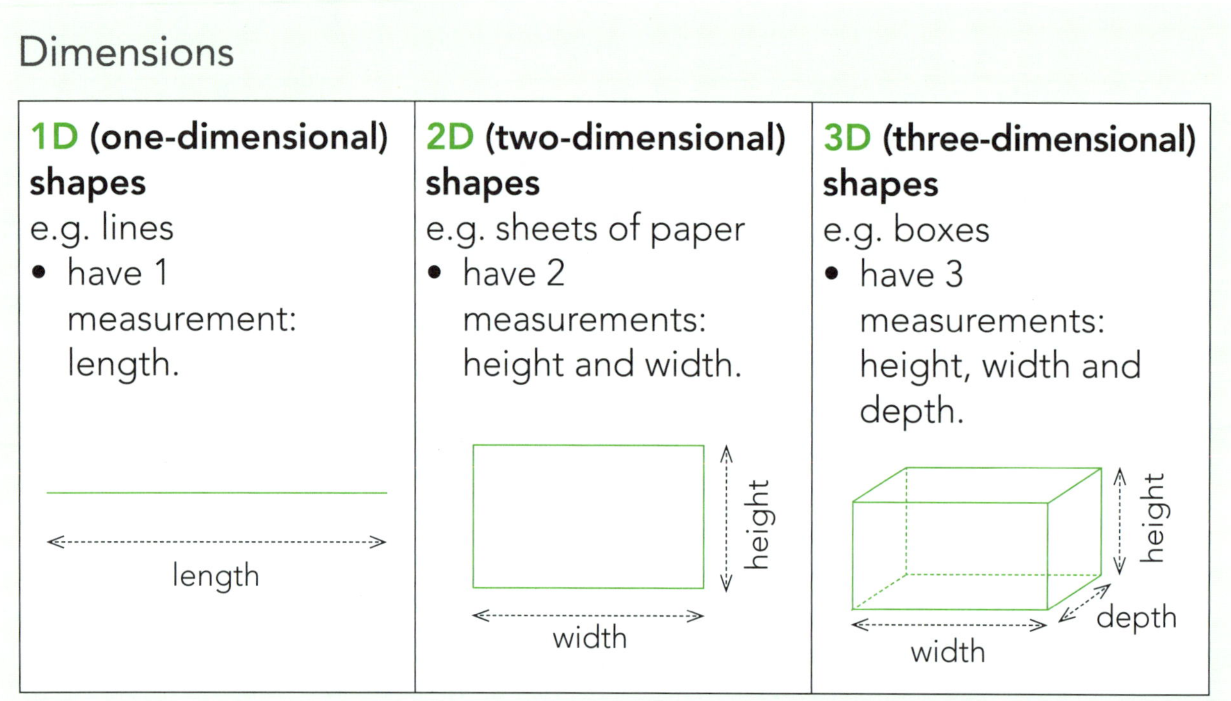

Dimensions

1D (one-dimensional) shapes	**2D (two-dimensional) shapes**	**3D (three-dimensional) shapes**
e.g. lines • have 1 measurement: length.	e.g. sheets of paper • have 2 measurements: height and width.	e.g. boxes • have 3 measurements: height, width and depth.

Circle the correct term for the shapes these figures represent.

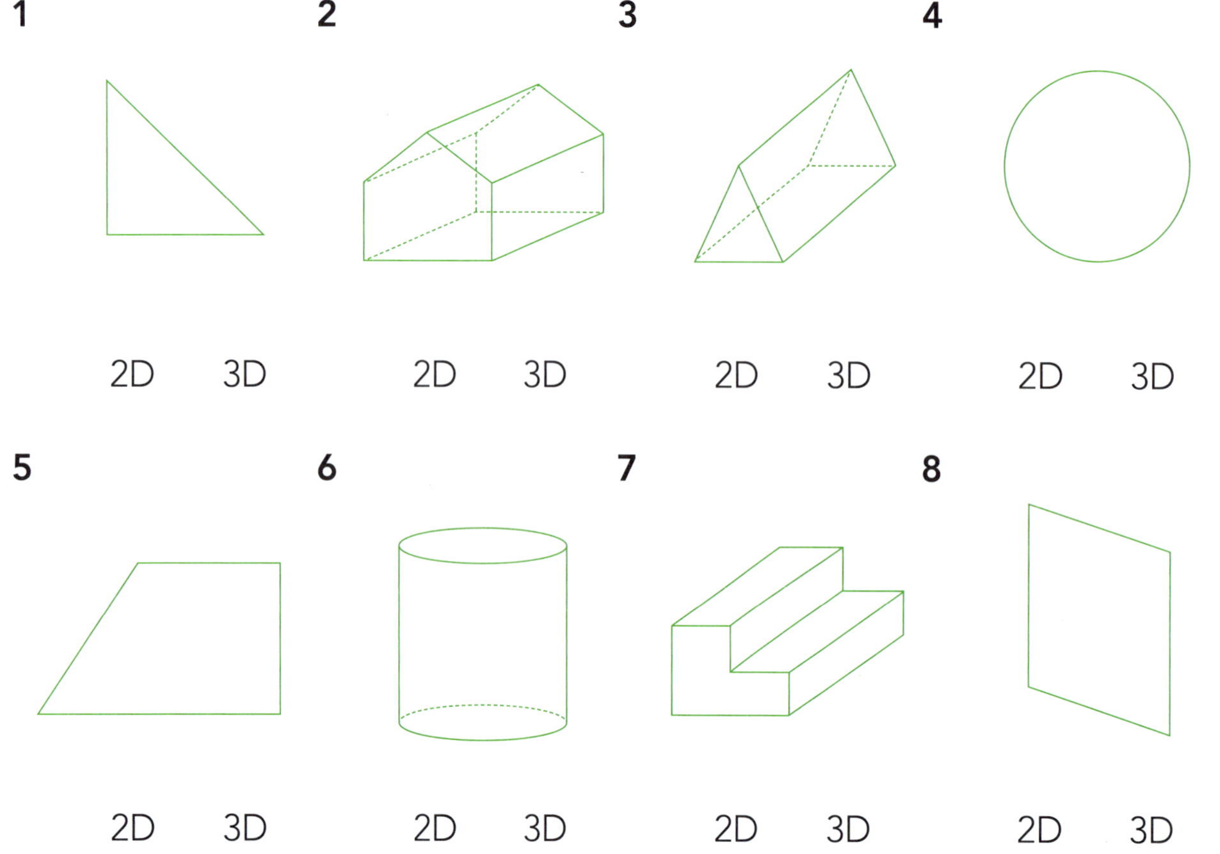

1 2D 3D

2 2D 3D

3 2D 3D

4 2D 3D

5 2D 3D

6 2D 3D

7 2D 3D

8 2D 3D

 ISBN: 9780170451970

Vertices, faces, sides and edges

- We talk about **one vertex** or **several vertices**.

2D shapes have vertices, one face and sides.

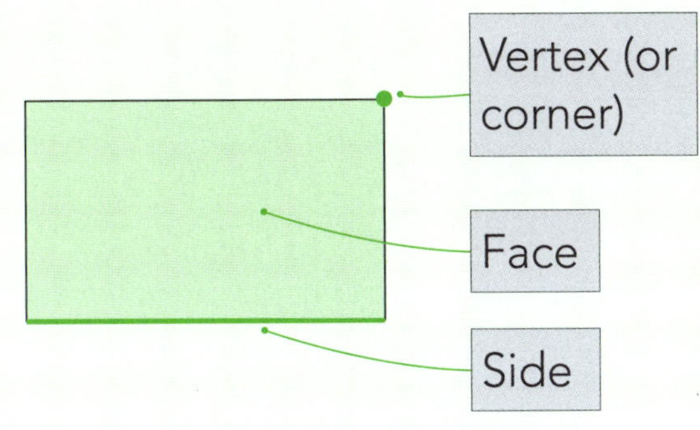

A rectangle has **4 sides** and **4 vertices**.

3D shapes have vertices, faces and edges.

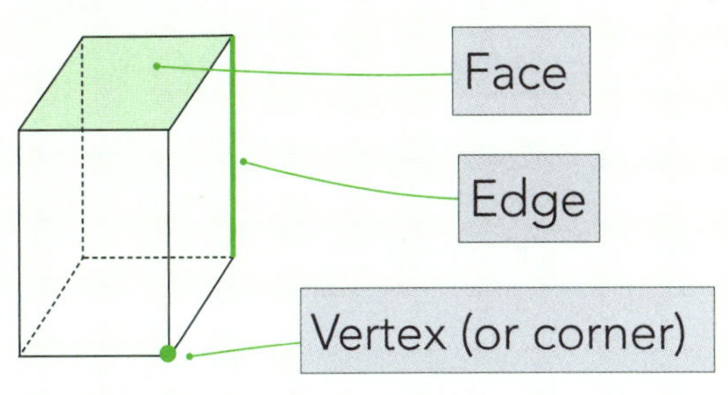

A cube has **6 faces**, **8 vertices** and **12 edges**.

Write down the numbers of vertices, edges and faces these 3D shapes have.

1

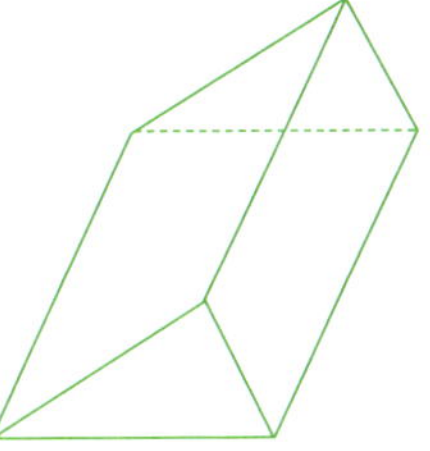

Vertices ________

Edges ________

Faces ________

2

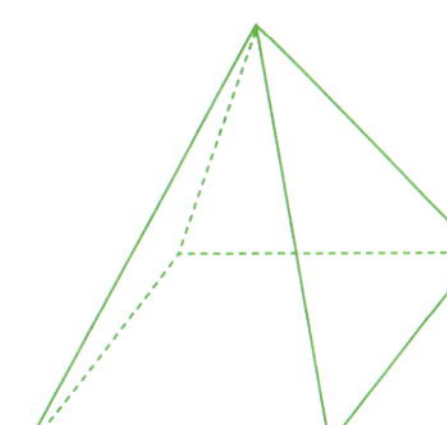

Vertices ________

Edges ________

Faces ________

3

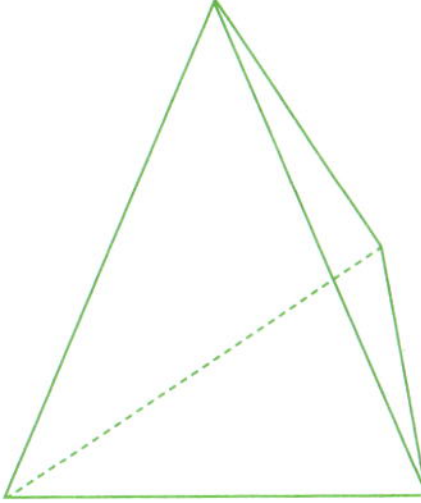

Vertices ________

Edges ________

Faces ________

4

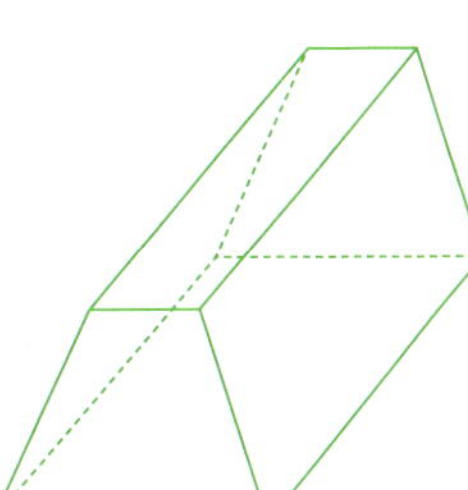

Vertices ________

Edges ________

Faces ________

5

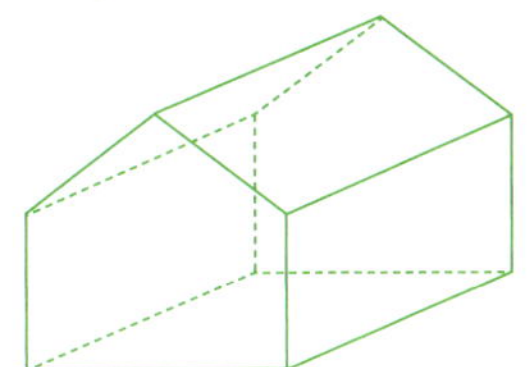

Vertices ________

Edges ________

Faces ________

6

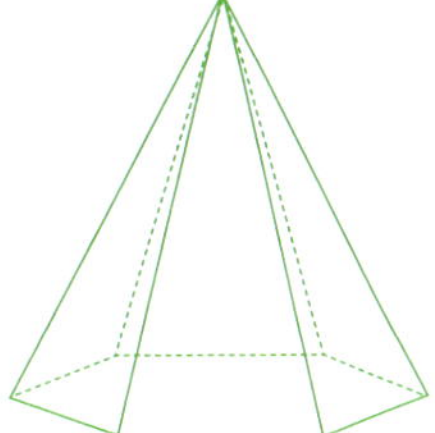

Vertices ________

Edges ________

Faces ________

ISBN: 9780170451970

Naming 3D shapes

- Some 3D shapes have specific names.

Use the terms in the box and match them to the shapes below. Some terms need to be used more than once.

Cylinder	Cube	Sphere
Pyramid	Cone	Cuboid

1 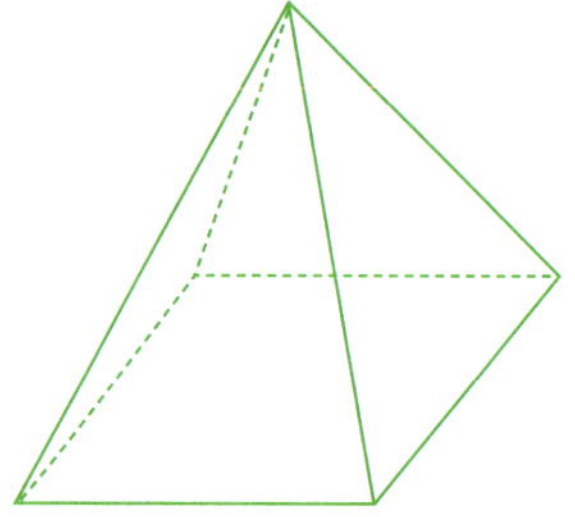

____

2 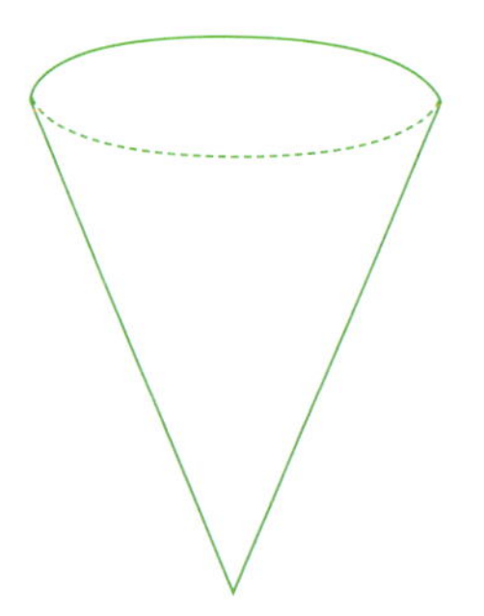

____

3 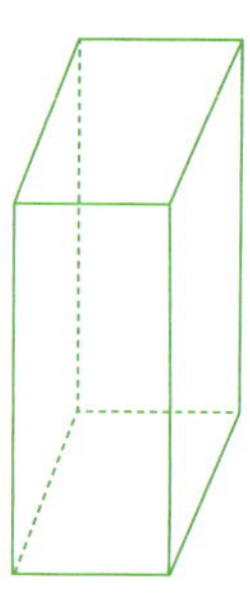

____

4 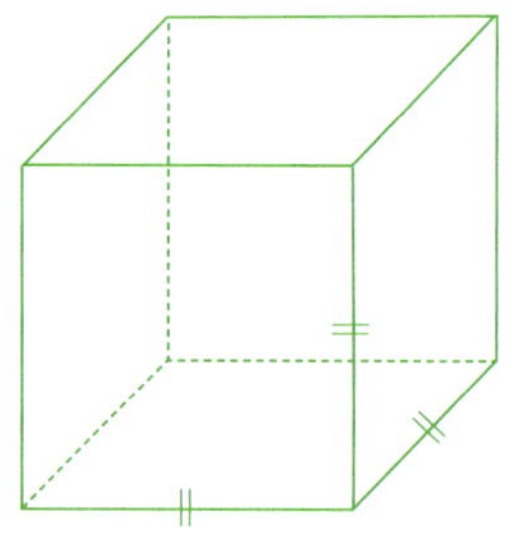

____

5 

____

6 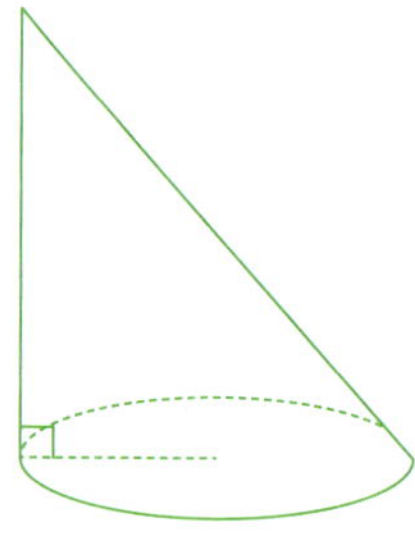

____

7 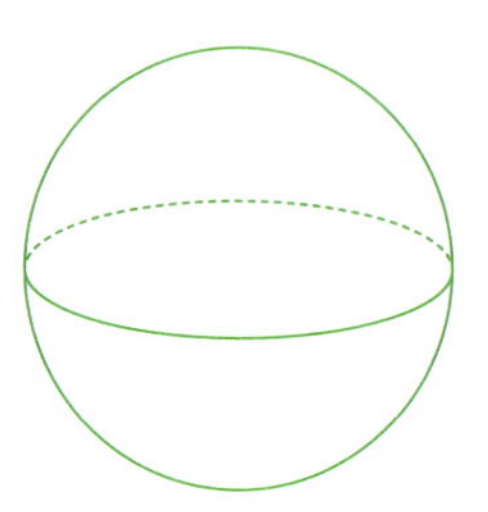

____

8 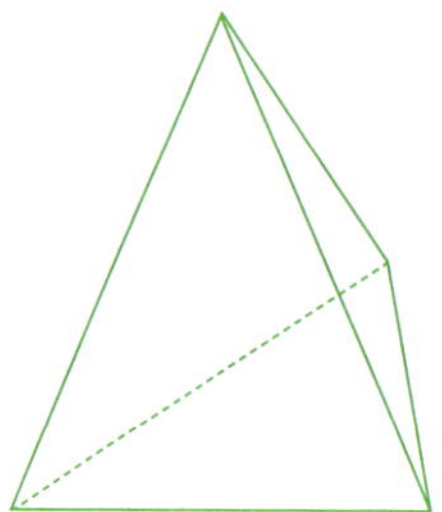

____

9 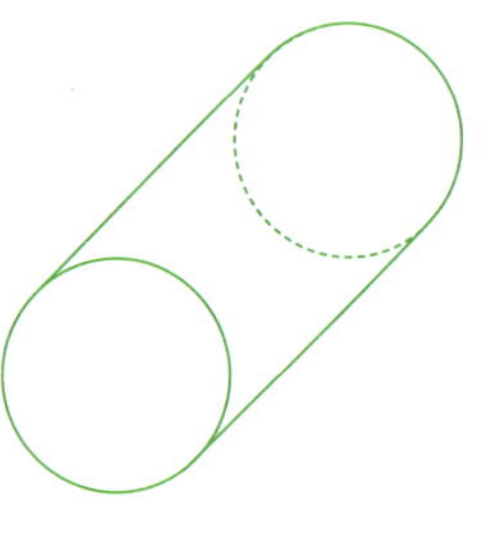

____

 ISBN: 9780170451970

Nets

- Nets are the two-dimensional version of three-dimensional shapes.
- When nets are cut out and folded correctly, they form a solid.

Example:
A closed cube is made up of 6 squares, which could be unfolded to look like the net on the far right.

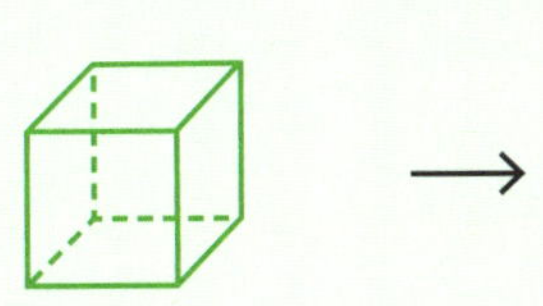

→

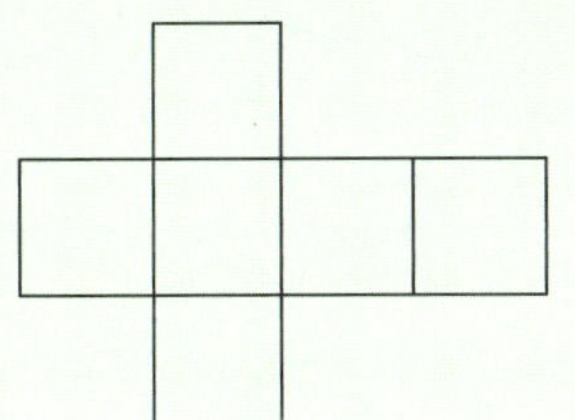

1 Complete the table.

Shape name	Picture	Number of rectangular or square faces	Number of triangular faces
Cube		6	0
Triangular prism			
Square-based pyramid			
Tetrahedron			
Octahedron			

ISBN: 9780170451970

2 Match each net to the solid it would make. The nets are not drawn to scale.

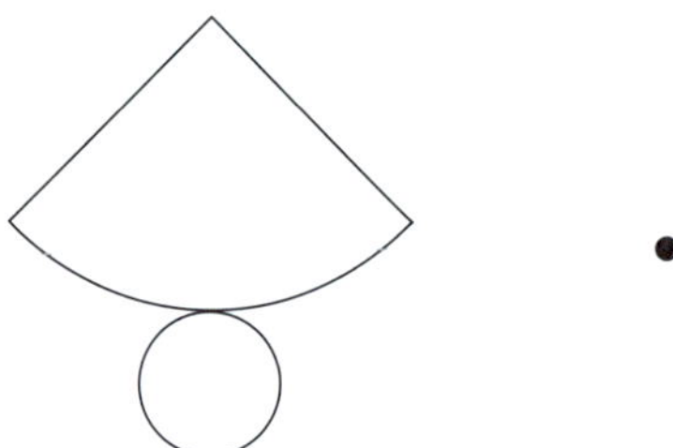
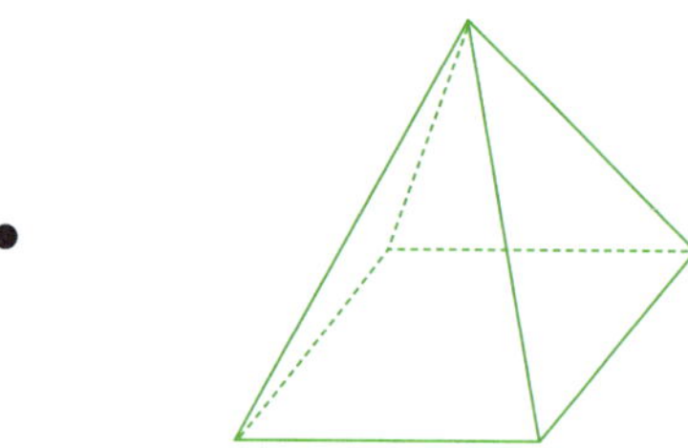
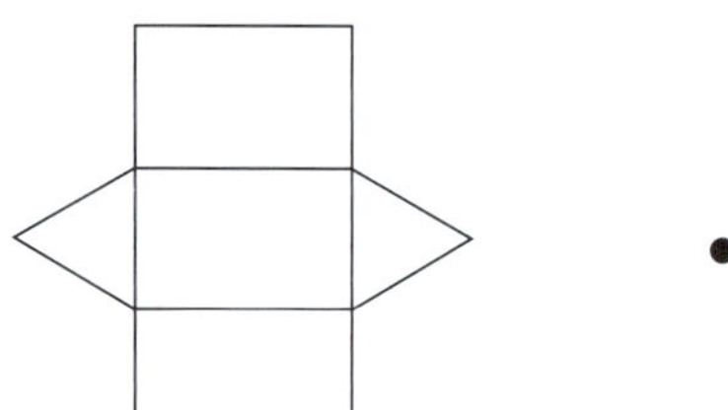
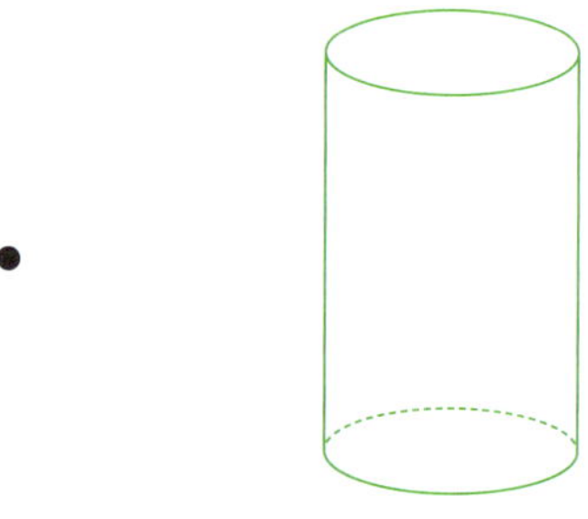

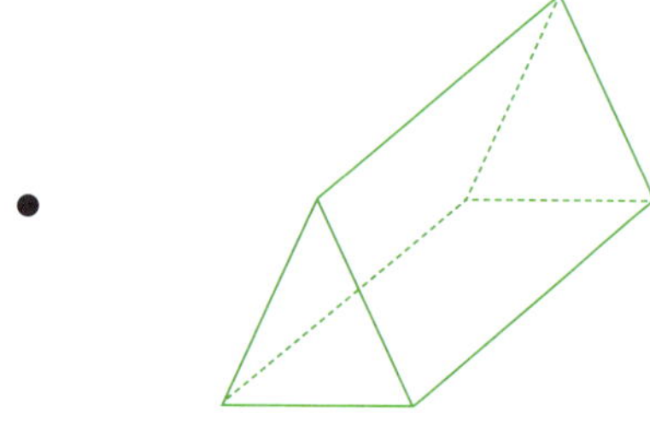
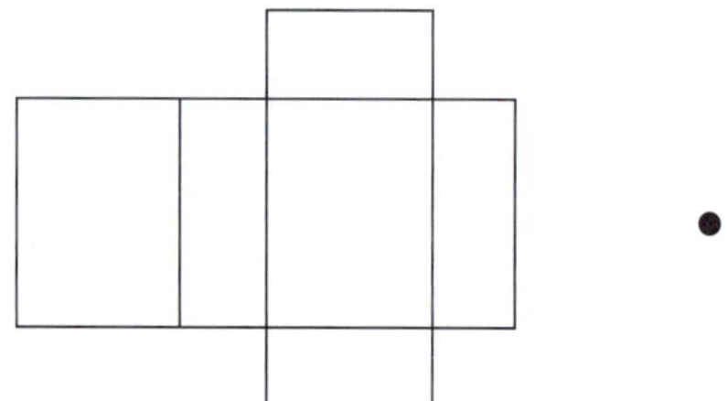
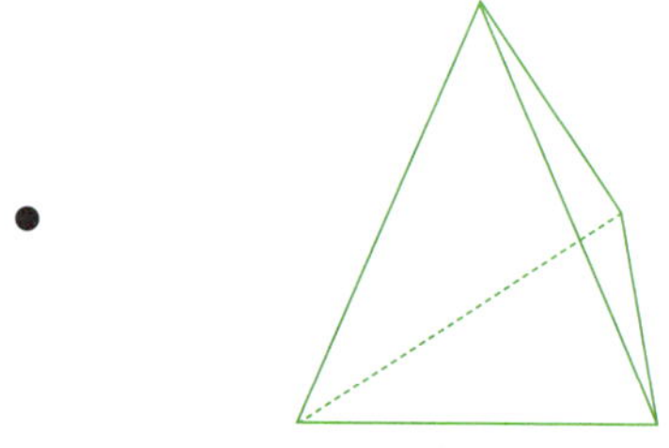
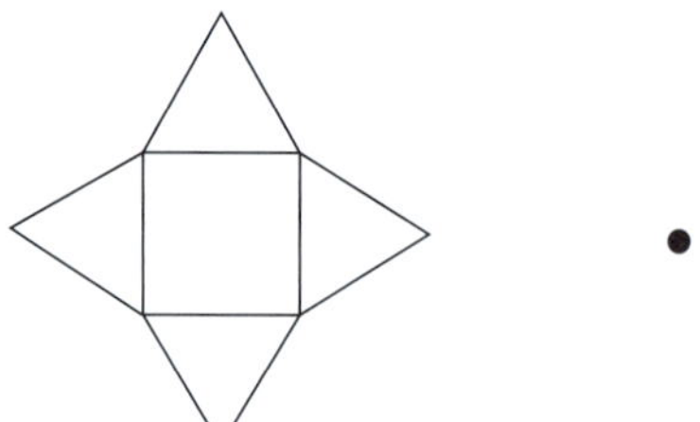
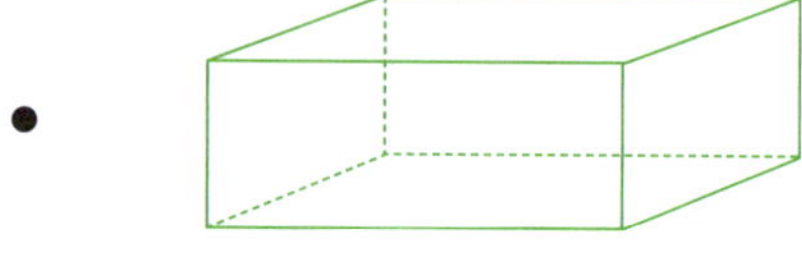
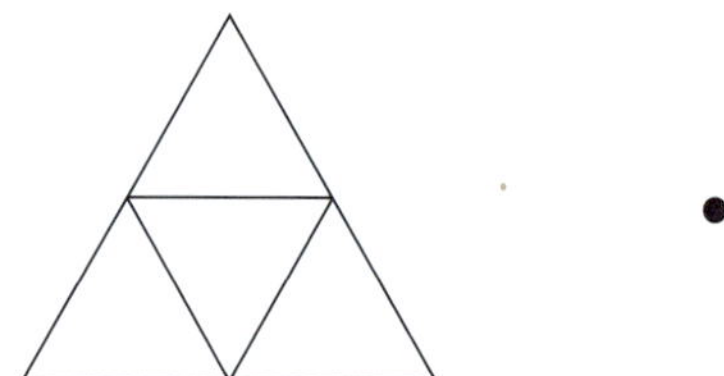
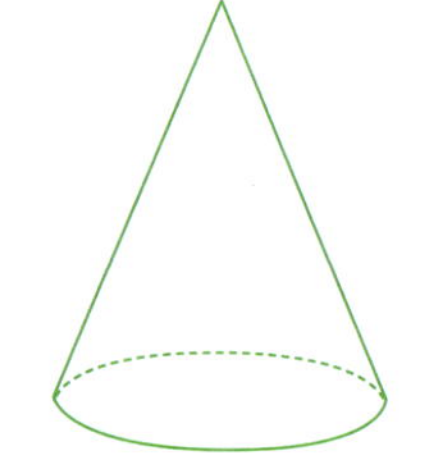

ISBN: 9780170451970

3 Tick the nets that could be folded to form a closed cube. If you are not sure, cut them out of squared paper and try them. Two have been done for you.

ISBN: 9780170451970

Isometrics

Copying isometric shapes

- The dots on isometric paper make it easy to draw 3D shapes.

One cube would look like this:

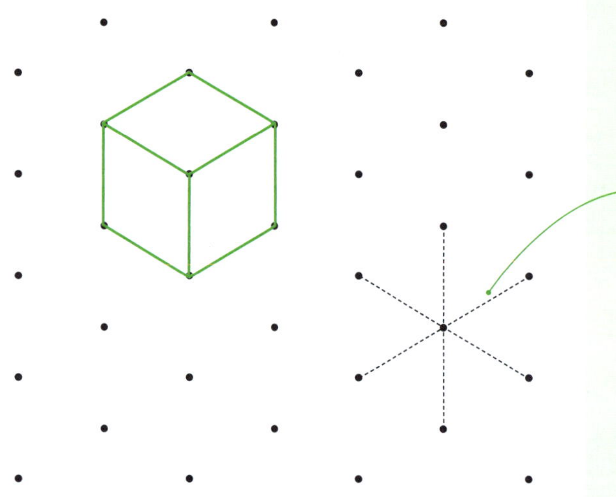

Notice that these are the only lines that can be used in an isometric drawing. There are **no horizontal lines**.

Copy these shapes using ruled lines. The first one has been started for you.

1

 ISBN: 9780170451970

2

3

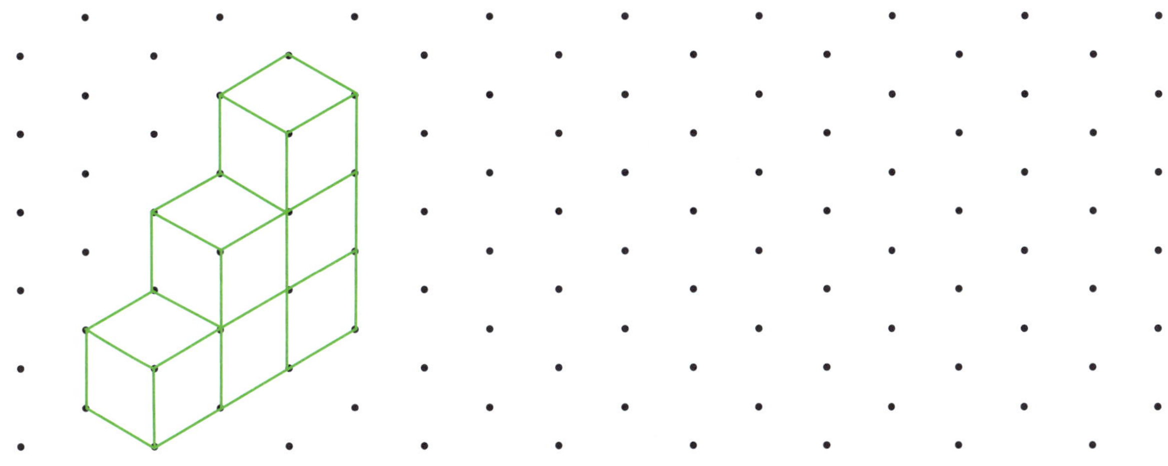

4

ISBN: 9780170451970

Drawing cuboids

Examples:

1 One cube with sides of 1 unit looks like this:

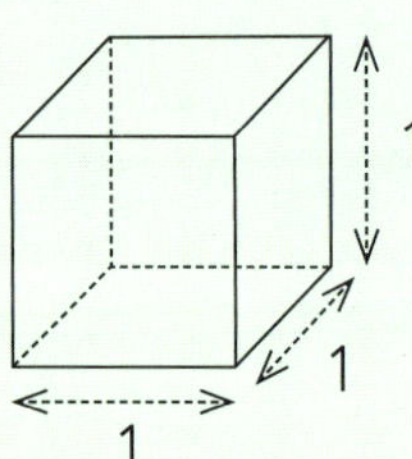

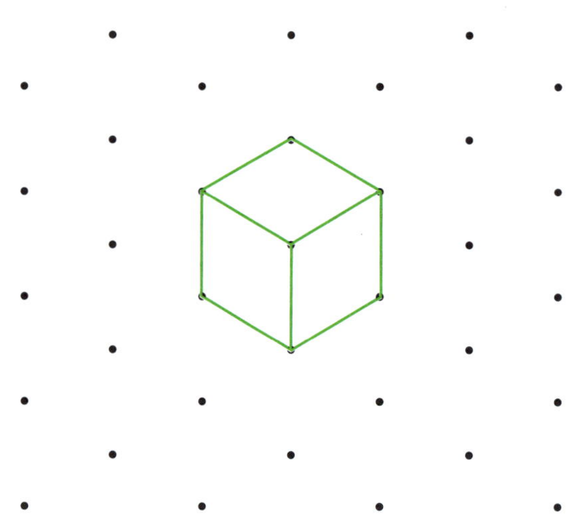

2 A cuboid with these units would look like this:

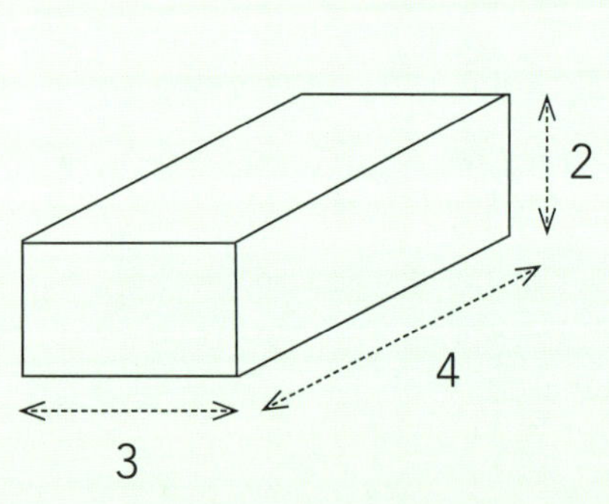

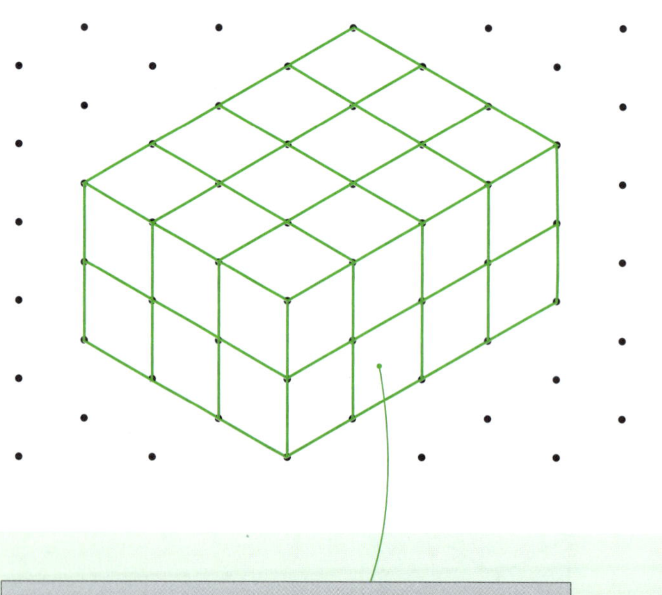

Notice that this cuboid is made up of 2 layers, each containing 12 blocks, so there are 24 blocks altogether.

ISBN: 9780170451970

Draw these cuboids on isometric paper.

1

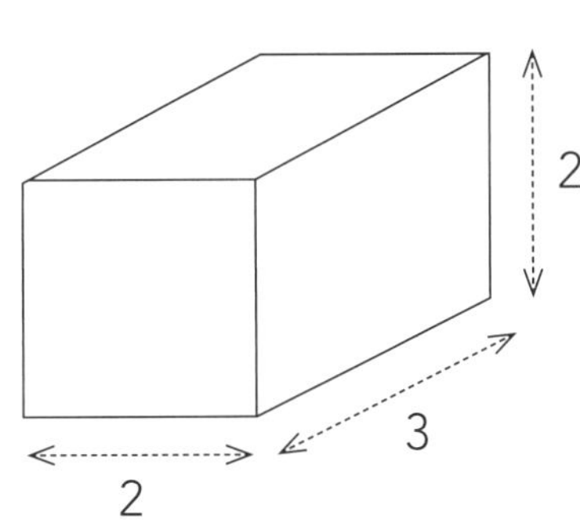

Number of blocks: ____________

2

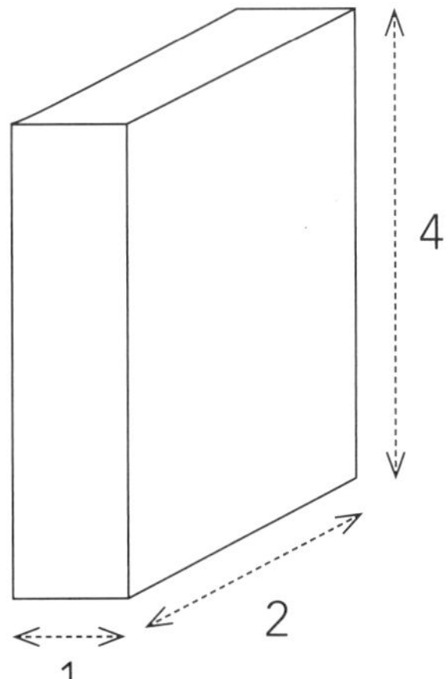

Number of blocks: ____________

3

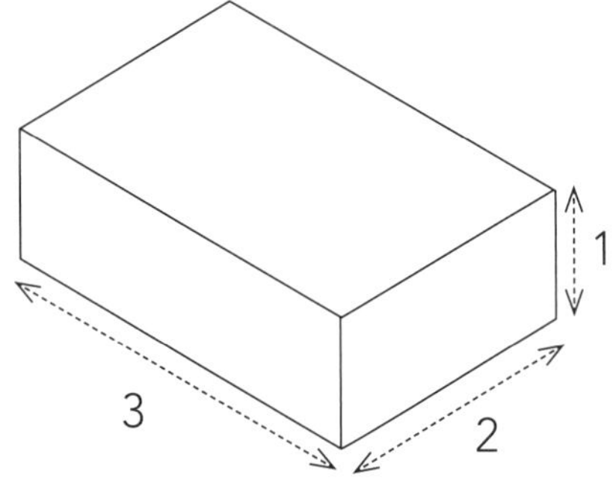

Number of blocks: ____________

ISBN: 9780170451970

Mix and match

Below are two different views of the same shape. Join the dots to connect diagrams of the same shape.

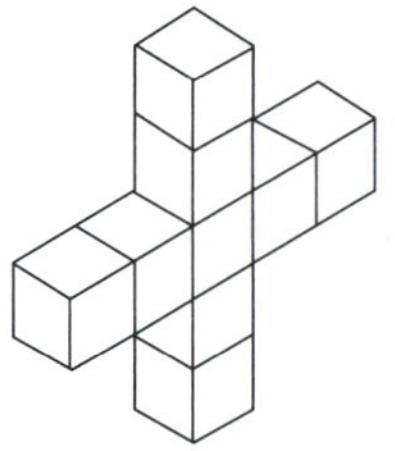 •  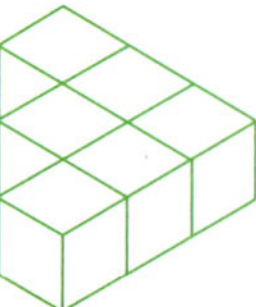

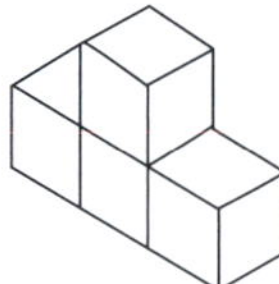 •  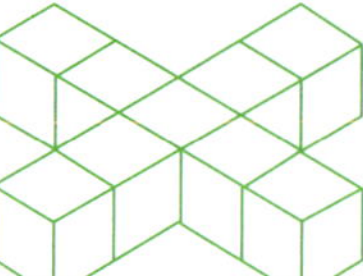

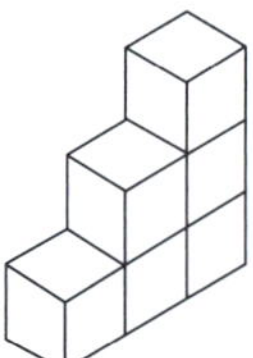 • • 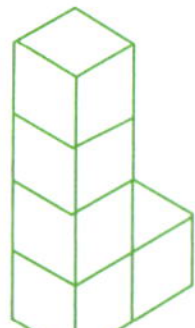

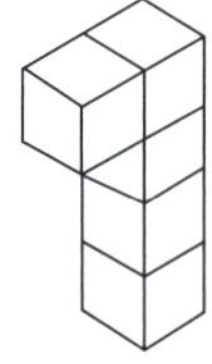 • • 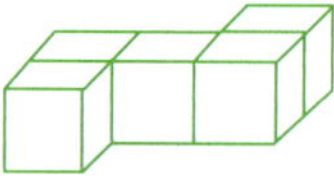

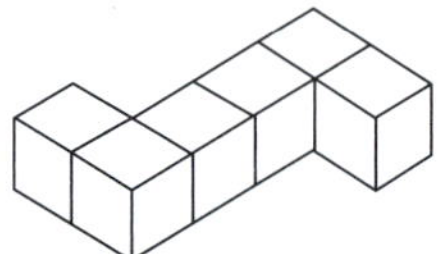 • • 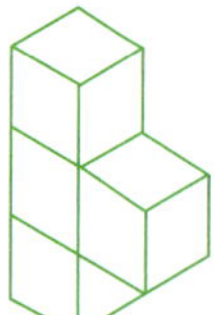

 ISBN: 9780170451970

Drawing isometric shapes from numbers in each column

- Some isometric shapes can also be represented by the numbers of blocks in each column.

Examples:

1

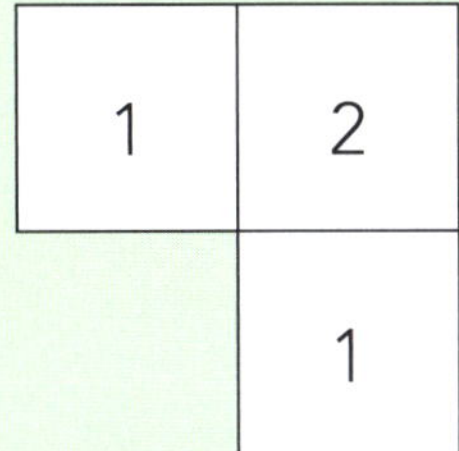

1	2
	1

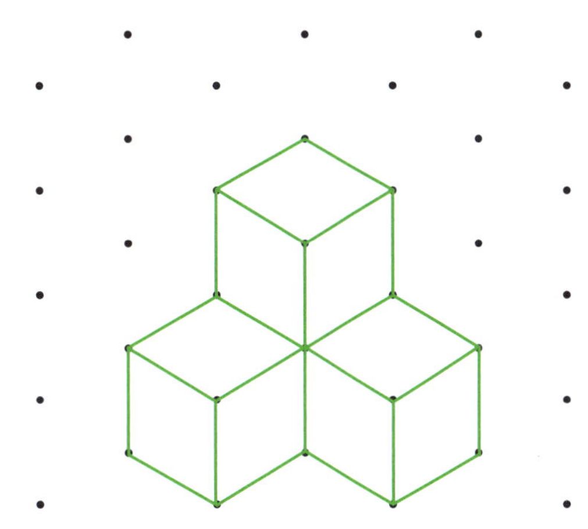

2

3	2	2
2	1	1

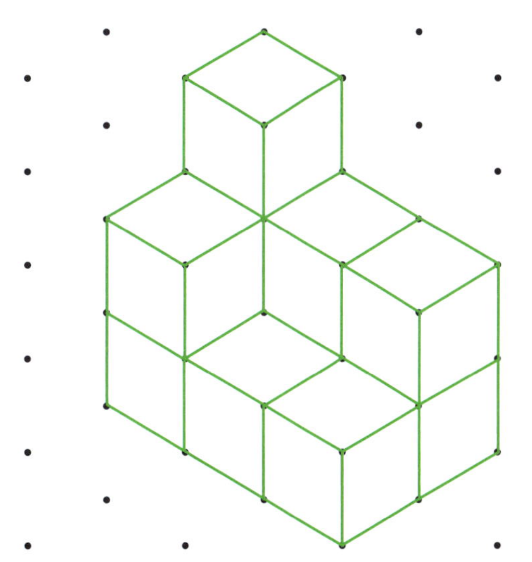

Write down the number of blocks in each column of these shapes. The bases of all the figures contain 6 blocks and are 3 blocks long and 2 blocks deep.

1

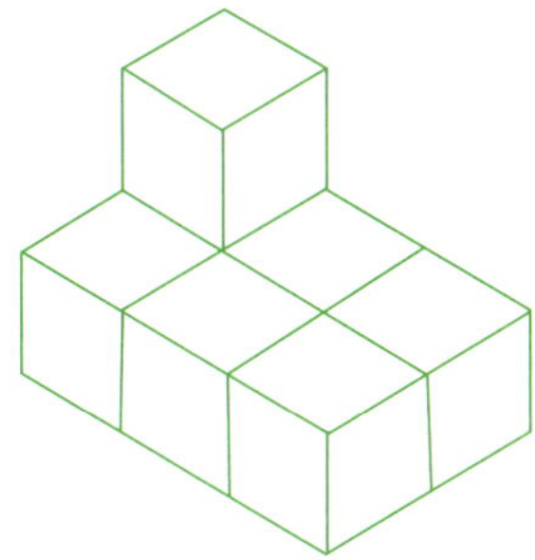

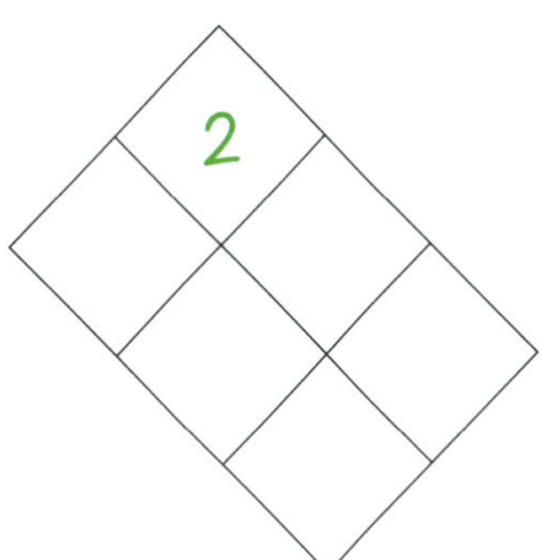

ISBN: 9780170451970

2

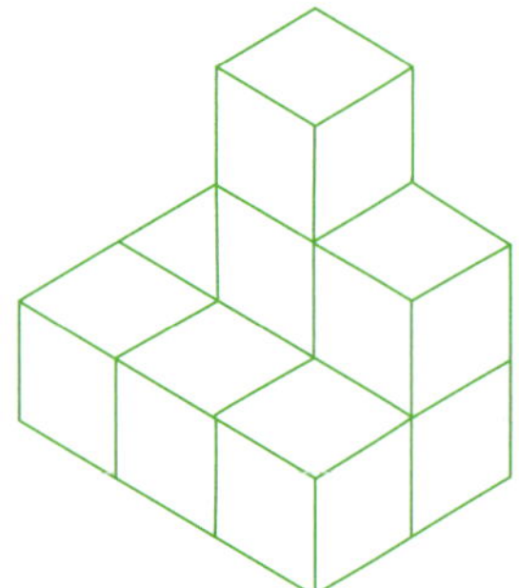

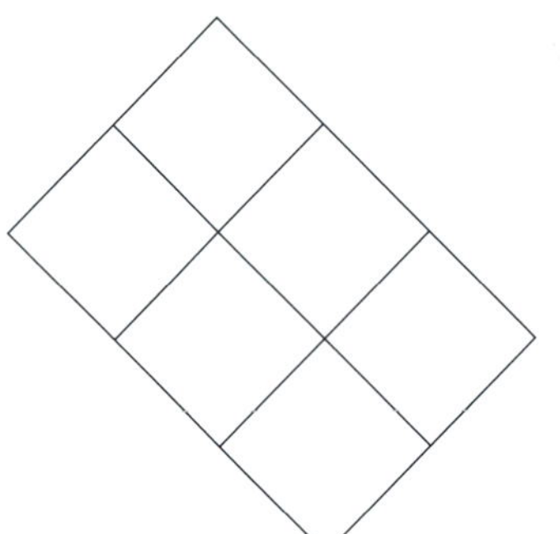

3

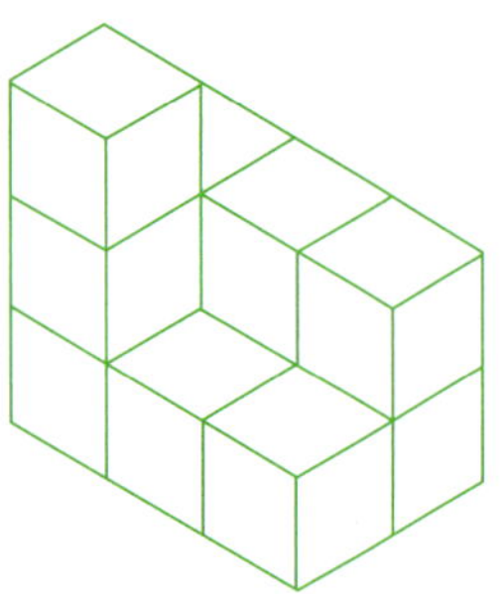

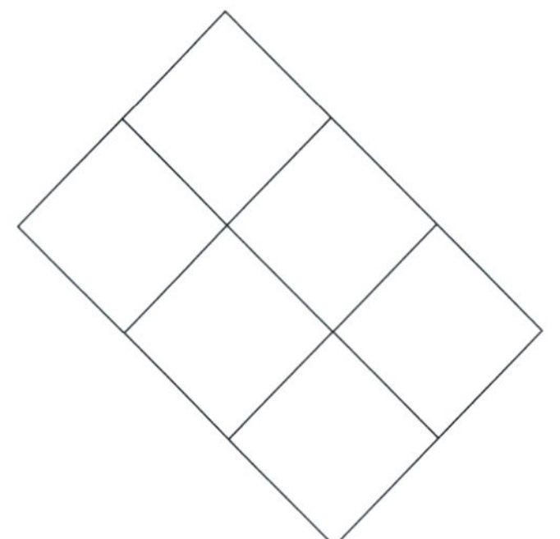

4

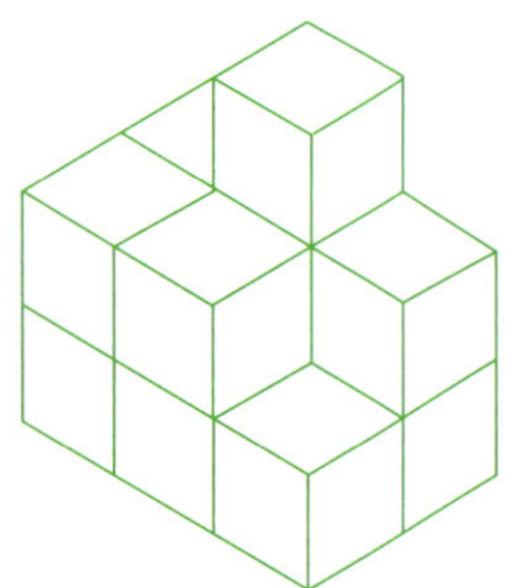

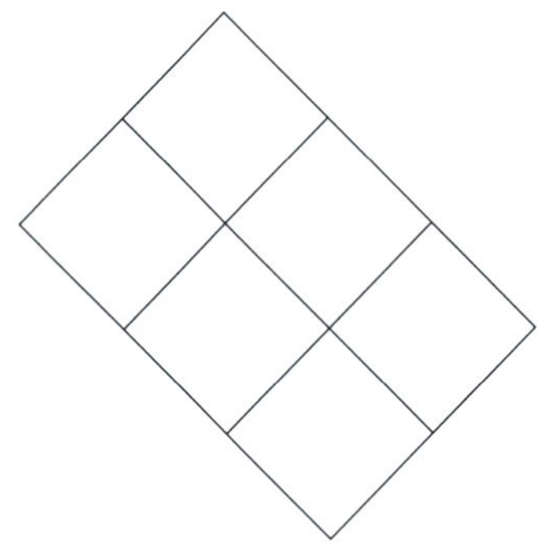

5

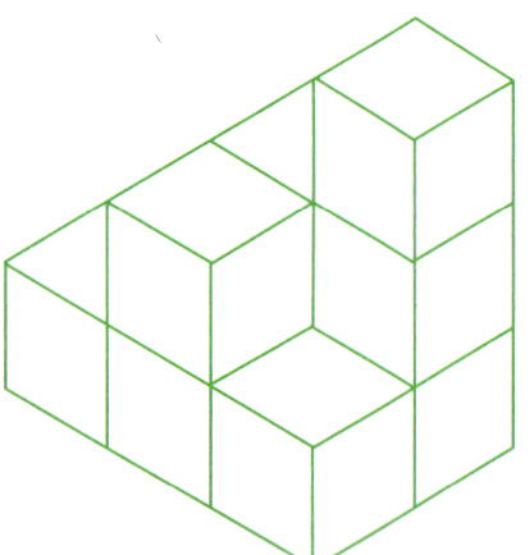

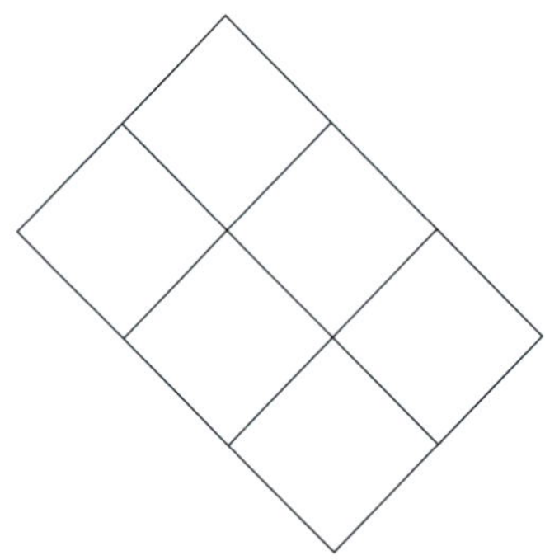

6

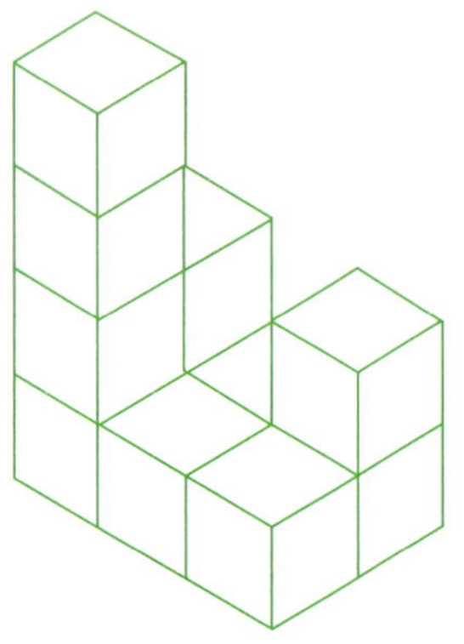

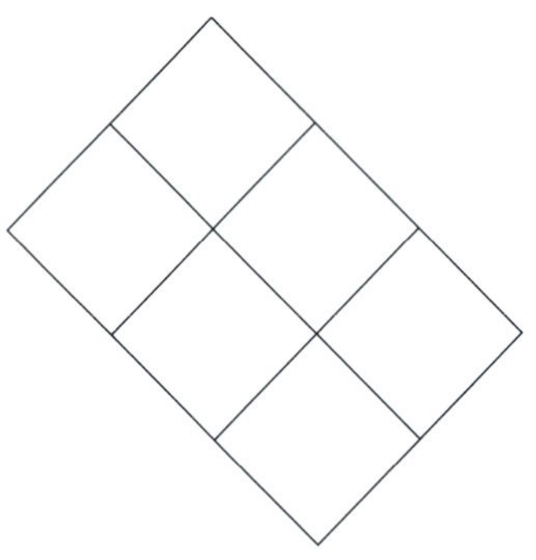

 ISBN: 9780170451970

7 Join the dots to connect each isometric drawing to its matching table.

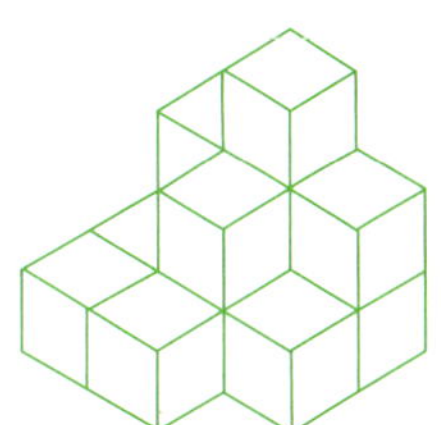

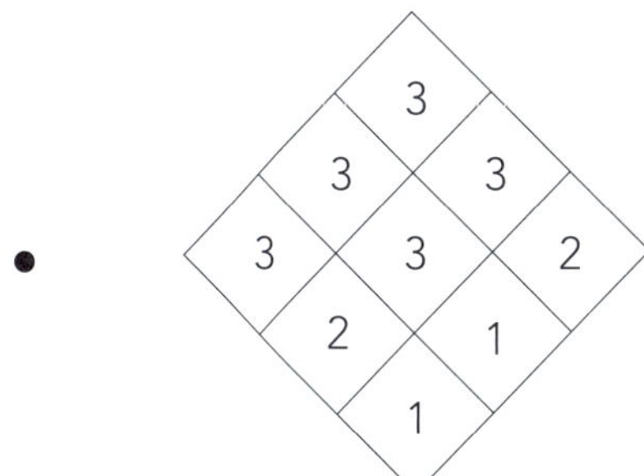

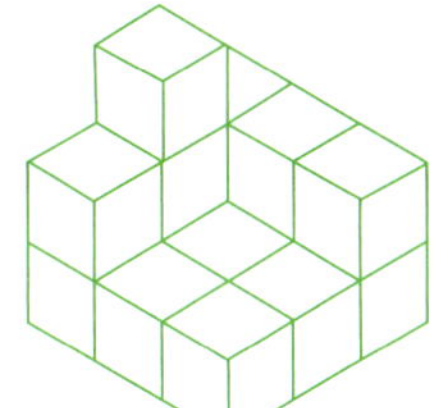

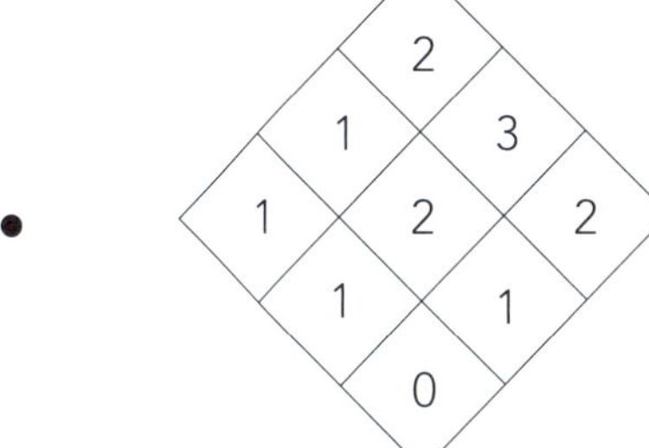

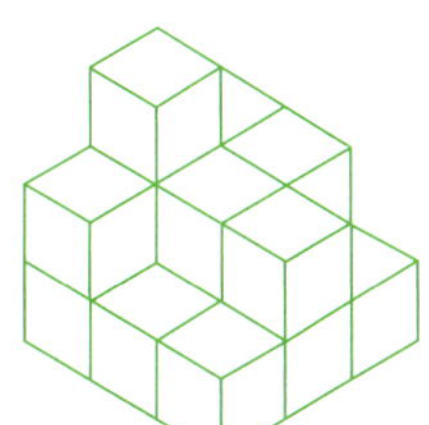

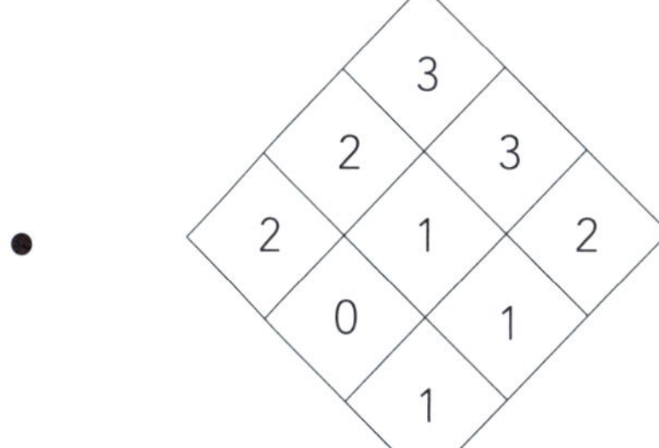

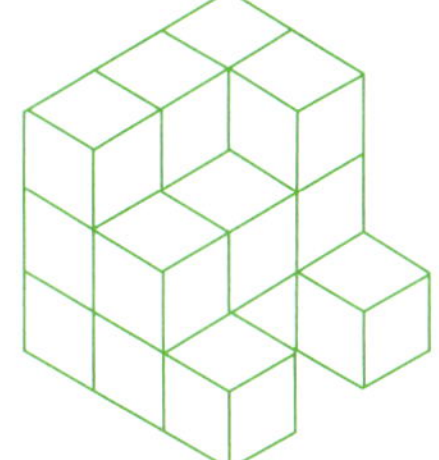

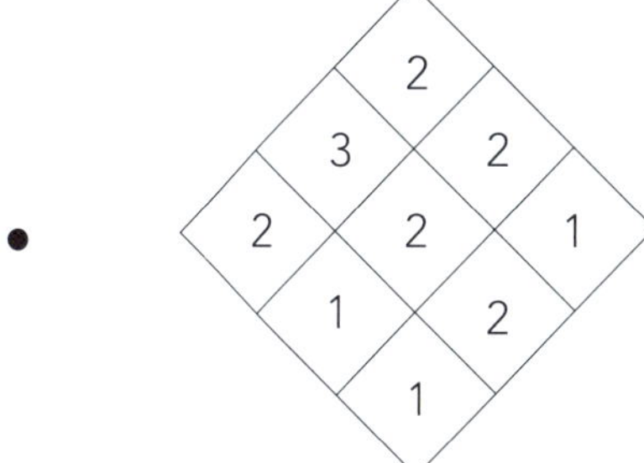

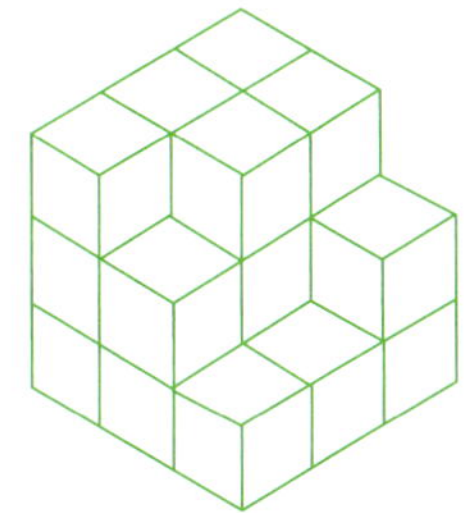

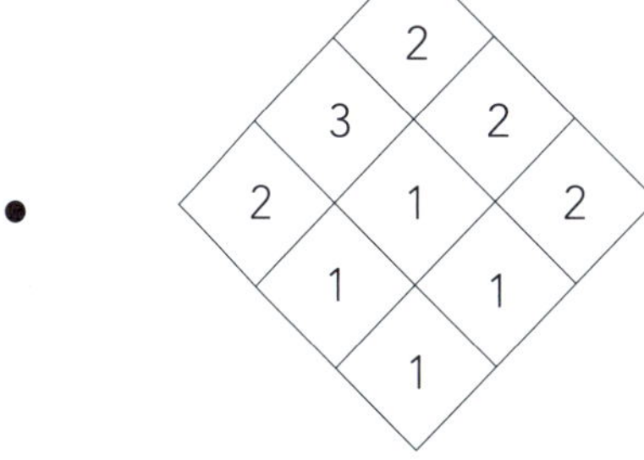

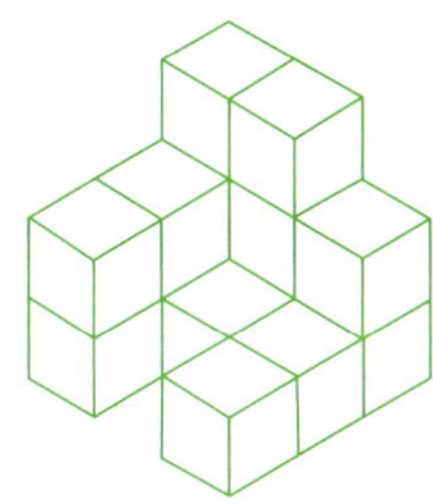

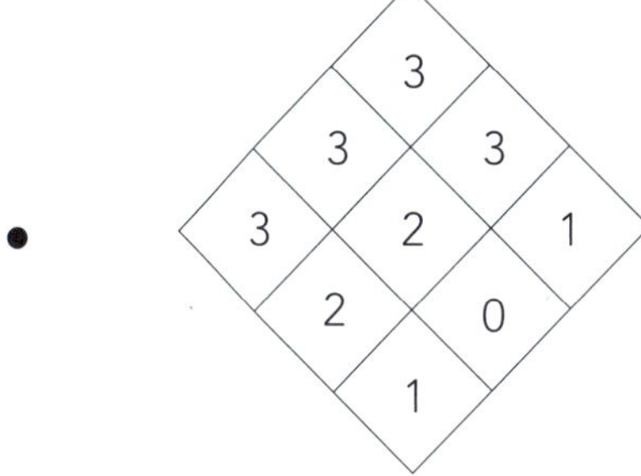

ISBN: 9780170451970

Different views of isometric diagrams

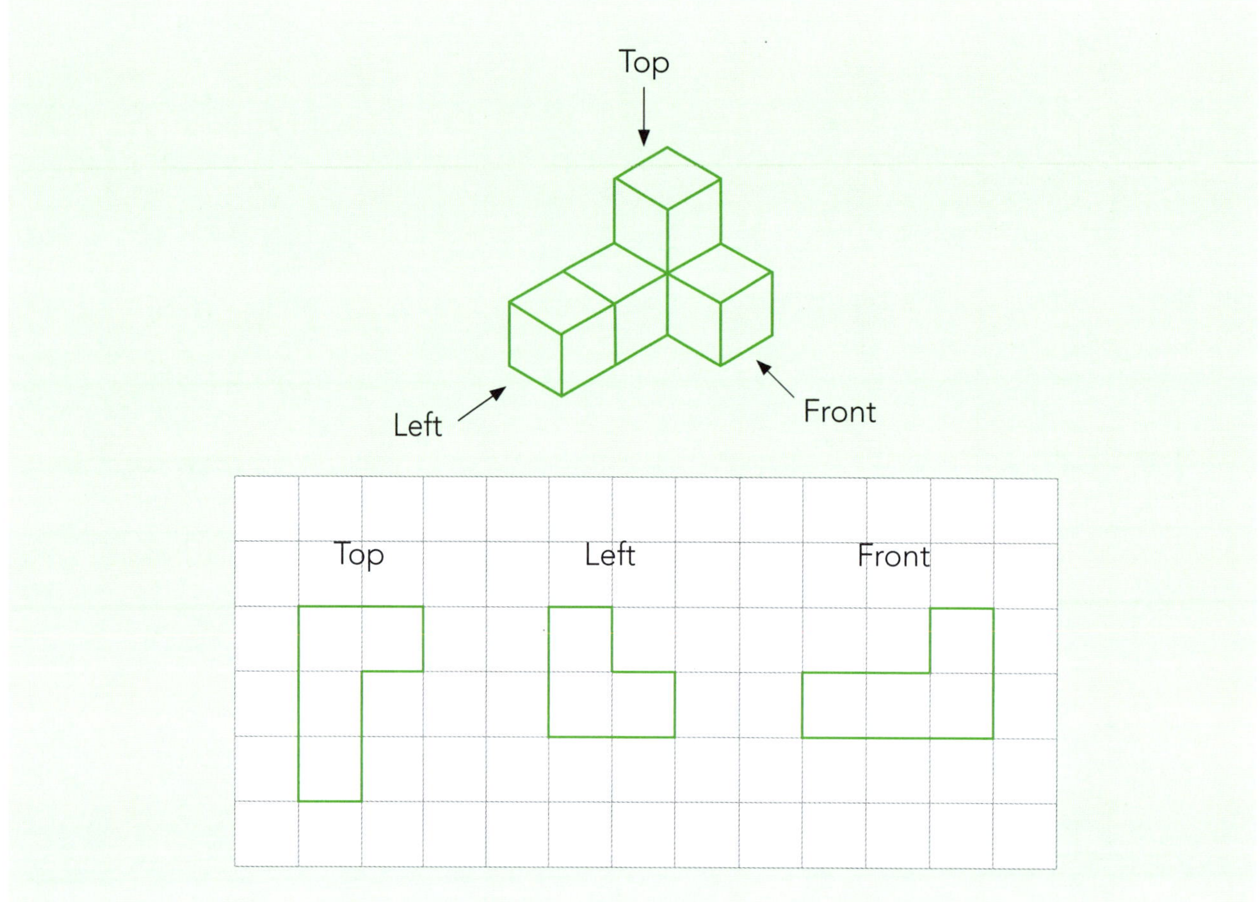

Match these shapes with their 2D views. There are no blocks hidden in behind.

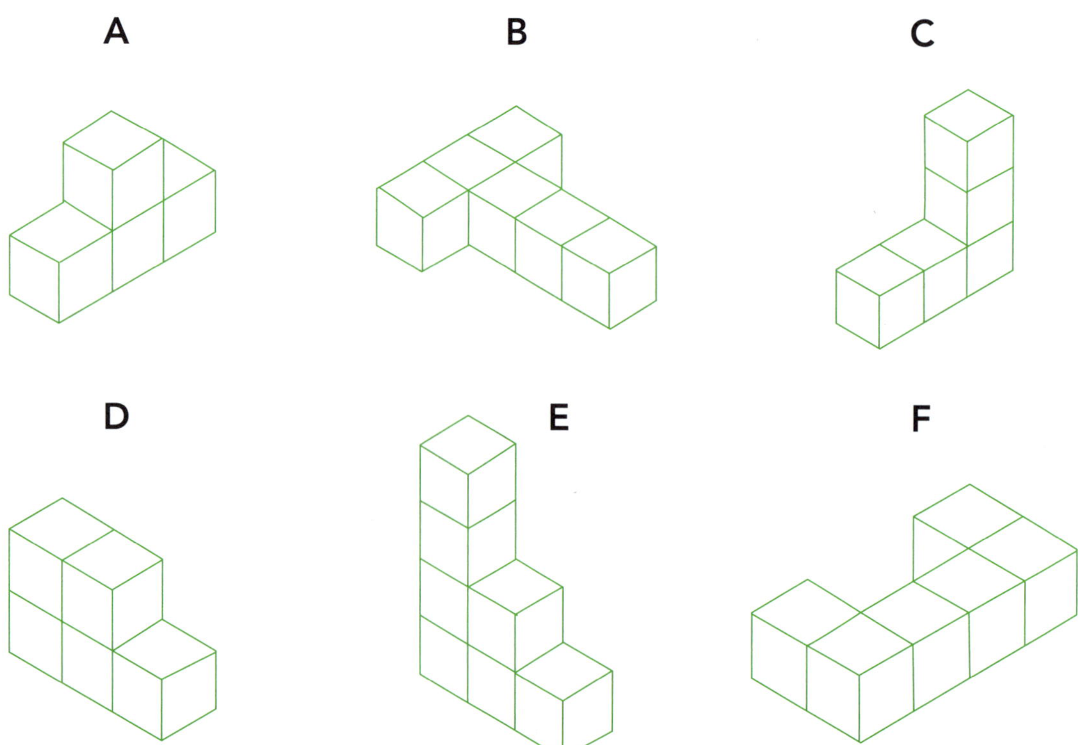

ISBN: 9780170451970

1 ________

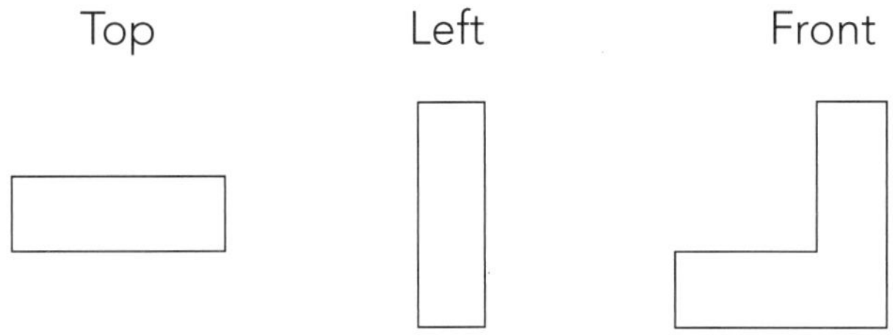

Top Left Front

2 ________

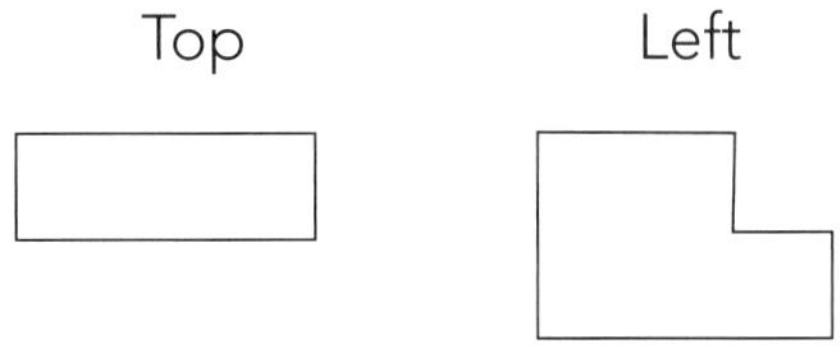

Top Left Front

3 ________

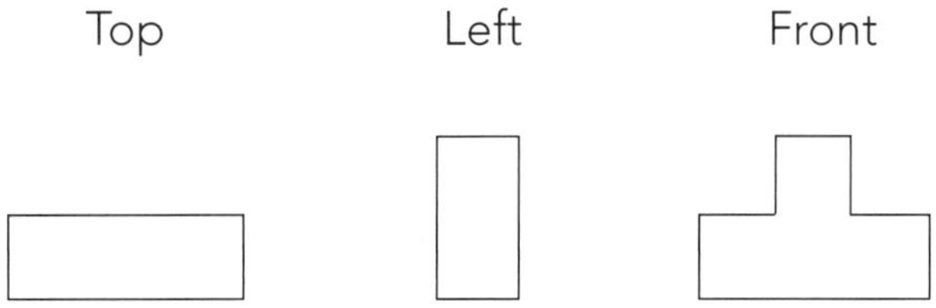

Top Left Front

4 ________

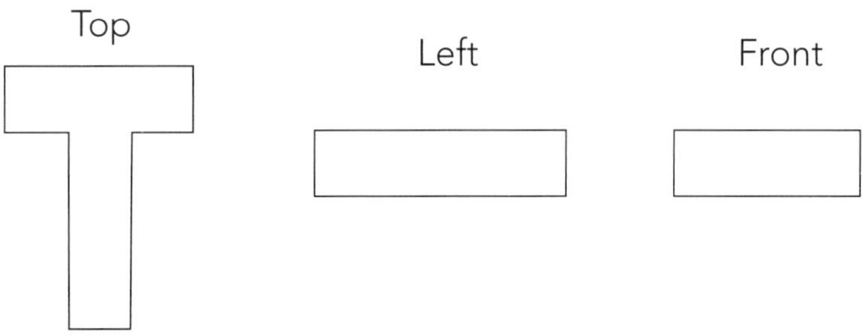

Top Left Front

5 ________

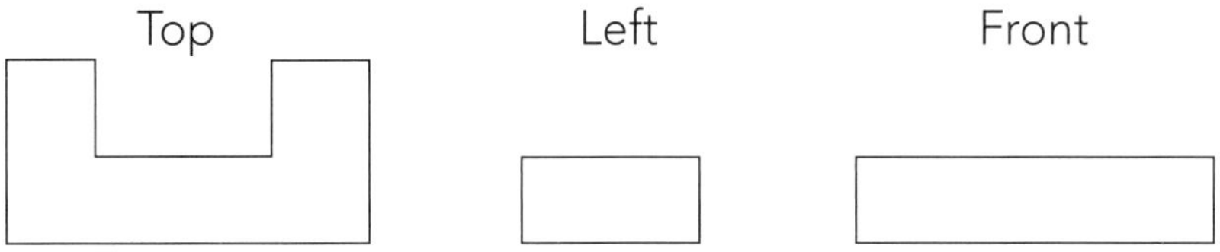

Top Left Front

6 ________

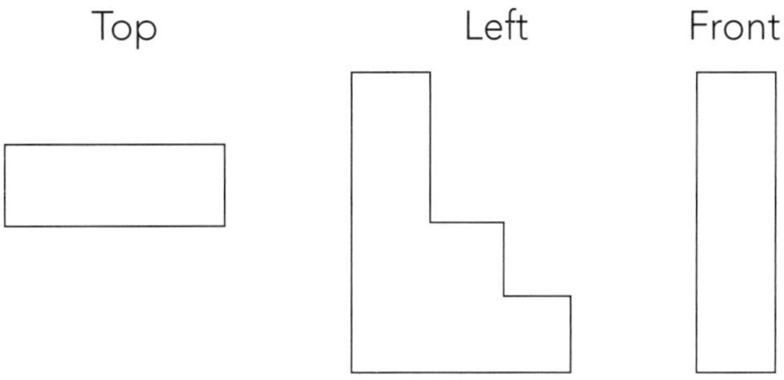

Top Left Front

ISBN: 9780170451970

Draw the top, left and front views of these shapes.

Top Left Front

7

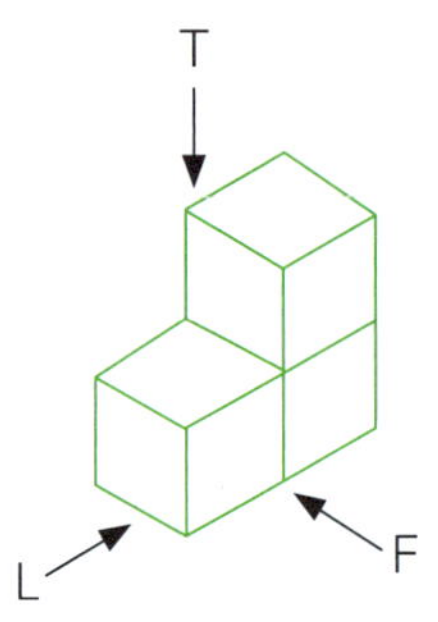

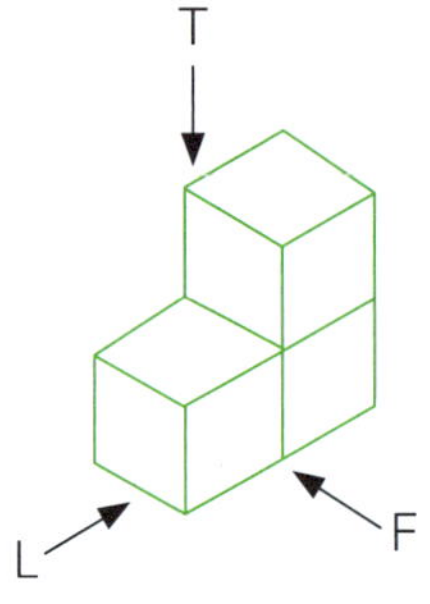

8

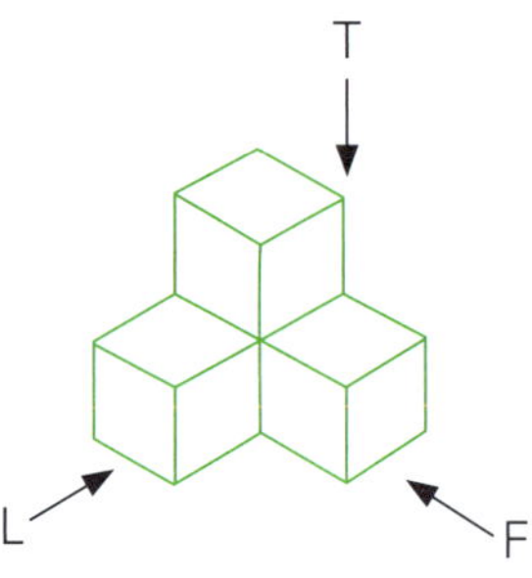

9

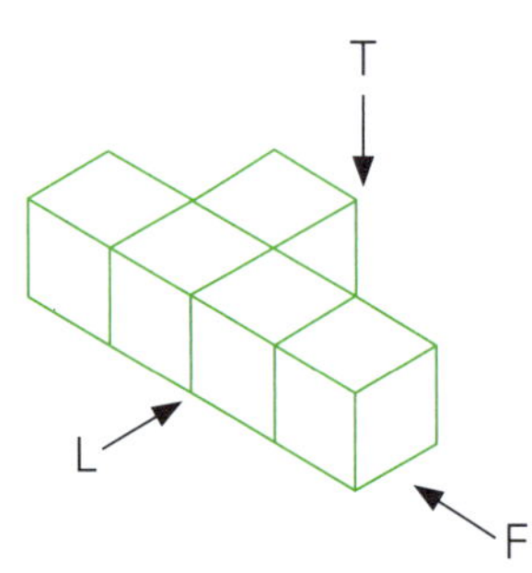

10

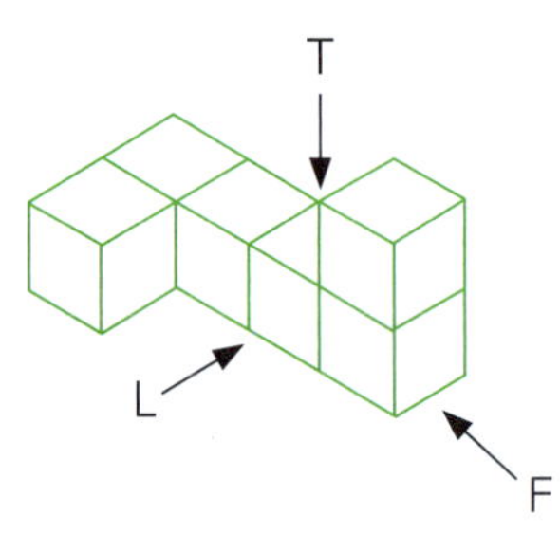

ISBN: 9780170451970

Position and orientation

Directions

- Directions can be given in terms of north, south, east and west.
- North is always given as the starting point.

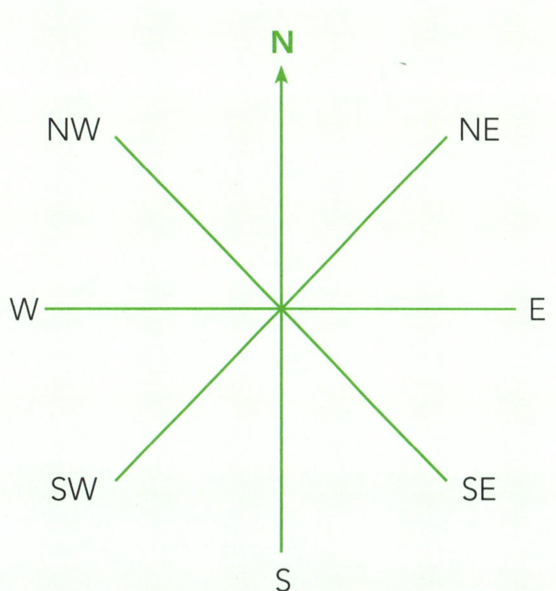

Examples:

1

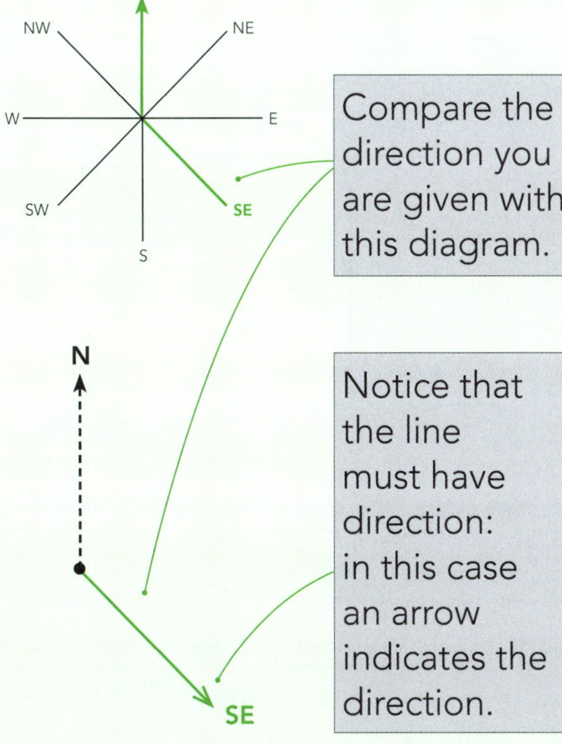

Compare the direction you are given with this diagram.

Notice that the line must have direction: in this case an arrow indicates the direction.

2

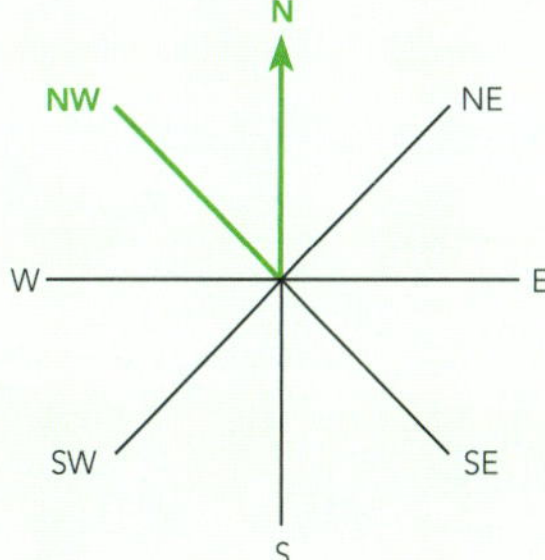

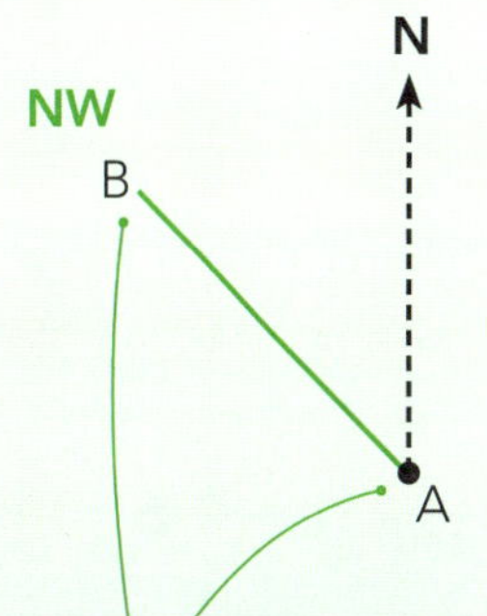

Sometimes the direction will be indicated by words, e.g. 'from A to B'.

ISBN: 9780170451970

Match the compass directions in the list to each of the diagrams. They are either in the direction of the arrow or from A to B.

~~W~~	NE	S	E	NW	SE	SW	N

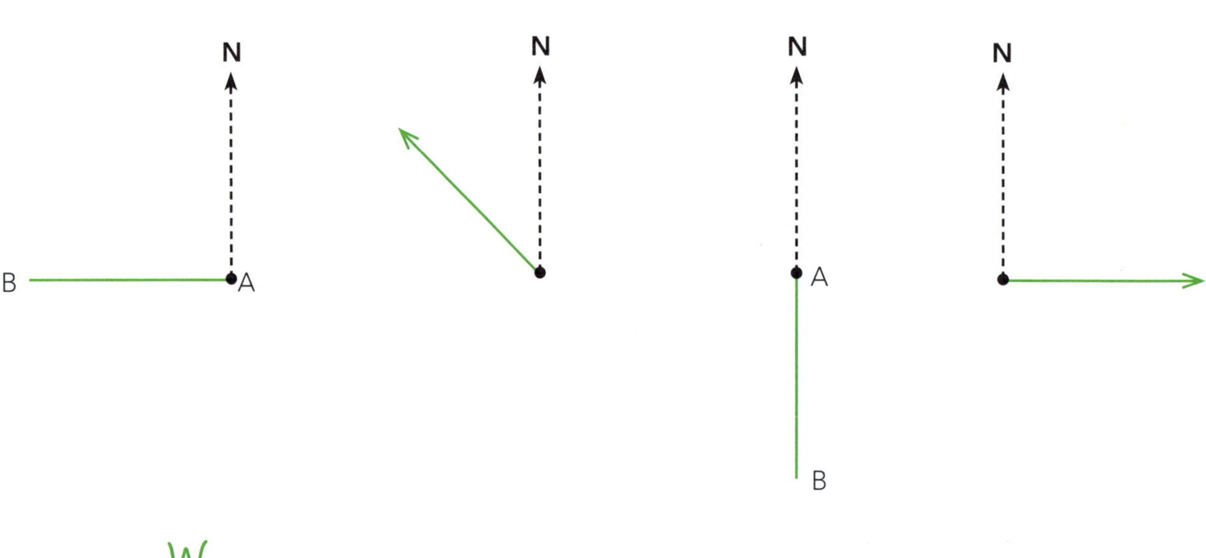

1 W 2 ______ 3 ______ 4 ______

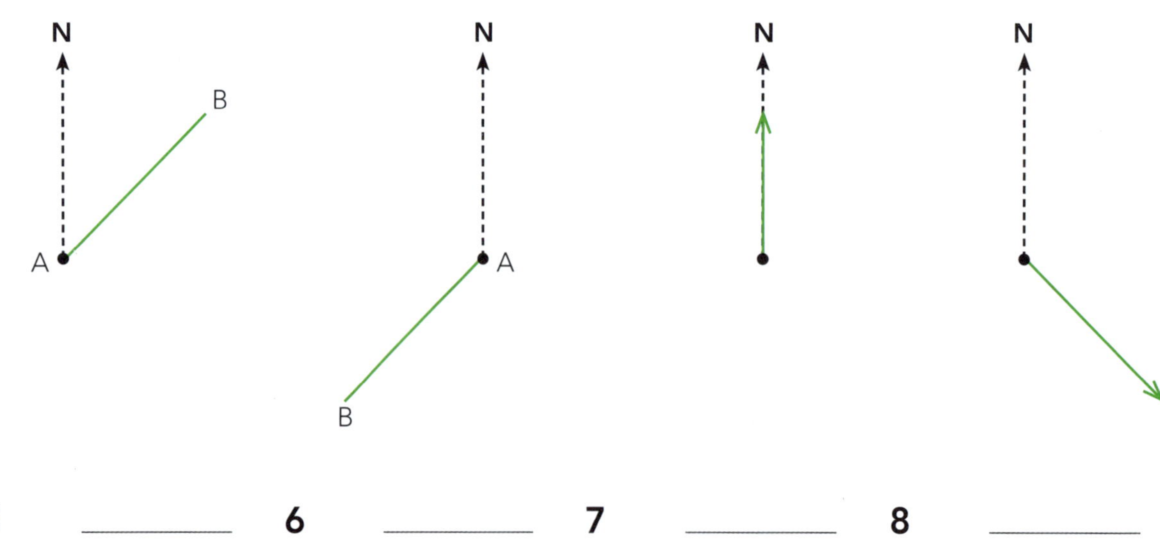

5 ______ 6 ______ 7 ______ 8 ______

 ISBN: 9780170451970

Location: grid references

- Grid references are used to identify **locations** on a map.
- Locations are specified by **two** coordinates.
- As with coordinates on graphs, **horizontal** coordinates are always given **before vertical** coordinates.

Locating squares

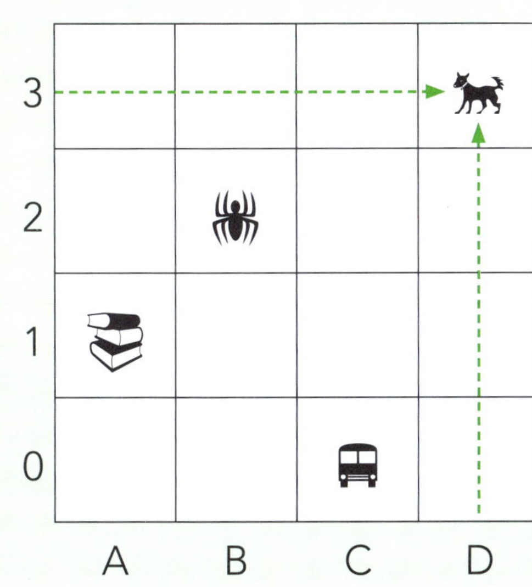

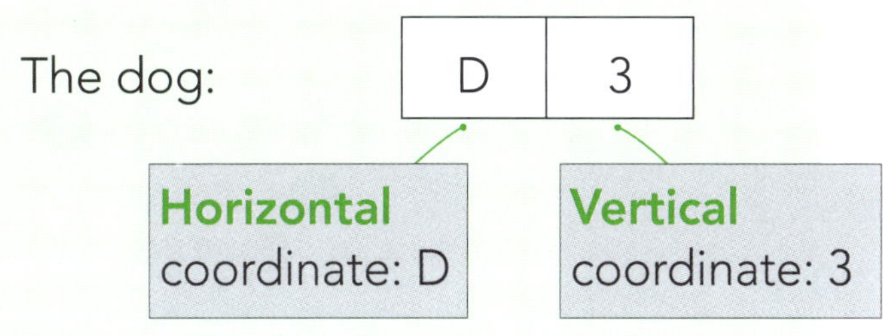

Check for yourself

The books:	A	1
The spider:	B	2
The bus:	C	0

7					
6					
5					
4					
3					
	P	Q	R	S	T

What would you find in the following squares?

1 S6 ______________________

2 Q3 ______________________

Write coordinates for the squares where you would find the following.

3 Clock __________

4 Hand __________

ISBN: 9780170451970

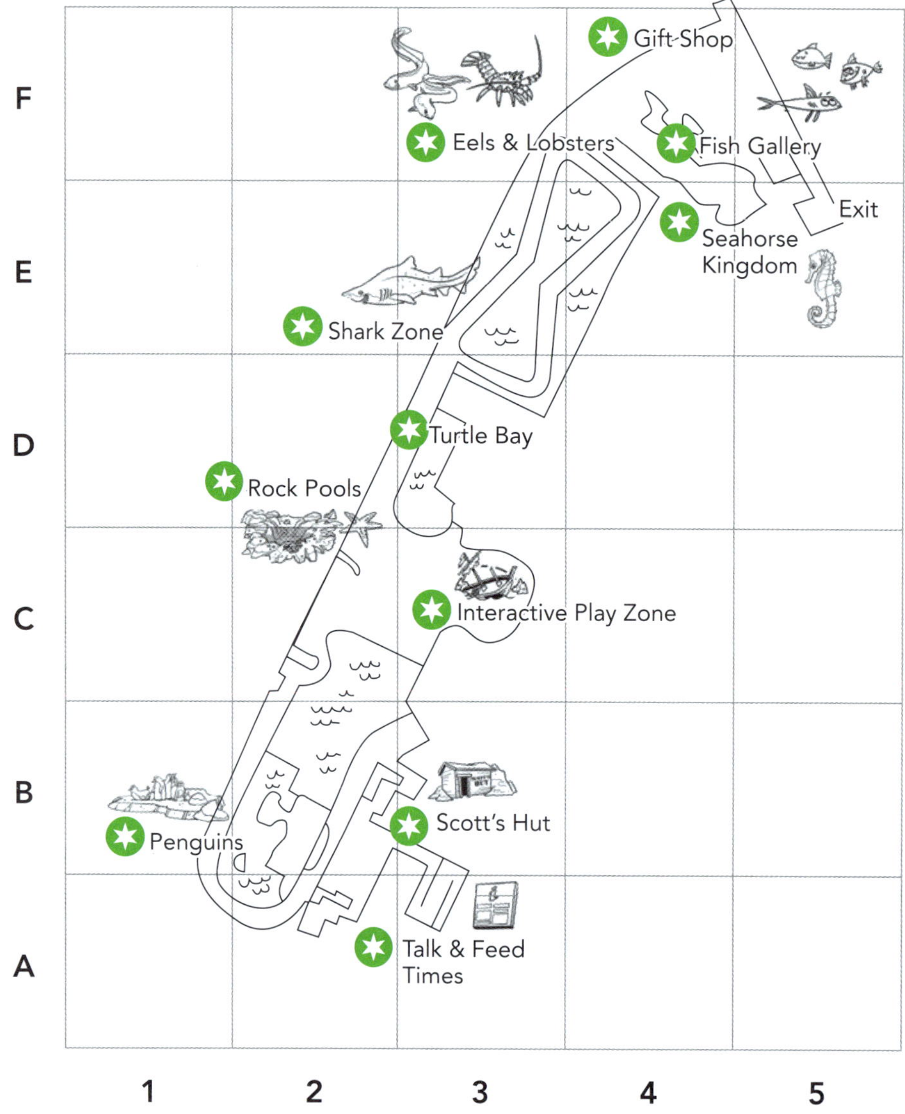

The locations of activities are indicated by asterisks. What would you find in the following squares?

5 3B ____________________ **6** 4E ____________________

7 1B ____________________ **8** 2E ____________________

Write grid references for the squares containing the asterisk for the following locations.

9 Eels and Lobsters ________ **10** Interactive Play Zone ________

11 Talk & Feed Times ________ **12** Fish Gallery ________

 ISBN: 9780170451970

Locating grid points

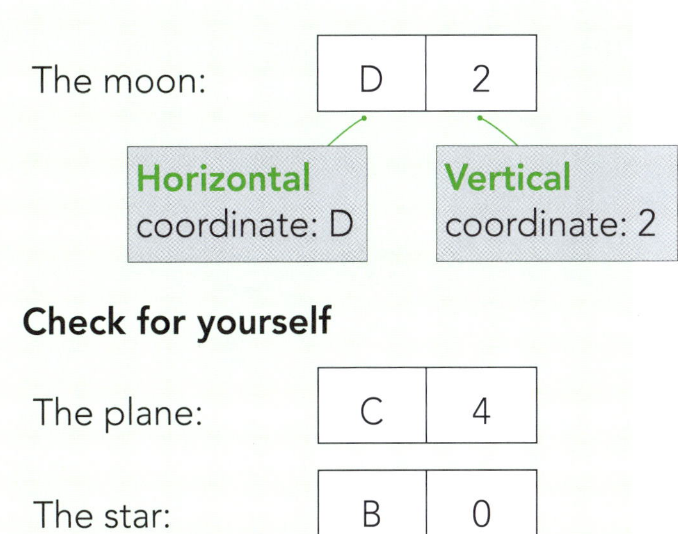

The moon: | D | 2 |

Horizontal coordinate: D

Vertical coordinate: 2

Check for yourself

The plane:	C	4
The star:	B	0
The tools:	E	1

What would you find at the following grid points?

1 V8 ______________________

2 Y5 ______________________

3 U8 ______________________

4 W7 ______________________

Write coordinates for the grid points where you would find the following.

5 Smiley face __________

6 Eye __________

7 The bicycle __________

8 The clock __________

ISBN: 9780170451970

The map shows the layout of a small zoo. All the displays and other locations are at the intersections of gridlines. The gridlines are 10 m apart. Use the map along with the key below to answer the following questions.

Key:

	Entrance		Toilets
	Restaurant		Giant totara
	Ice-cream stall		Tuatara
	Insect house		Farmyard
	Kiwi house		Duck pond
	Aviary (bird house)		Bat cave
	Geckos and skinks		Information centre

ISBN: 9780170451970

What would you find at the following grid references?

9 F8 ______________________

10 D5 ______________________

11 E3 ______________________

12 G6 ______________________

13 D11 ______________________

14 D3 ______________________

Write grid references for the following locations.

15 The kiwi house __________

16 The geckos and skinks __________

17 The duck pond __________

18 The giant totara __________

19 The farmyard __________

20 The tuatara __________

What would you find if you followed the following instructions?

21 From the entrance, you walk due north. ______________________

22 From the farmyard, you walk due south. ______________________

23 From the restaurant, you walk due west. ______________________

24 From the geckos and skinks, you walk northeast. ______________________

25 From the farmyard, you walk northwest. ______________________

26 From the giant totara, you walk northwest. ______________________

At which grid references is Dani standing when she is at the following?

27 South of the bat cave and east of the kiwi house. __________

28 Southeast of the farmyard and north of the tuatara. __________

29 Northeast of the aviary and southeast of the bat cave. __________

30 Southwest of the ice-cream stall and north of the information centre. __________

ISBN: 9780170451970

Paths and directions

This version of the zoo map has the paths on it. The routes for numbers 1 and 7 are shown on the map.

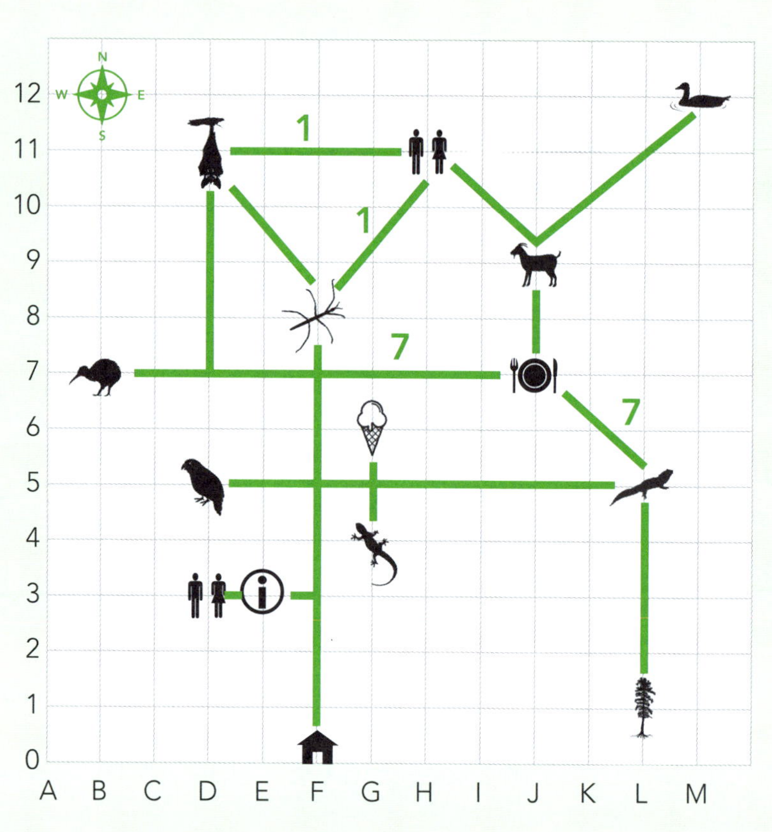

Where would you be if you followed these routes?

1 From the bat cave, walk east and then southwest. *The insect house*

2 From the entrance, walk north. Take the second turning to the left, and walk in a westerly direction. __________

3 From the giant totara, walk north and then northwest. __________

4 From the insect house, walk south. At the second intersection walk in an easterly direction, then take the first path that heads north. __________

5 From the duck pond, walk southwest, turn right and walk northwest and then west. __________

6 From the northern toilets, walk southeast, then south and then southeast. __________

ISBN: 9780170451970

Use directions to describe the following routes. Include the names of locations that you pass on the way.

7 From the tuatara to the kiwi house via the restaurant.

From the tuatara, walk northwest to the restaurant and then west.

8 From the duck pond to the nearest toilets.

9 The shortest route from the entrance to the bat cave.

10 From the entrance to the geckos and skinks.

11 The shortest route from the giant totara to the insect house.

12 From the information centre to the farmyard.

ISBN: 9780170451970

This map shows part of Greymouth.

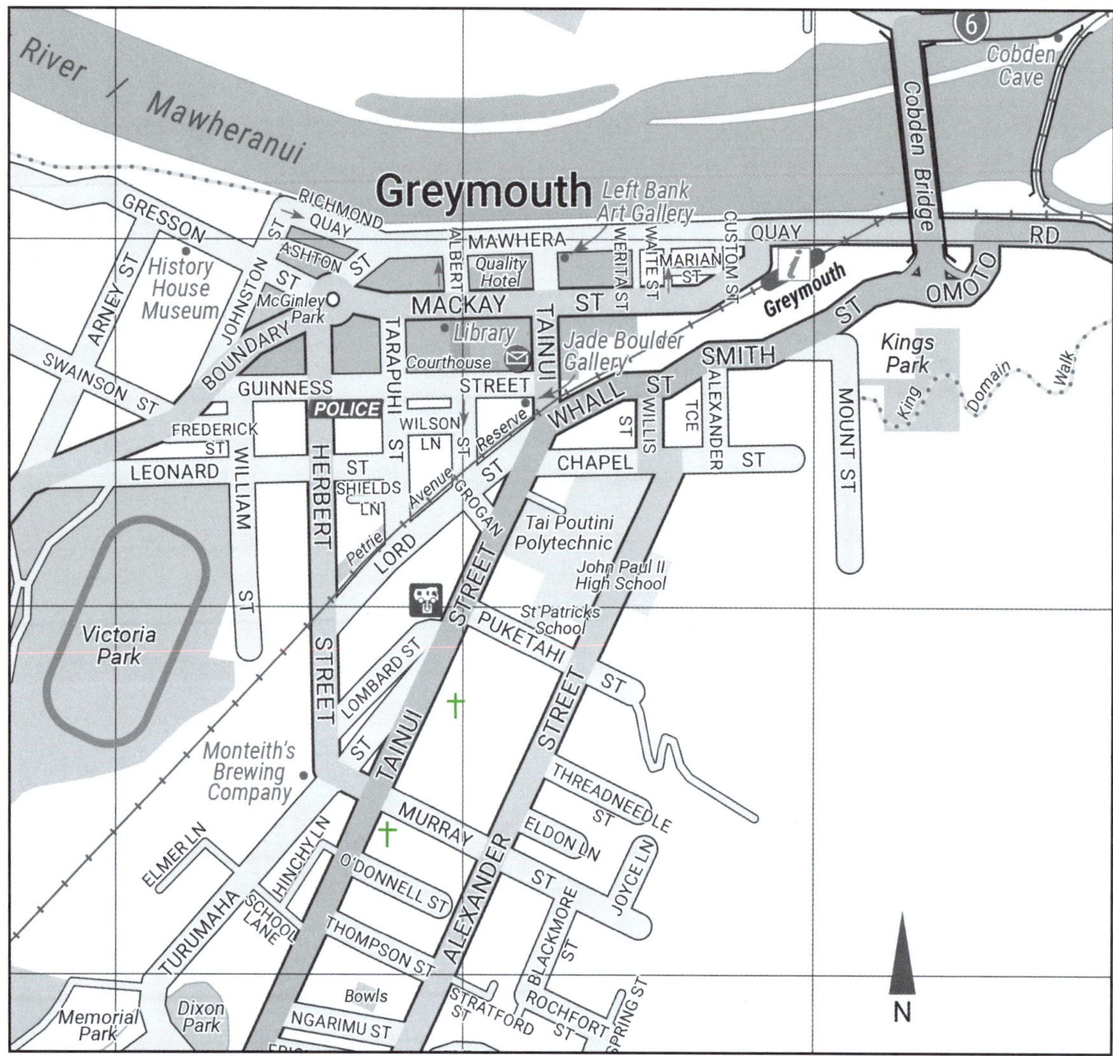

Key:

	Post Office		Church
	Information centre		Railway station
	Caravan park	6	State Highway number

Scale: 1 cm = 100 m

This means that 1 cm on the map = 100 m on the ground.

Examples:

1 Murray Street is 4 cm long on the map ⇒ it is 4 x 100 m = 400 m long.

2 Ngarimu Street is 1.6 cm long on the map ⇒ it is 1.6 x 100 m = 160 m long.

 ISBN: 9780170451970

Estimate the following lengths or distances.

		Length on map	Length on ground
13	Threadneedle Street	________ cm	________ m
14	Puketahi Street	________ cm	________ m
15	Cobden Bridge (including the crossing of Mawhera Quay)	________ cm	________ m
16	Guinness Street	________ cm	________ m
17	School Lane	________ cm	________ m

Where would you be if you followed these routes?

18 From the bowls club in Ngarimu Street, you went to the corner of Tainui Street, then turned right and went about 450 m. ____________________

19 From the Post Office you went north along Tainui Street for about 60 m, then you turned right and followed the road for about 300 m. ____________________

20 From the library, go west along Mackay Street about 200 m, then head south along Herbert Street for about 500 m. Turn left into Lombard Street and go about 200 m. ____________________

Use directions and approximate distances to describe the following routes. Include the names of locations that you pass on the way.

21 From the library, via Mackay Street to State Highway 6.

____

____

____

22 From the History House Museum to Dixon Park.

____

____

____

ISBN: 9780170451970

Transformation geometry

- A transformation (e.g. translation, reflection, rotation, enlargement) is the changing or moving of a figure by following certain rules.
- The transformed figure is called the **image**.
- A transformation may change the position, size, shape or orientation of the object.

Translation	Reflection
The figure is **shifted**.	The figure is **reflected in a mirror** line.
Rotation	**Enlargement**
The figure **rotates around a point**.	The figure **gets bigger or smaller**.

 ISBN: 9780170451970

Translation

- When translated, the figure is **shifted**.
- We can describe a shift using the terms **up**, **down**, **left** and **right**.

Example: Describe the shift for each of these letters.
Note: Throughout the book, the **green figure** is the **original** and the **grey figure** is the **image**.

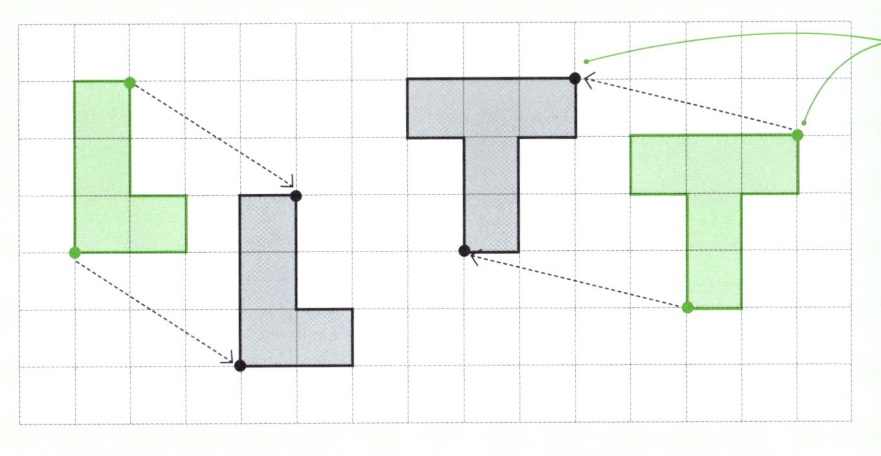

When drawing arrows to show a translation, be sure you **choose equivalent points** on the shape. In this case we have chosen the point on the top right of the T.

The **L** has moved **three squares to the right** and **two squares down**.

The **T** has moved **four squares to the left** and **one square up**.

1

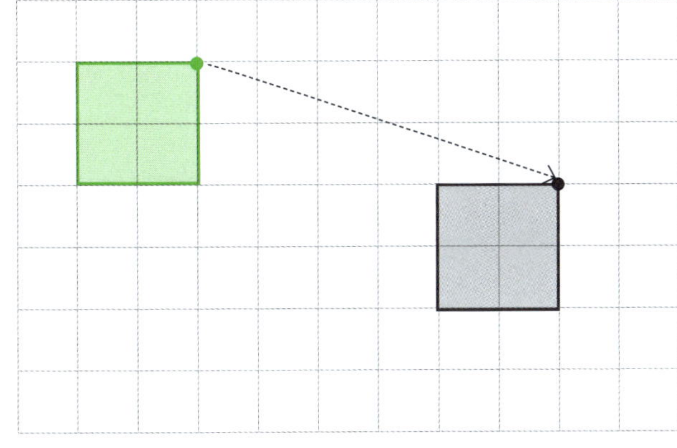

The square has moved __6__ square(s) to the __right__ and __2__ square(s) __down__.

ISBN: 9780170451970

2

The rectangle has moved

________ square(s) to the

________ and ________

square(s) ________.

3

The triangle has moved

________ square(s) to the

________ and ________

square(s) ________.

4

Hint: Choose points that are on intersections of the grid.

____

____

____

____

5

____

____

____

____

6

____

____

____

____

 ISBN: 9780170451970

Reflection

- The figure is **reflected in a mirror** line.

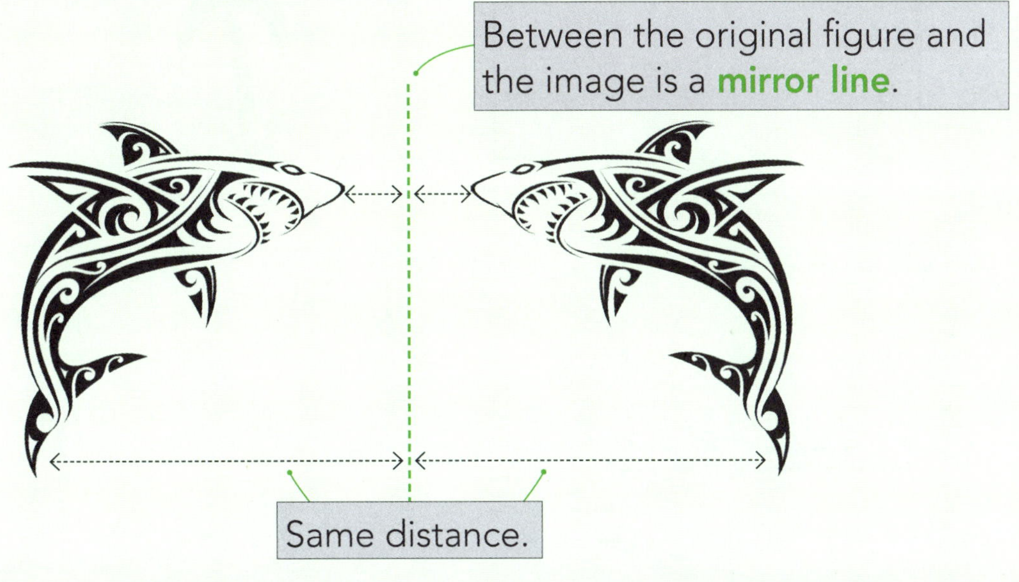

Example: Draw the mirror line for each of these reflections.

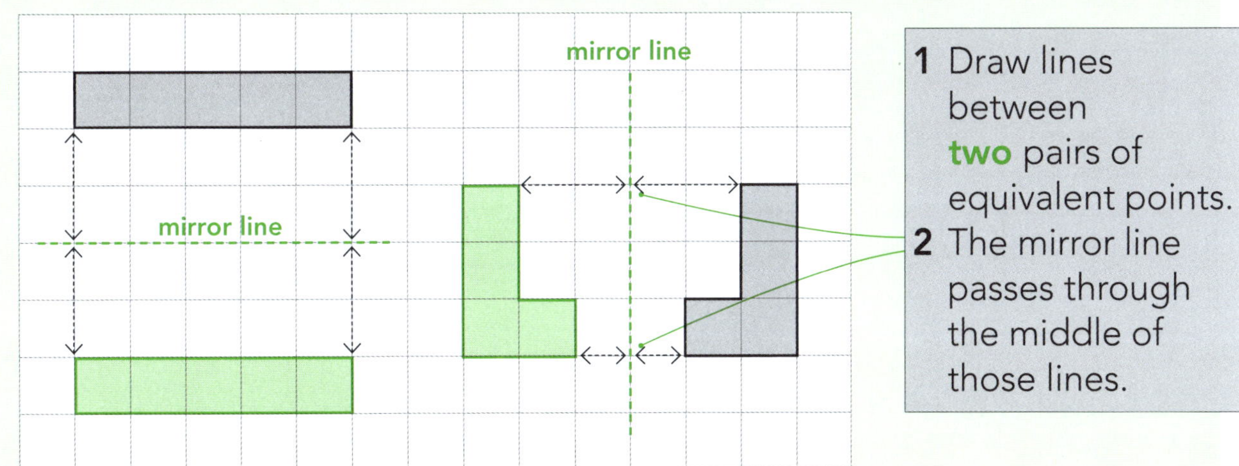

Draw mirror lines for the following reflections.

1

2

3

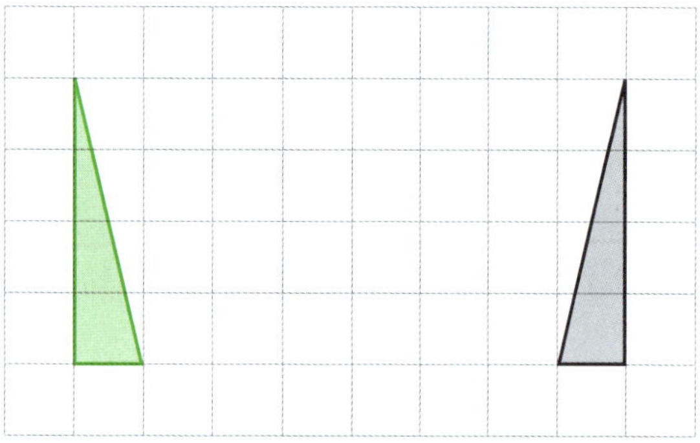

4

5

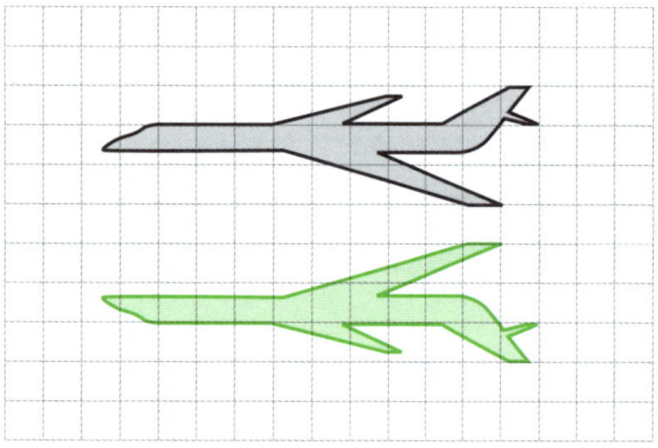

6

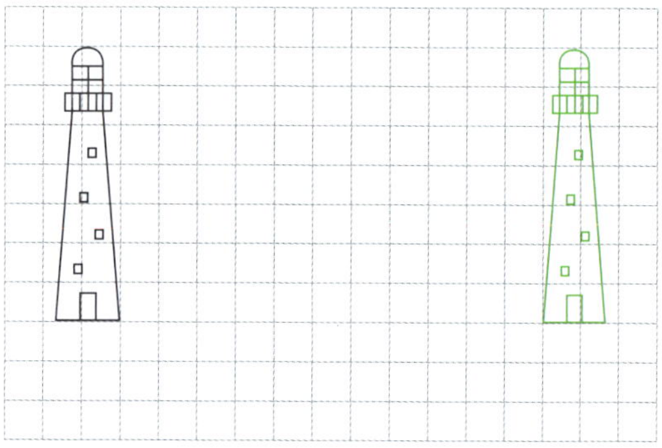

7

8

 ISBN: 9780170451970

Line symmetry

- Some figures form reflections of themselves in a mirror line.
- They are said to have **line symmetry**.
- **Each mirror line** that can be drawn through a figure is known as **a line of symmetry**.
- The **order** of line symmetry is the **number of lines of symmetry** in a figure.

This figure has **one** line of symmetry.

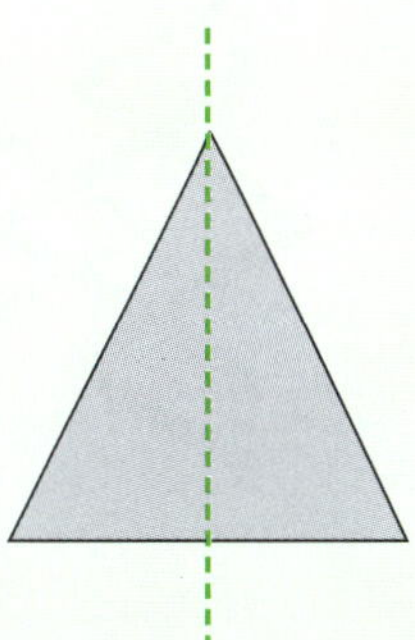

Order of line symmetry = 1

This figure has **two** lines of symmetry.

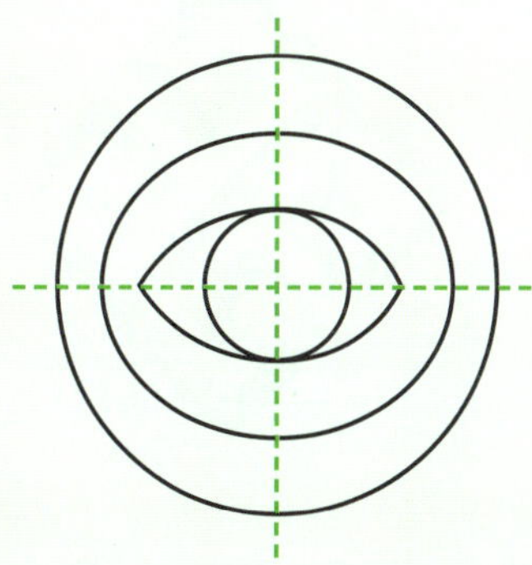

Order of line symmetry = 2

Draw any lines of symmetry on these figures and write the order of line symmetry for each.

1

Order of line symmetry = ________

2

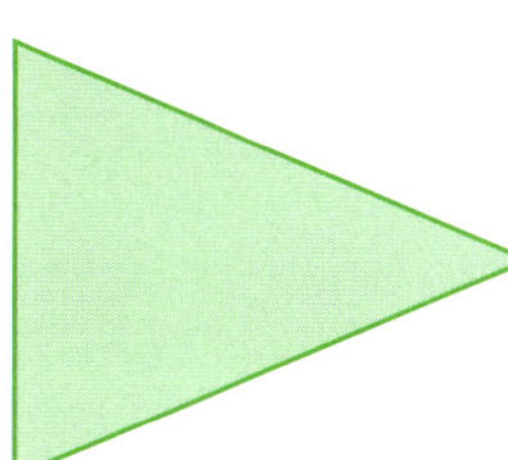

Order of line symmetry = ________

3

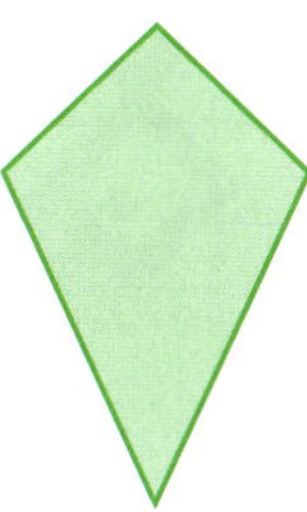

Order of line symmetry = ________

4

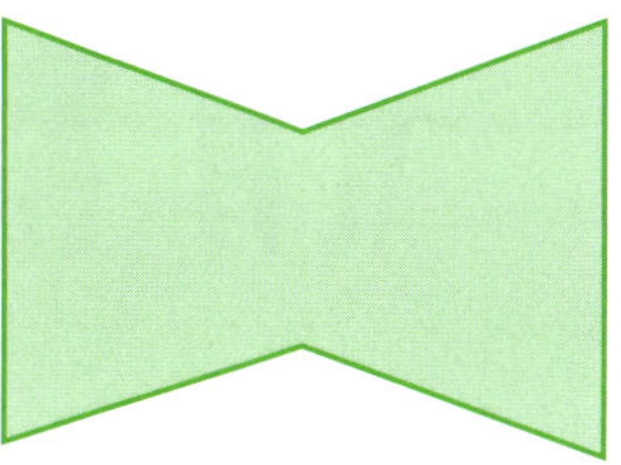

Order of line symmetry = ________

ISBN: 9780170451970

5

Order of line symmetry = ________

6

Order of line symmetry = ________

7

Order of line symmetry = ________

8

Order of line symmetry = ________

9

Order of line symmetry = ________

10

Order of line symmetry = ________

11

Order of line symmetry = ________

12

Order of line symmetry = ________

 ISBN: 9780170451970

Challenge 3

These figures have more than two lines of symmetry. Draw them and write the order of line symmetry for each.

1

Order of line symmetry = ________

2

Order of line symmetry = ________

3

Order of line symmetry = ________

4

Order of line symmetry = ________

5

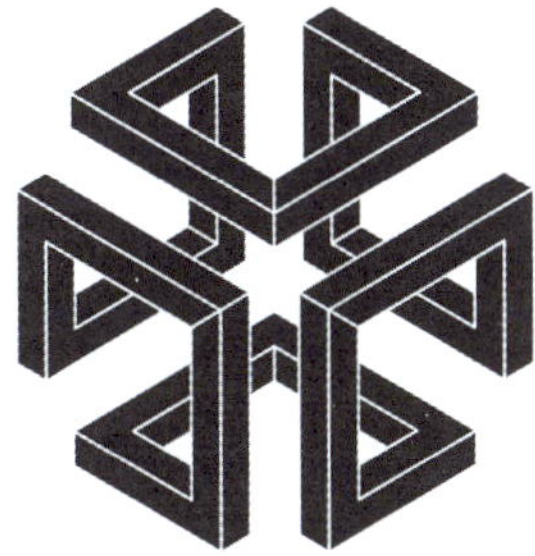

Order of line symmetry = ________

6

Order of line symmetry = ________

ISBN: 9780170451970

Rotation

- The figure **rotates around a point**.
- The **point** is known as the **centre of rotation**.
- Rotations, unless specified otherwise, are always measured in a **clockwise direction**.

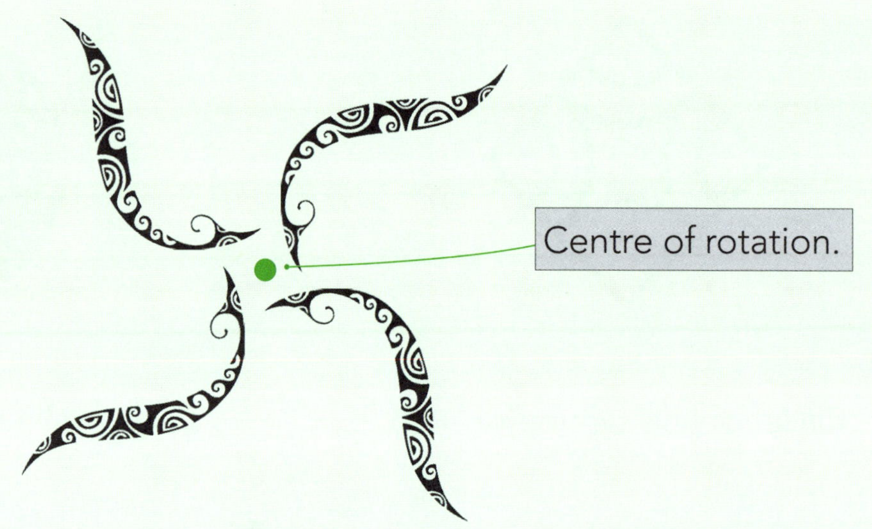

We will use only these angles:

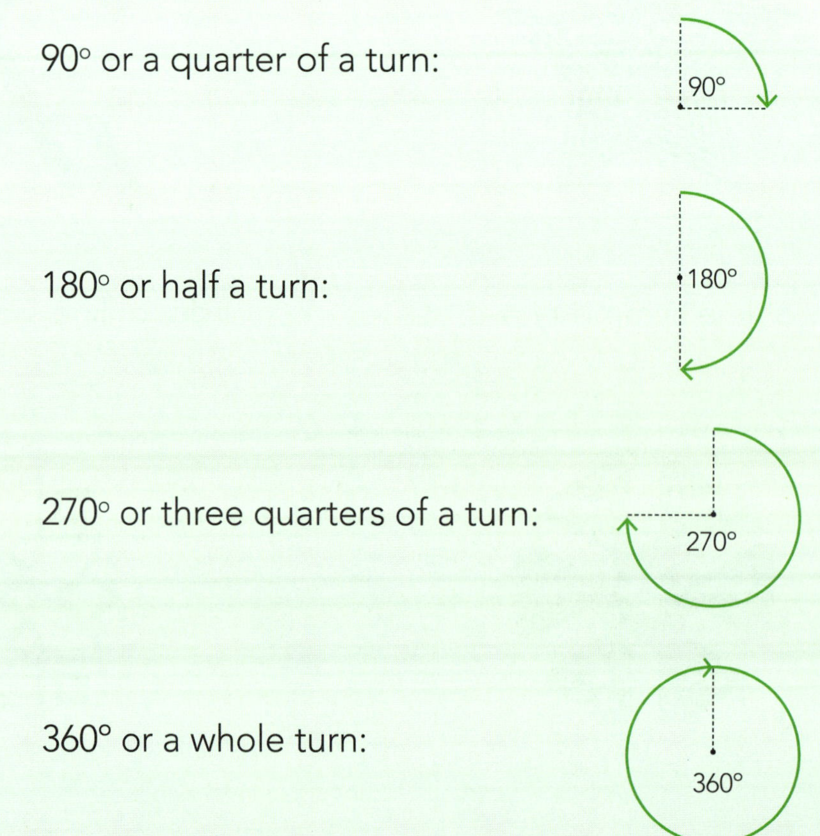

ISBN: 9780170451970

Using angles of rotation

Examples: Write the angle of rotation for each of the following.

Remember: 1 The green figure is the **original**, so **start** your angle there.
2 The grey figure is the **image**.
3 Rotations are in a **clockwise** direction.

Remember: Unless you are told otherwise, angles are always measured in a **clockwise** direction.

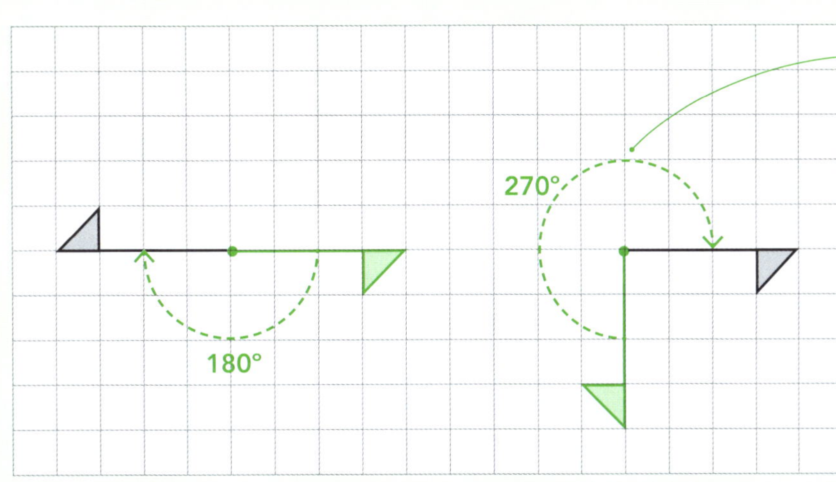

Write the angle of rotation for each of the following.

1

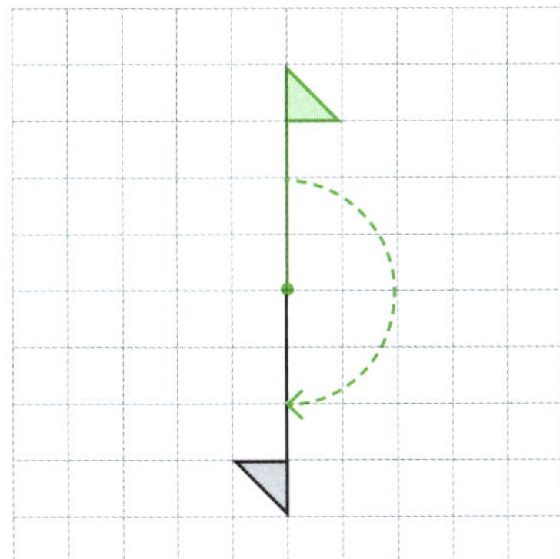

Angle = ________°

2

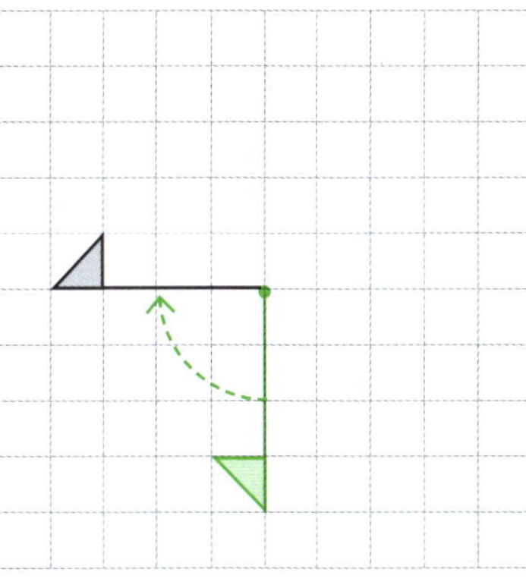

Angle = ________°

3

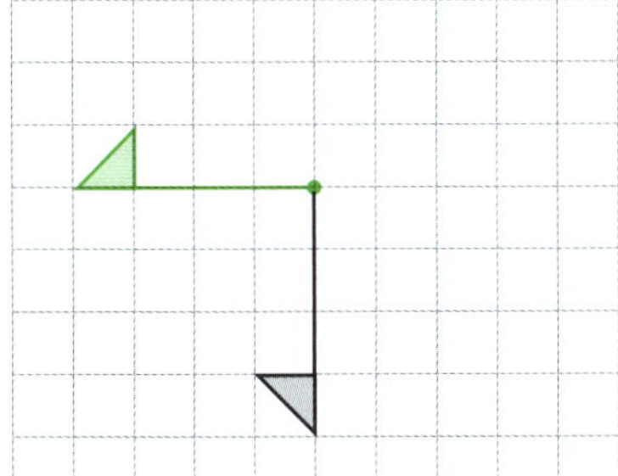

Angle = ________°

4

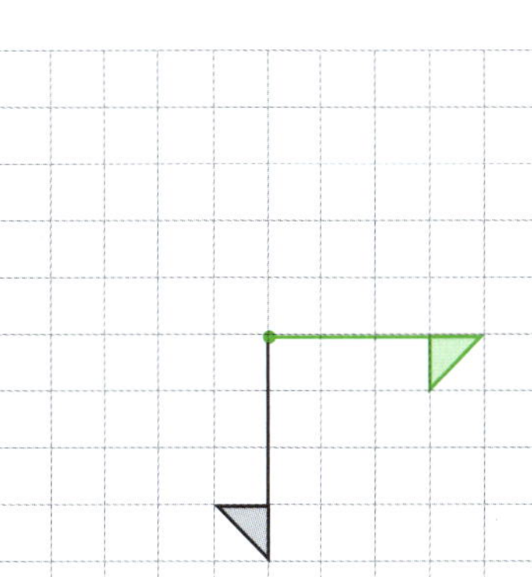

Angle = ________°

ISBN: 9780170451970

Enlargement

- The figure **gets bigger or smaller**.
- The **scale factor** tells us how much larger or smaller the lines in the figure become.

$$\text{scale factor} = \frac{\textbf{length of image}}{\textbf{length of original figure}}$$

Examples:

The lines in the image are **three times** as long as those in the original. The image has a scale factor of **3**.

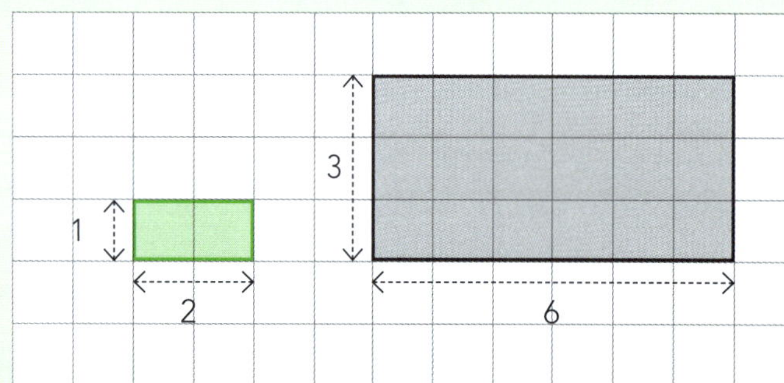

$$\text{scale factor} = \frac{3}{\mathbf{1}} = \frac{6}{\mathbf{2}} = 3$$

The lines in the image are **twice** as long as those in the original. The image has a scale factor of **2**.

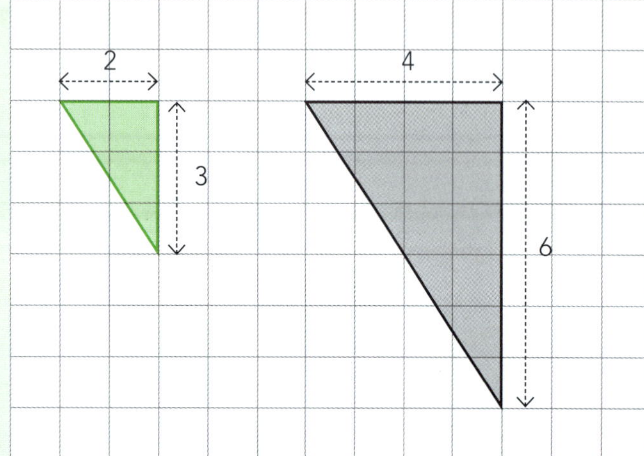

$$\text{scale factor} = \frac{4}{\mathbf{2}} = \frac{6}{\mathbf{3}} = 2$$

ISBN: 9780170451970

Write the scale factor for these enlargements.

1

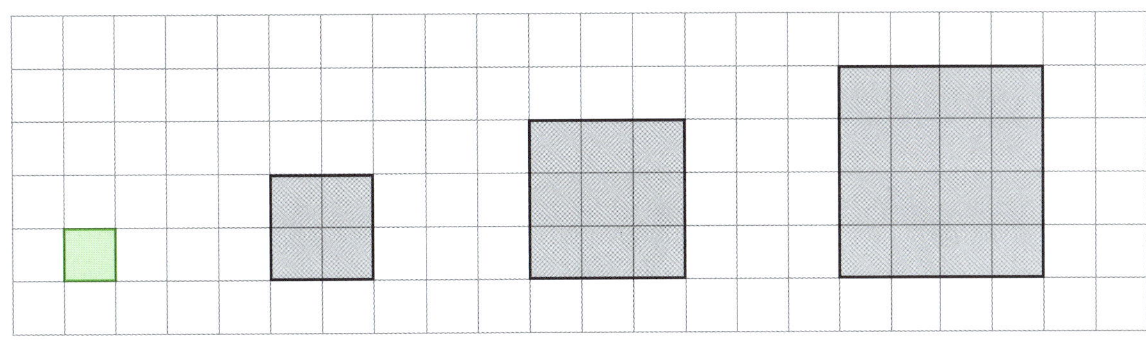

scale factor = ______   scale factor = ______   scale factor = ______

2

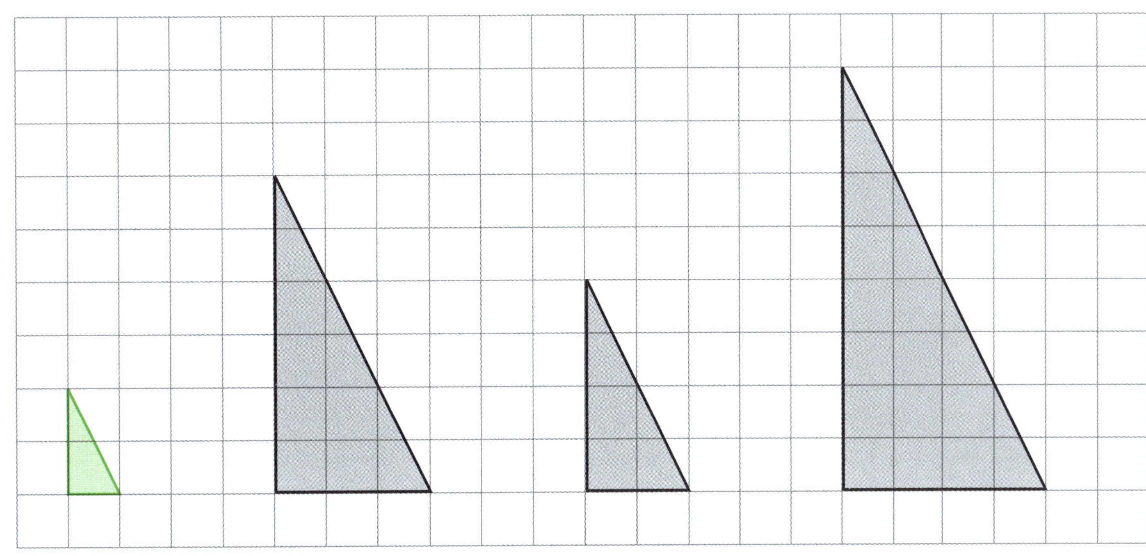

scale factor = ______   scale factor = ______   scale factor = ______

3

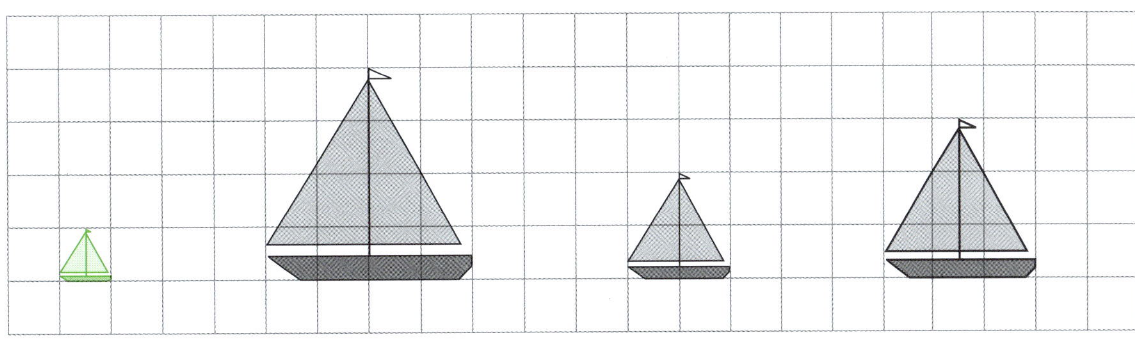

scale factor = ______   scale factor = ______   scale factor = ______

ISBN: 9780170451970

Mixing it up

Circle the correct transformation for each of these pairs of images.

1

Translated Reflected

Rotated Enlarged

2

Translated Reflected

Rotated Enlarged

3

Translated Reflected

Rotated Enlarged

4

Translated Reflected

Rotated Enlarged

5

Translated Reflected

Rotated Enlarged

ISBN: 9780170451970

6

Translated Reflected

Rotated Enlarged

7

Translated Reflected

Rotated Enlarged

8

Translated Reflected

Rotated Enlarged

9

Translated Reflected

Rotated Enlarged

10

Translated Reflected

Rotated Enlarged

ISBN: 9780170451970

Challenge 4

Write down the letter(s) that you think are represented by these logos. Describe the transformations including symmetries in each, if any. If there is reflective symmetry, draw the mirror line.

1 Letter(s): ______

Transformation:

______

______

2 Letter(s): ______

Transformation:

______

______

3 Letter(s): ______

Transformation:

______

______

4 Letter(s): ______

Transformation:

______

______

5 Letter(s): ______

Transformation:

______

______

6 Letter(s): ______

Transformation:

______

______

7 Letter(s): ______

Transformation:

______

______

8 Letter(s): ______

Transformation:

______

______

9 Letter(s): ______

Transformation:

______

______

10 Letter(s): ______

Transformation:

______

______

ISBN: 9780170451970

Revision 1

1 Highlight the word(s) that can be used to describe this shape.

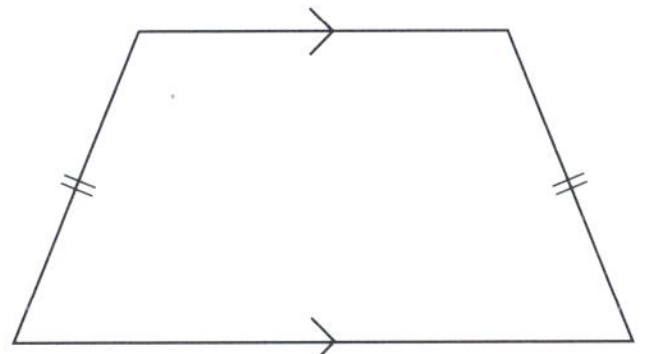

quadrilateral isosceles regular polygon

2 Select the *best* term to describe each of the following figures.

Irregular quadrilateral	Polygon	Trapezium	Isosceles triangle
Irregular triangle	Pentagon	Scalene triangle	Parallelogram

a

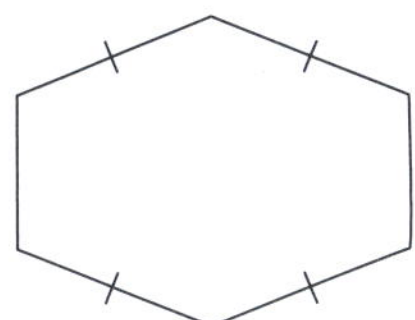

____

b

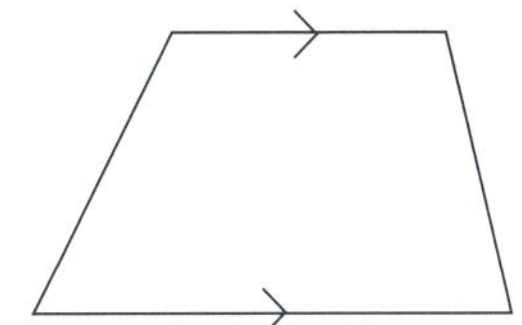

____

c

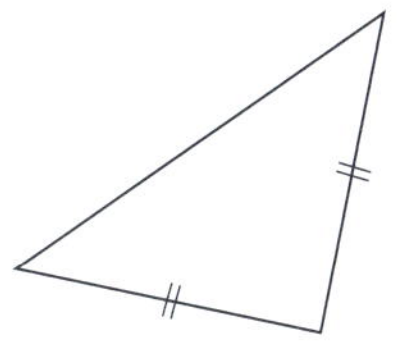

____

3 **a** Name the marked angle using any of the letters A, B, C, D.

$\angle$ ______

b What type of angle is this? ______________

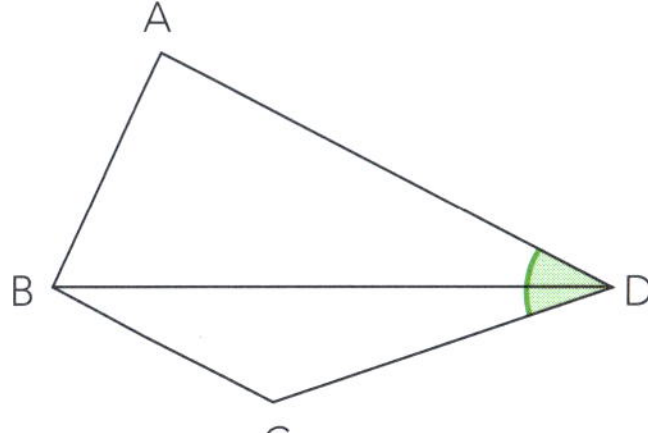

4 Calculate the size of the marked angles.

a

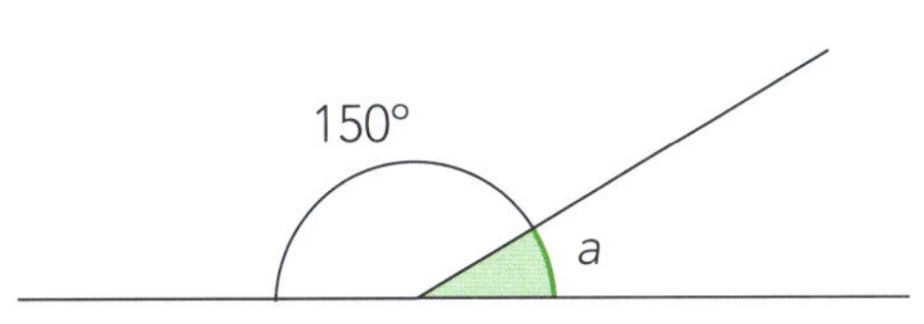

____

____

b

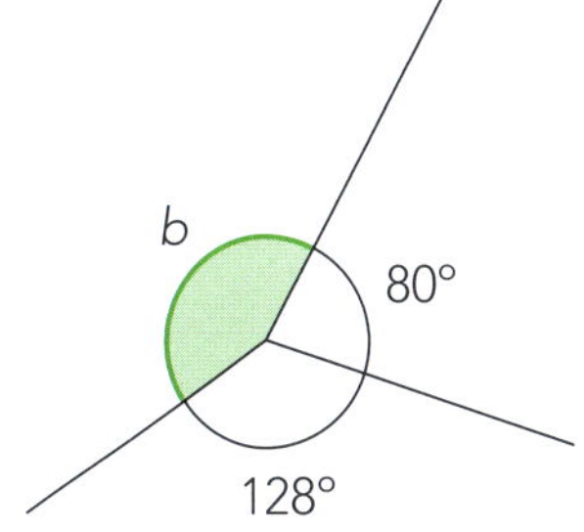

____

____

c

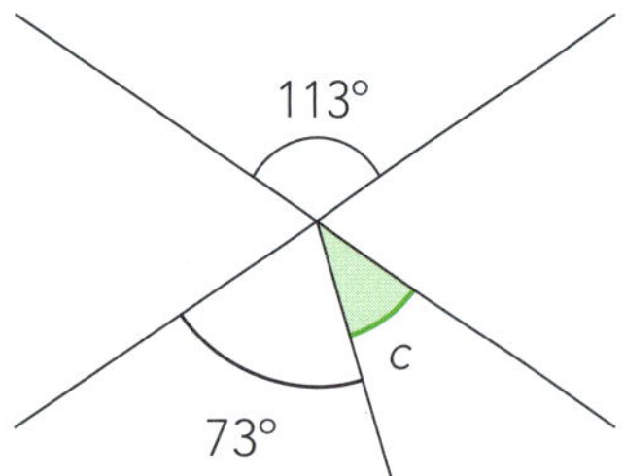

d

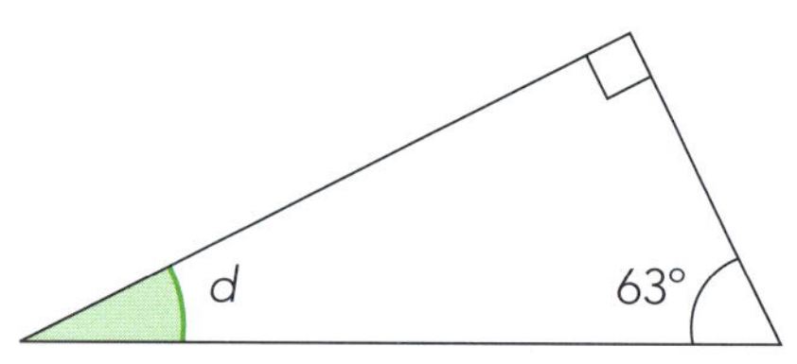

______________________ ______________________

______________________ ______________________

5 Write down the numbers of vertices, edges and faces this 3D shape has.

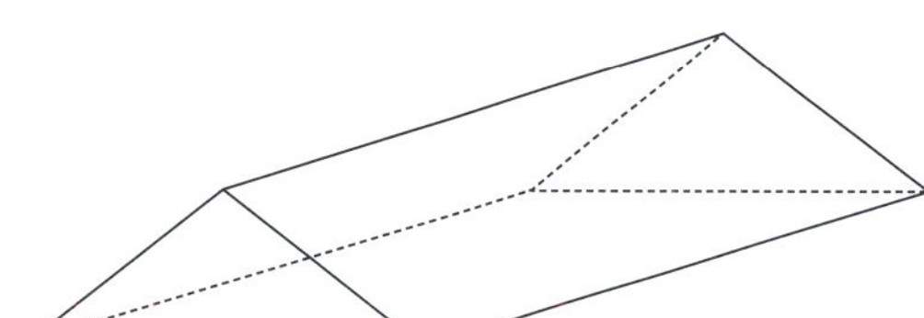

Vertices ________

Edges ________

Faces ________

6

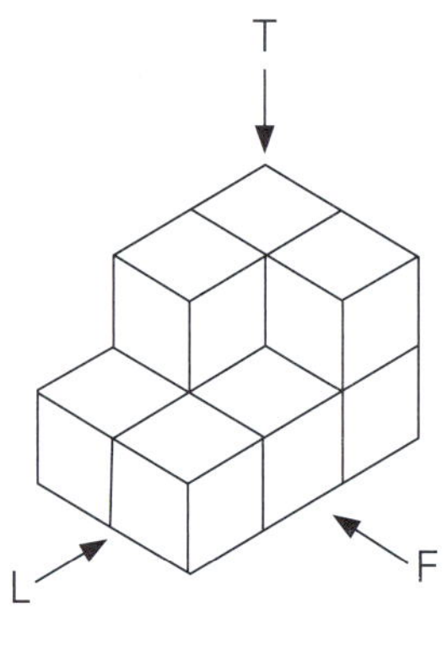

a Draw this shape on the isometric grid.

b Write the number of blocks in each column.

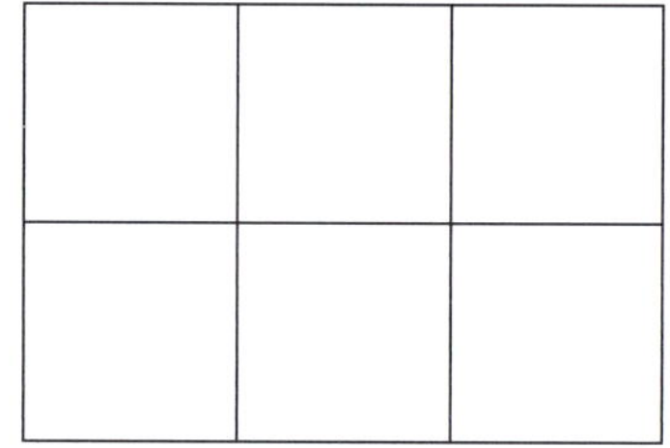

c Draw the top, left and front views of this shape.

Top Left Front

ISBN: 9780170451970

7

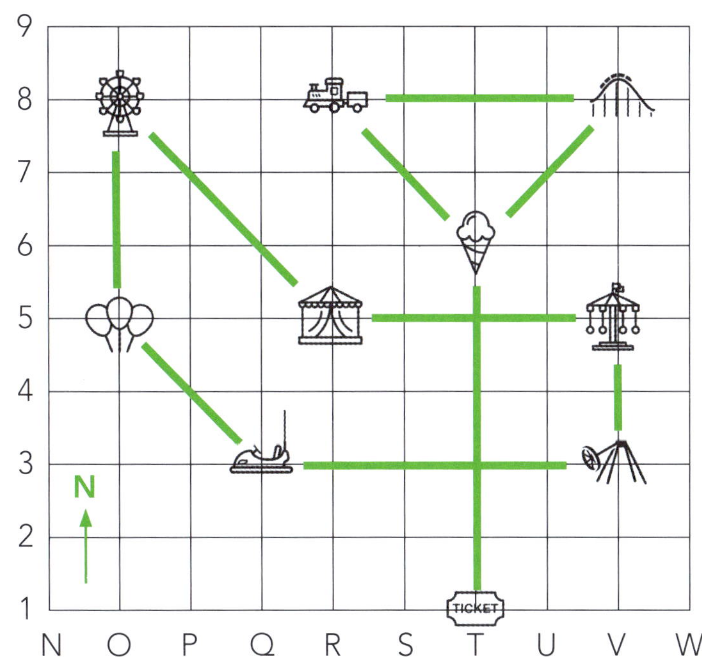

Key
Balloons
Ferris wheel
Stage
Merry-go-round
Bumper cars
Pendulum ride
Rollercoaster
Train
Ice creams

a What would you find at the grid point V5? ________________

b Write the grid point for the location of the train. ________________

c In what direction should you walk if you wanted to get from the rollercoaster to the ice creams? ________________

d Where would you get to if you walked southeast from the balloons? ________________

e Name a symbol that has one line of symmetry. ________________

8 The green stick figure has been translated and then rotated around the green point. Describe these transformations.

a The translation:

____

____

b The rotation:

____

____

ISBN: 9780170451970

Revision 2

1 Highlight the word(s) that can be used to describe this shape.

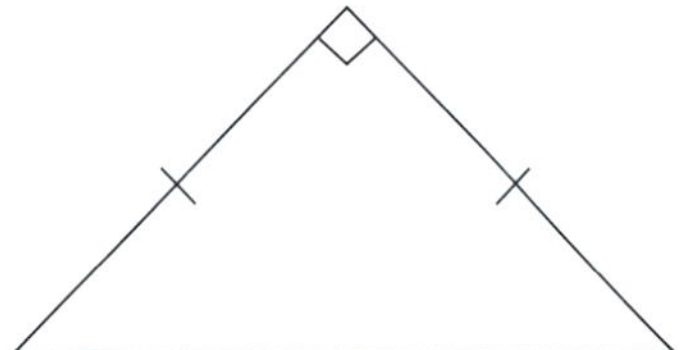

isosceles regular polygon parallel

2 Select the *best* term to describe each of the following figures.

Isosceles triangle	Polygon	Hexagon	Irregular triangle
Irregular quadrilateral	Arrowhead	Scalene triangle	Parallelogram

a 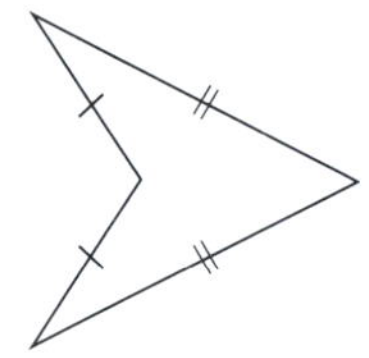

____

b 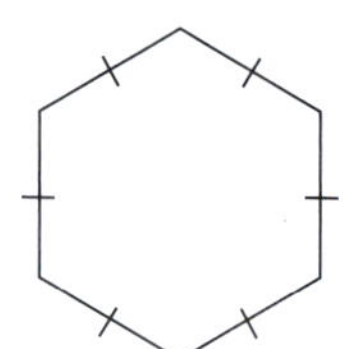

____

c 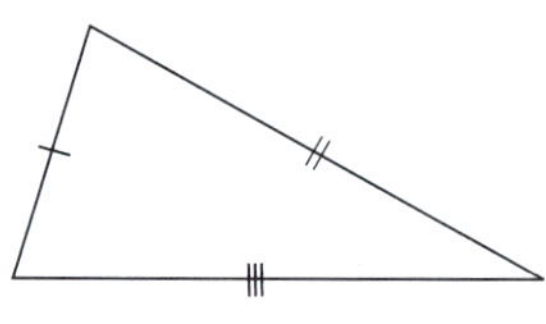

____

3 **a** Name the marked angle using any of the letters A, B, C, D. ∠ ________

b What type of angle is this? ________________

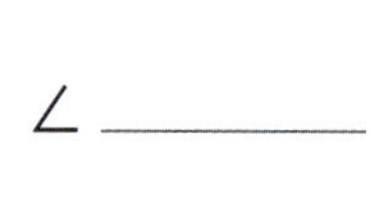

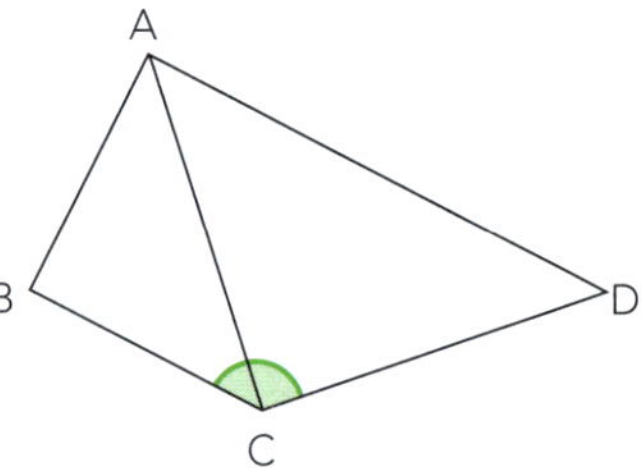

4 Calculate the size of the marked angles.

a 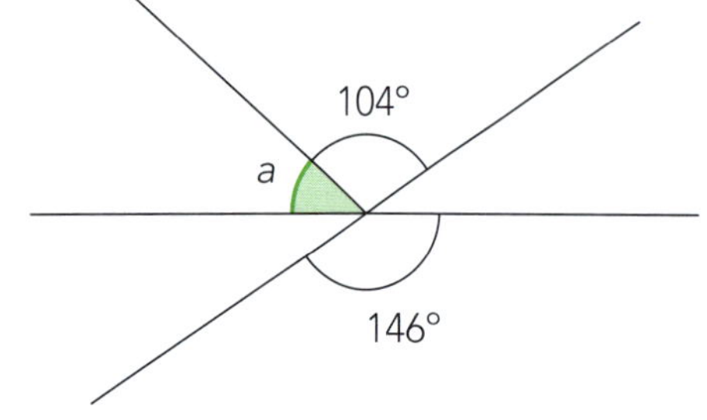

____

____

b 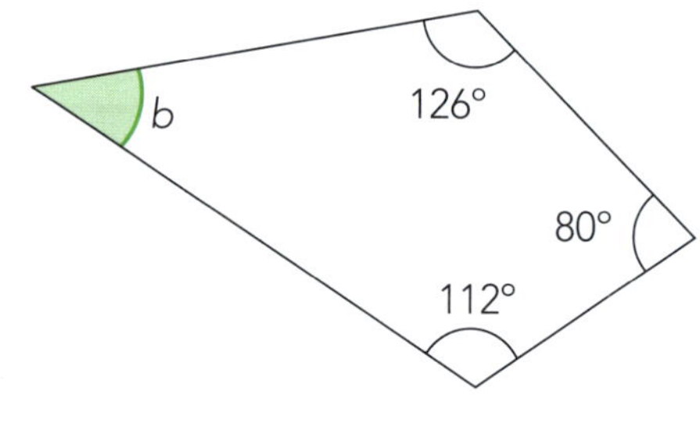

____

____

ISBN: 9780170451970

c

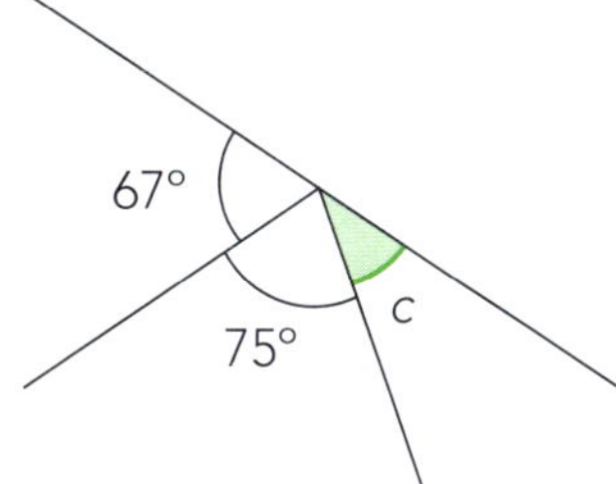

d

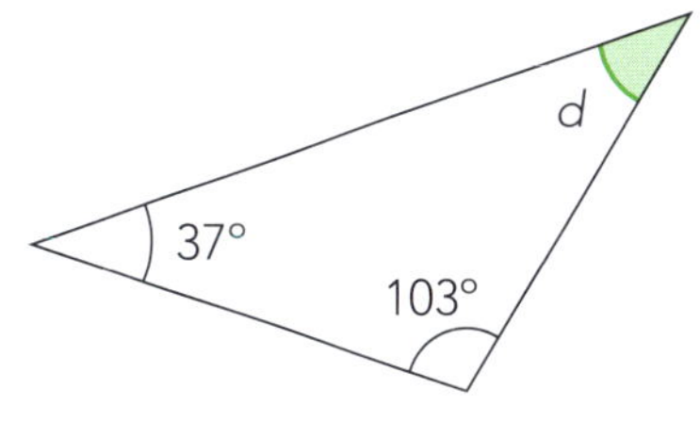

______________________ ______________________

______________________ ______________________

5 Write down the numbers of vertices, edges and faces this 3D shape has.

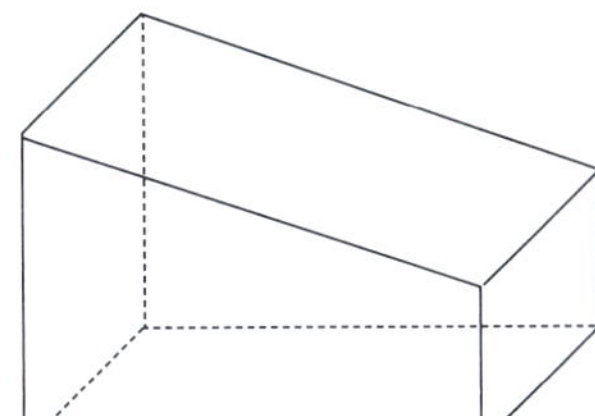

Vertices ________

Edges ________

Faces ________

6

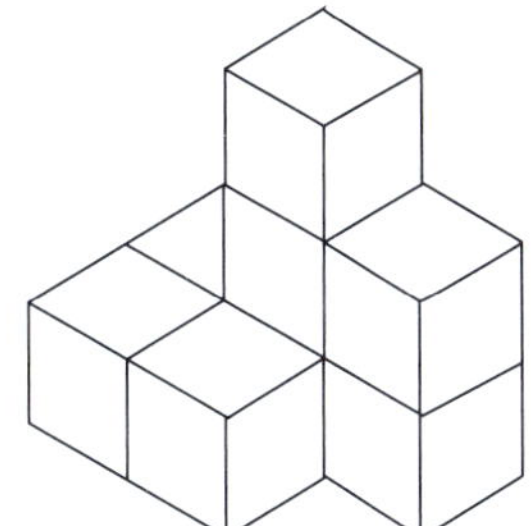

a Draw this shape on the isometric grid.

b Write the number of blocks in each column.

c Draw the top, left, front and right views of this shape.

Top Left Front

7

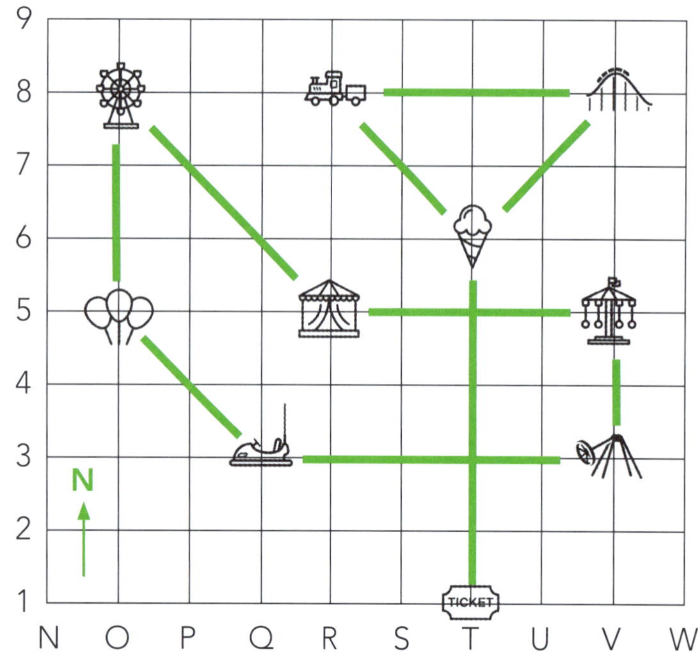

Key	
Balloons	
Ferris wheel	
Stage	
Merry-go-round	
Bumper cars	
Pendulum ride	
Rollercoaster	
Train	
Ice creams	

a What would you find at the grid point Q3? ________________

b Write the grid point for the location of the balloons. ________________

c In what direction should you walk if you wanted to get from the stage to the ferris wheel? ________________

d Where would you get to if you walked southwest from the rollercoaster? ________________

e Name a symbol that has no lines of symmetry. ________________

8 The green truck has been reflected and then enlarged.

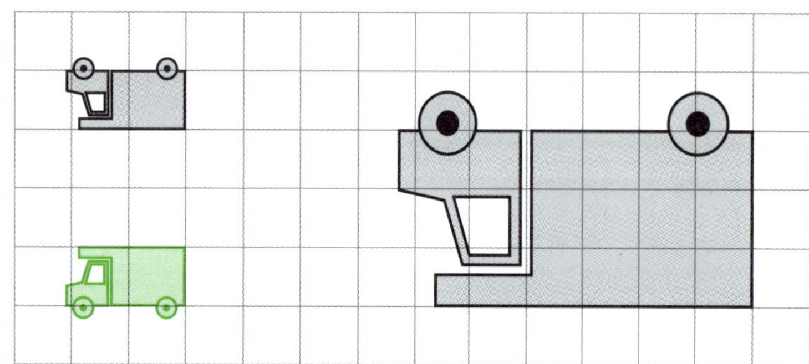

a Draw the mirror line for the reflection.

b Write the scale factor for the enlargement.

Scale factor = __________

 ISBN: 9780170451970

Answers

Shapes (pp. 6–14)

Polygons (p. 6)

1	Polygon	2	Not a polygon
3	Not a polygon	4	Polygon
5	Not a polygon	6	Polygon

Shape language (pp. 7–9)

1	triangle	polygon	regular
2	polygon	quadrilateral	
3	symmetrical	regular	polygon
4	quadrilateral	polygon	irregular
5	irregular	triangle	
6	symmetrical		

7 These are some shapes you could have drawn. Check with your teacher if you have something different.

8 These are some shapes you could have drawn. Check with your teacher if you have something different.

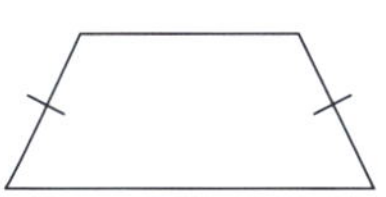

9 These are some shapes you could have drawn. Check with your teacher if you have something different.

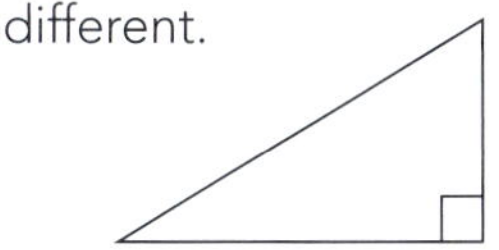
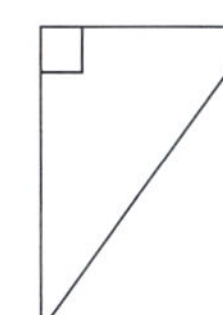

Naming triangles (pp. 10–11)

1	Isosceles	2	Right-angled, scalene
3	Equilateral	4	Scalene
5	Isosceles		
6	Right-angled, isosceles		
7	Scalene	8	Isosceles
9	12		

Naming quadrilaterals (p. 12)

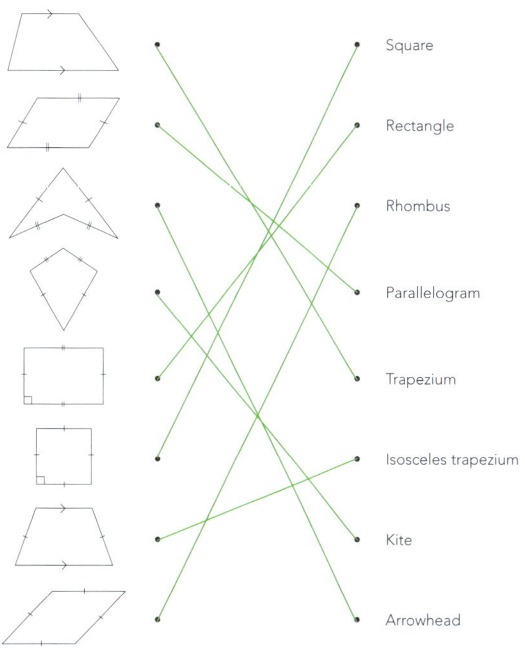

Naming other 2D shapes (p. 13)

1	pentagon	2	hexagon
3	heptagon	4	circle
5	semicircle	6	octagon
7	nonagon	8	decagon

Challenge 1 (p. 14)

Number of rectangles = 14
Number of quadrilaterals = 12

Angles (pp. 15–37)

Matching angles (p. 16)

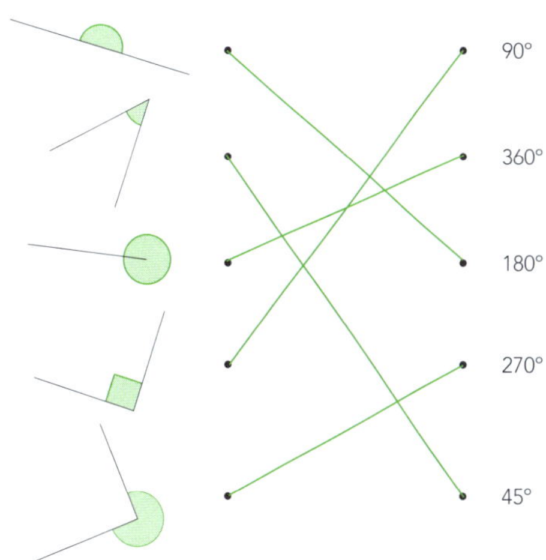

ISBN: 9780170451970

Estimating angles (pp. 17–18)

1	80°	**2**	40°
3	320°	**4**	120°
5	20°	**6**	200°
7	250°	**8**	170°

Types of angles (pp. 19–20)

1	Right angle	**2**	Acute angle
3	Straight angle	**4**	Reflex angle
5	Obtuse angle	**6**	Acute angle
7	Right angle	**8**	Straight angle
9	Obtuse angle	**10**	Reflex angle

Naming angles (pp. 21–22)

1	$\angle b$	**2**	$\angle BAD$
3	$\angle a$	**4**	$\angle ABD$
5	$\angle CBA$	**6**	$\angle d$

7

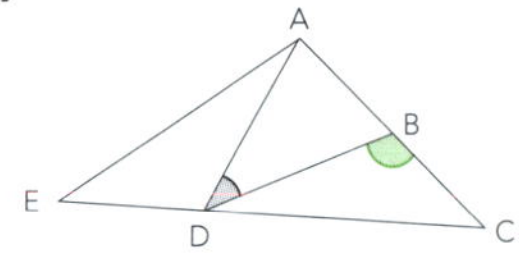
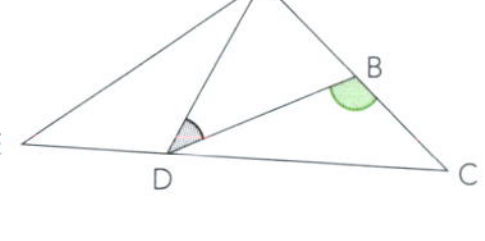

Shaded angle: $\angle DBC$ or $\angle CBD$

8

Shaded angle: $\angle CFD$ or $\angle DFC$

9

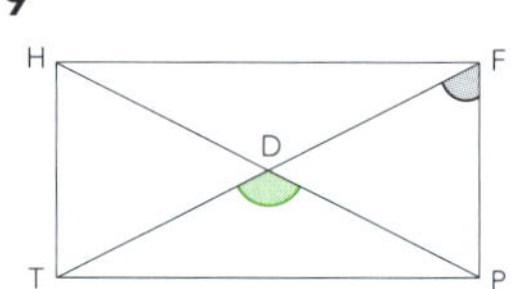

Shaded angle: $\angle TDP$ or $\angle PDT$

10

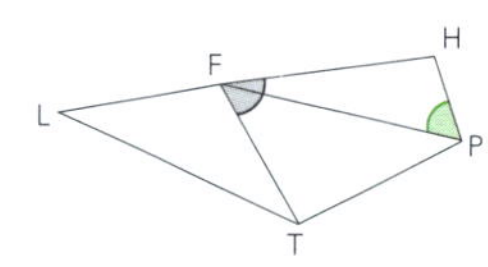

Shaded angle: $\angle FPH$ or $\angle HPF$

11

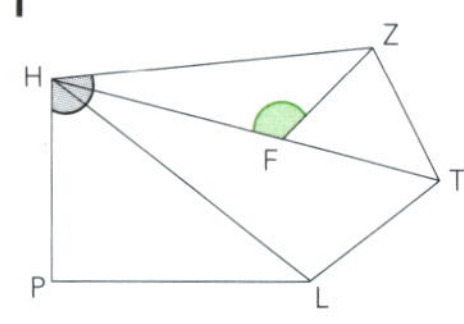
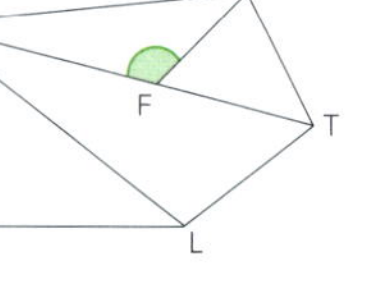

Shaded angle: $\angle HFZ$ or $\angle ZFH$

12

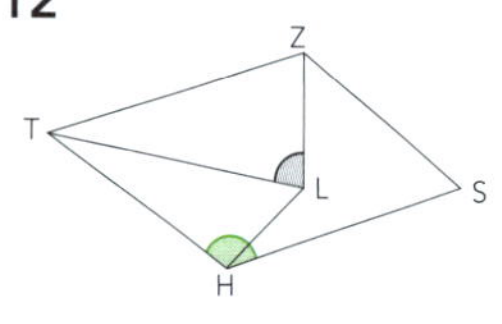

Shaded angle: $\angle TJS$ or $\angle SJT$

Angles in a right angle (pp. 23–24)

1	$a = 50^\circ$	**2**	$g = 60^\circ$
3	$z = 35^\circ$	**4**	$y = 15^\circ$
5	$f = 56^\circ$	**6**	$p = 71^\circ$
7	$h = 35^\circ$	**8**	$k = 30^\circ$
9	$b = 31^\circ$	**10**	$k = 15^\circ$
11	$\angle DFE = 12^\circ$	**12**	$\angle PUQ = 16^\circ$

Angles on a line (pp. 25–26)

1	$a = 70^\circ$	**2**	$f = 135^\circ$
3	$y = 100^\circ$	**4**	$x = 75^\circ$
5	$b = 43^\circ$	**6**	$a = 110^\circ$
7	$z = 40^\circ$	**8**	$g = 91^\circ$
9	$y = 56^\circ$	**10**	$h = 48^\circ$
11	$\angle DCI = 50^\circ$	**12**	$\angle JMK = 34^\circ$

Angles at a point (pp. 27–28)

1	$a = 160^\circ$	**2**	$x = 210^\circ$
3	$d = 40^\circ$	**4**	$z = 310^\circ$
5	$c = 140^\circ$	**6**	$y = 170^\circ$
7	$p = 235^\circ$	**8**	$x = 42^\circ$
9	$b = 142^\circ$	**10**	$b = 101^\circ$
11	$\angle CDB = 114^\circ$	**12**	$\angle VZW = 113^\circ$

Vertically opposite angles (pp. 29–30)

1	$y = 130^\circ$	**2**	$b = 85^\circ$
3	$a = 45^\circ$	**4**	$x = 75^\circ$
5	$c = 110^\circ$	**6**	$f = 60^\circ$
7	$g = 40^\circ$	**8**	$p = 34^\circ$
9	$d = 57^\circ$	**10**	$y = 45^\circ$
11	$\angle MPN = 45^\circ$	**12**	$\angle WXV = 21^\circ$

Angles in a triangle (pp. 31–32)

1	$z = 50^\circ$	**2**	$a = 50^\circ$
3	$b = 60^\circ$	**4**	$z = 66^\circ$
5	$k = 58^\circ$	**6**	$b = 40^\circ$
7	$h = 66^\circ$	**8**	$a = 45^\circ$
9	$x = 110^\circ$	**10**	$p = 78^\circ$
11	$\angle EHG = 121^\circ$	**12**	$\angle UVW = 83^\circ$

Angles in a quadrilateral (pp. 33–34)

1	$b = 110^\circ$	**2**	$d = 90^\circ$
3	$a = 68^\circ$	**4**	$y = 103^\circ$
5	$z = 76^\circ$	**6**	$c = 79^\circ$
7	$d = 33^\circ$	**8**	$g = 76^\circ$
9	$\angle EFG = 69^\circ$	**10**	$\angle KJN = 60^\circ$

Mixing it up (pp. 35–36)

1	$g = 48^\circ$	**2**	$x = 130^\circ$
3	$p = 112^\circ$	**4**	$f = 105^\circ$
5	$z = 108^\circ$	**6**	$p = 65^\circ$
7	$c = 126^\circ$	**8**	$b = 85^\circ$
9	$y = 20^\circ$	**10**	$m = 52^\circ$
11	$k = 64^\circ$	**12**	$f = 48^\circ$

Challenge 2 (p. 37)

$a = 75^\circ$	$b = 69^\circ$	$c = 39^\circ$
$d = 39^\circ$	$e = 46^\circ$	$f = 76^\circ$
$g = 45^\circ$	$h = 111^\circ$	$i = 69^\circ$

2D and 3D shapes (pp. 38–43)

2D and 3D language (p. 38)

1	2D	**2**	3D
3	3D	**4**	2D
5	2D	**6**	3D
7	3D	**8**	2D

 ISBN: 9780170451970

Vertices, faces, sides and edges (p. 39)

1 Vertices 6
Edges 9
Faces 5

2 Vertices 5
Edges 8
Faces 5

3 Vertices 4
Edges 6
Faces 4

4 Vertices 8
Edges 12
Faces 6

5 Vertices 10
Edges 15
Faces 7

6 Vertices 7
Edges 12
Faces 7

Naming 3D shapes (p. 40)

1 Pyramid
2 Cone
3 Cuboid
4 Cube
5 Cylinder
6 Cone
7 Sphere
8 Pyramid
9 Cylinder

Nets (pp. 41–43)

1

Shape name	Picture	Number of rectangular or square faces	Number of triangular faces
Cube		6	0
Triangular prism		3	2
Square-based pyramid		1	4
Tetrahedron		0	4
Octahedron		0	8

2

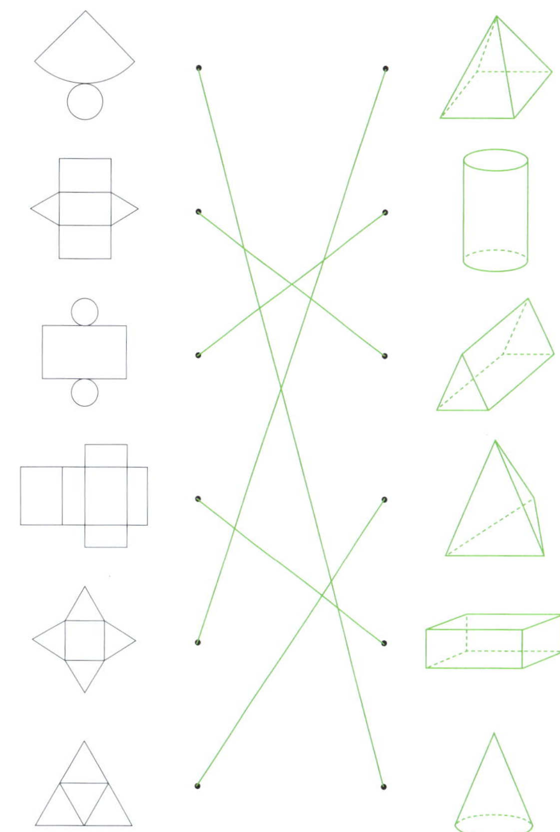

3

ISBN: 9780170451970

Isometrics (pp. 44–54)

Copying isometric shapes (pp. 44–45)

Get a teacher or classmate to check your work.

Drawing cuboids (pp. 46–47)

1 Number of blocks: 12

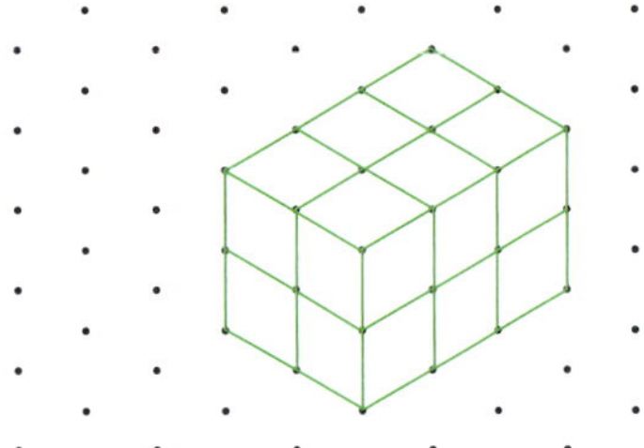

2 Number of blocks: 8

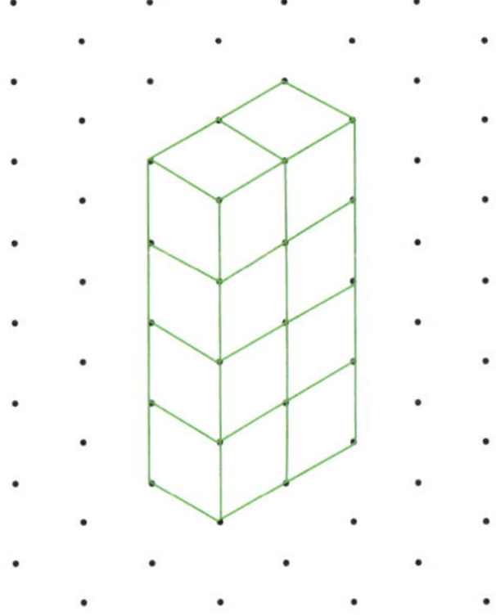

3 Number of blocks: 6

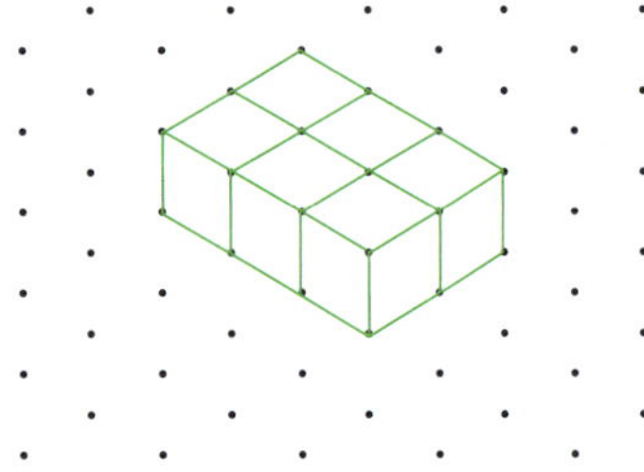

Mix and match (p. 48)

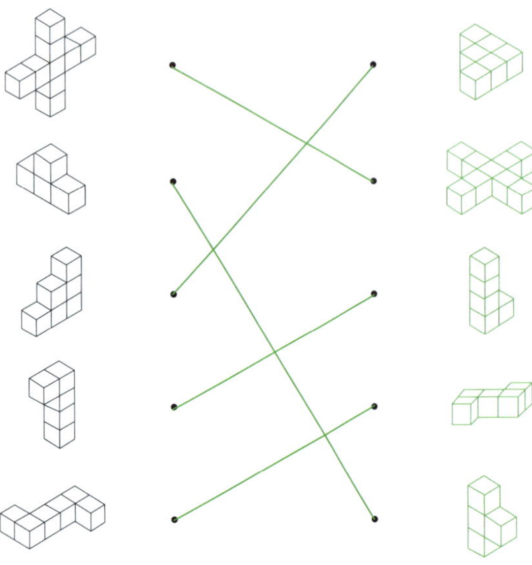

Drawing isometric shapes from numbers in each column (pp. 49–51)

1

2
1 1
1 1
1

2

1
1 3
1 2
1

3

2
3 2
1 2
1

4

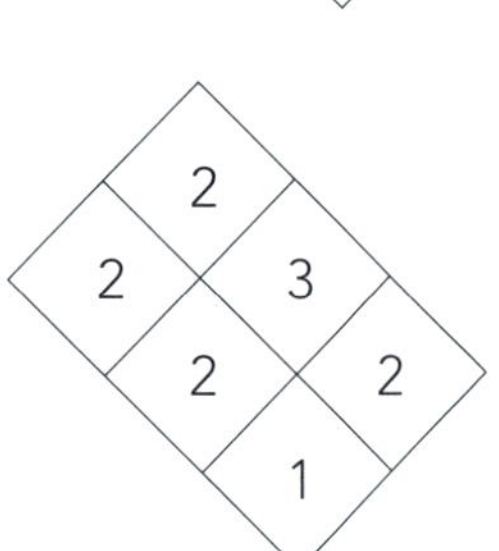

5

1
1 2
2 3
1

6

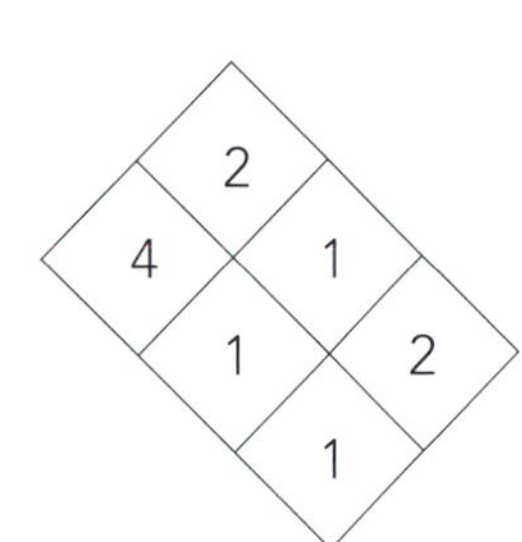

7

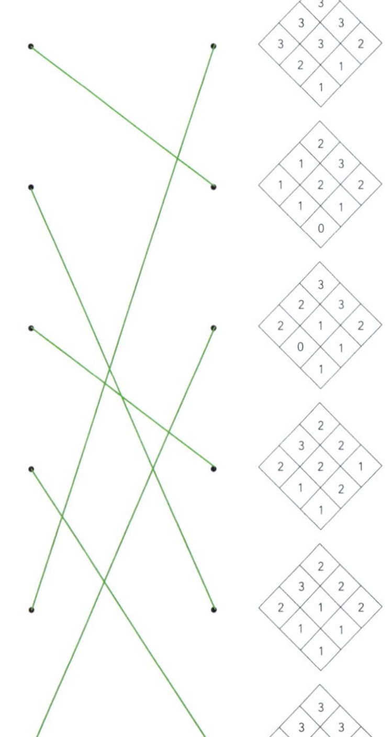

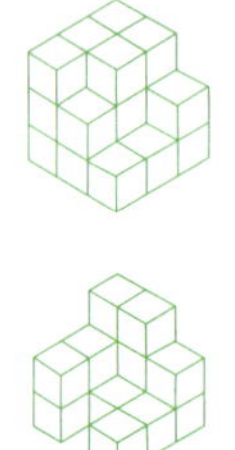

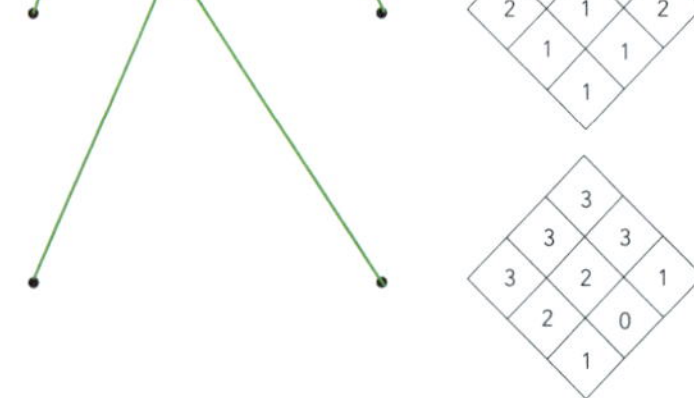

Different views of isometric drawings (pp. 52–54)

1	C	**2**	D
3	A	**4**	B
5	F	**6**	E

 ISBN: 9780170451970

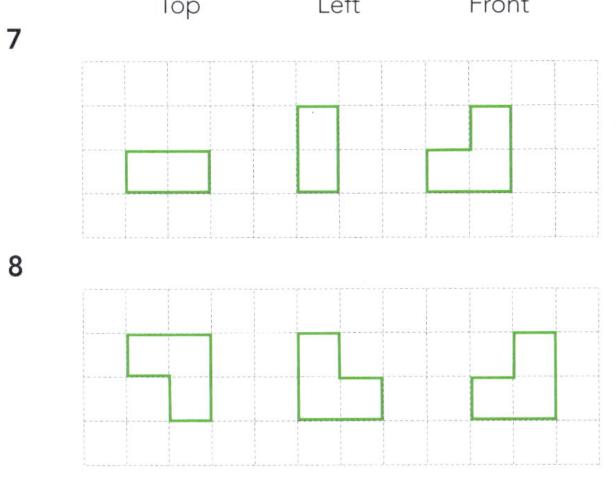

9

10

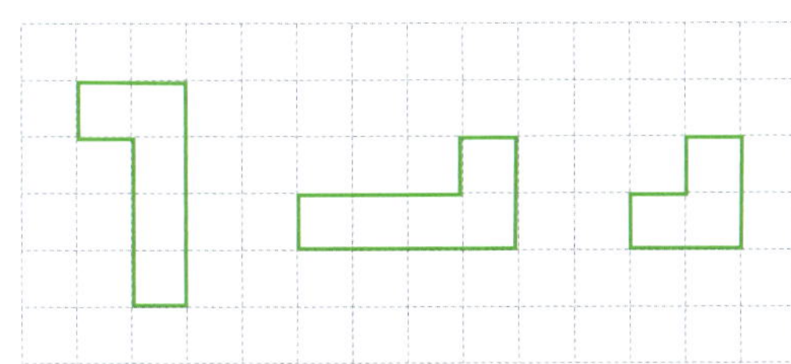

Position and orientation (pp. 55–65)

Directions (pp. 55–56)

1	W	**2**	NW	**3**	S	**4**	E
5	NE	**6**	SW	**7**	N	**8**	SE

Location: grid references (pp. 57–61)

Locating squares

1	Star	**2**	Letter
3	R7	**4**	T5
5	Scott's Hut	**6**	Seahorse Kingdom
7	Penguins	**8**	Shark Zone
9	3F	**10**	3C
11	2A	**12**	4F

Locating grid points

1	Spider's web	**2**	Ship's wheel
3	Star	**4**	Hand
5	X6	**6**	U5
7	V4	**8**	X8
9	Insect house	**10**	Aviary
11	Information centre	**12**	Ice-cream stall
13	Bat cave	**14**	Toilets
15	B7	**16**	G4
17	M12	**18**	L1
19	J9	**20**	L5
21	Insect house	**22**	Restaurant
23	Kiwi house	**24**	Restaurant
25	Toilets	**26**	Ice-cream stall
27	D7	**28**	L7
29	G8	**30**	E4

Paths and directions (pp. 62–65)

1	The insect house	**2**	The aviary
3	The restaurant	**4**	The ice-cream stall
5	The bat cave	**6**	The tuatara

7 From the tuatara, walk northwest to the restaurant and then west.

8 From the duck pond, walk southeast to the farmyard, then turn right and walk in a north-westerly direction.

9 From the entrance, walk north to the insect house and then northwest.

10 From the entrance, walk north to the second intersection, then turn right and walk east. Then turn right again and walk south.

11 From the giant totara, walk north to the tuatara, then northwest to the restaurant. Then walk west to an intersection, where you turn right and walk north.

12 From the information centre, walk east, turn left, and walk north to the second intersection. Then turn right and walk east to the restaurant. From there, turn left and walk north.

Note: For Q**13–17** your answers may be different from these. If so, get your teacher or neighbour to check them. Allow ± 0.1 cm and ± 10 m either side of these distances.

13	1.5 cm	150 m	**14**	2.6 cm	260 m
15	2.8 cm	280 m	**16**	4.3 cm	430 m
17	0.8 cm	80 m			

18 A church

19 The information centre

20 The caravan park

21 From the library, go east along Mackay Street for about 550 m to the intersection with Mawhera Quay. Turn right and go about 200 m and then cross the Cobden Bridge. At the end of the bridge turn right.

22 From the museum, go right along Gresson Street for about 200 m to the roundabout. Turn right and head south for about 600 m along Herbert Street. Turn right into Turumaha Street and go about 400 m. Dixon Park is on your left.

Transformation geometry (pp. 66–79)

Translation (pp. 67–68)

1 The square has moved **6** square(s) to the **right** and **2** square(s) **down**.

2 The rectangle has moved **6** square(s) to the **left** and **2** square(s) **down**.

3 The triangle has moved three square(s) to the left and four square(s) up.

4 The stickman has moved seven square(s) to the right and two square(s) up.

5 The ship has moved seven square(s) to the left and zero square(s) up or down.

6 The dice has moved four square(s) to the left and four square(s) down.

Reflection (pp. 69–70)

1

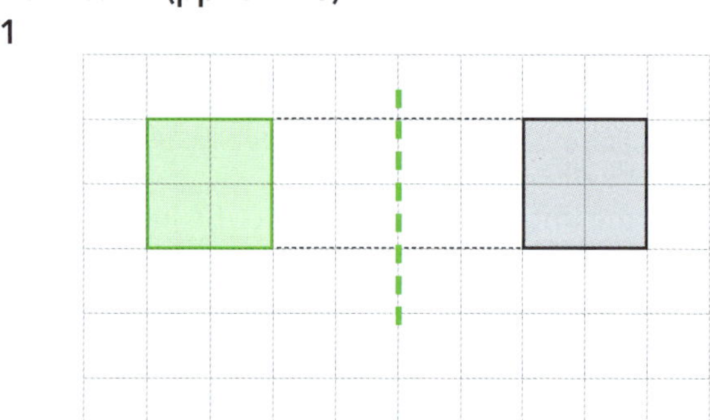

2

3

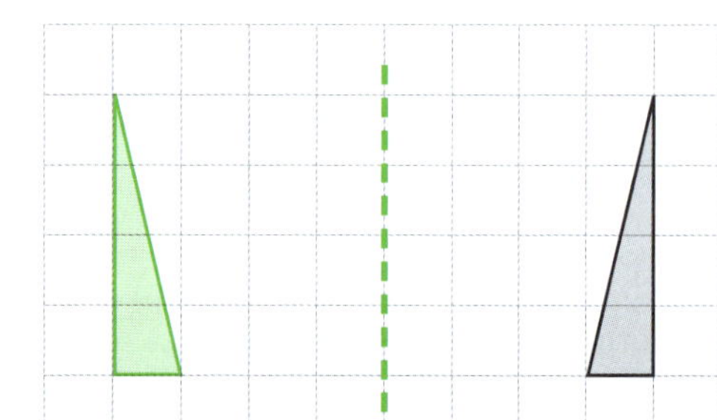

4

5

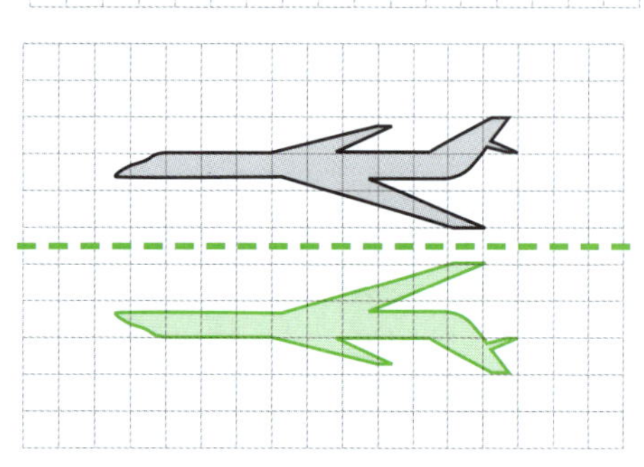

6

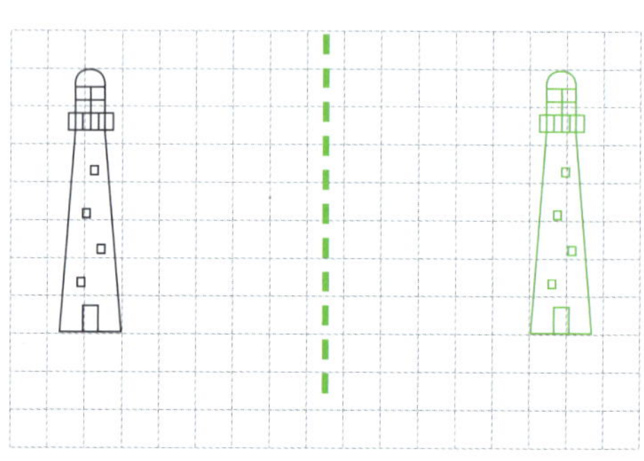

7

8

Line symmetry (pp. 71–72)

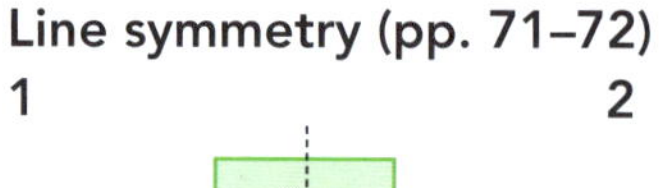

1

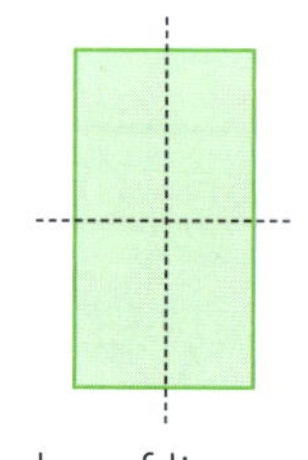

Order of line symmetry = 2

2

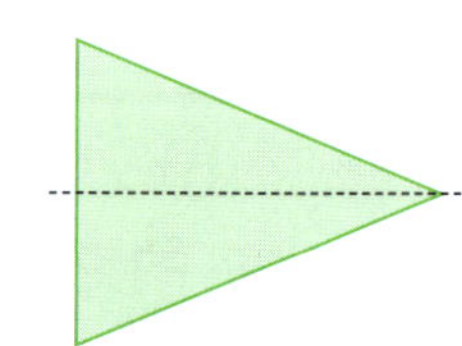

Order of line symmetry = 1

3

Order of line symmetry = 2

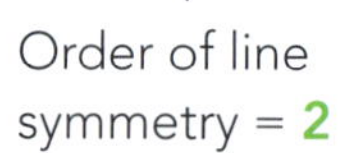

4

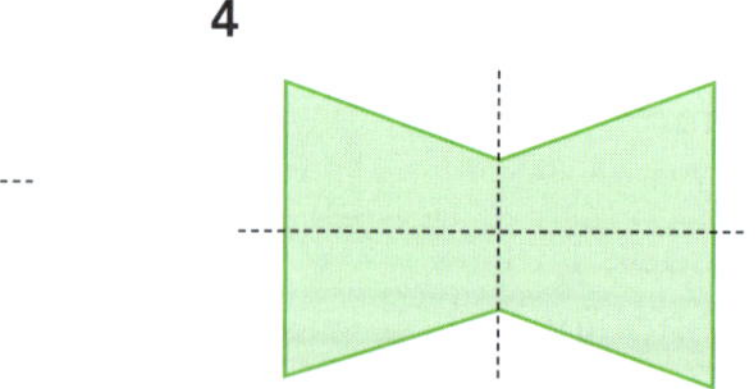

Order of line symmetry = 2

5

Order of line symmetry = 1

6

Order of line symmetry = 1

 ISBN: 9780170451970

7

Order of line symmetry = **2**

8

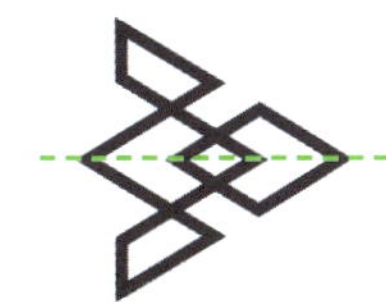

Order of line symmetry = **1**

9

Order of line symmetry = **2**

10

Order of line symmetry = **1**

11

Order of line symmetry = **1**

12

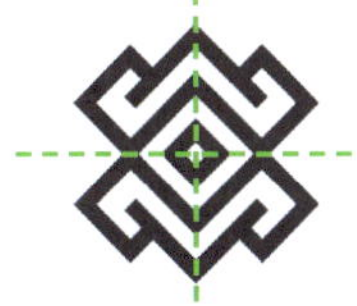

Order of line symmetry = **2**

Challenge 3 (p. 73)

1

Order of line symmetry = **4**

2

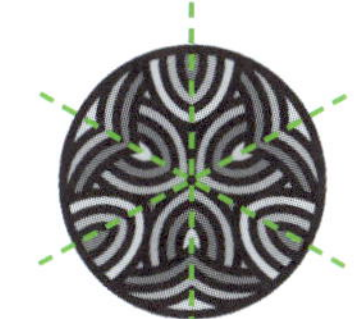

Order of line symmetry = **3**

3

Order of line symmetry = **5**

4

Order of line symmetry = **3**

5

Order of line symmetry = **3**

6

Order of line symmetry = **4**

Rotation (pp. 74–75)

1 Angle = 180° **2** Angle = 90°
3 Angle = 270° **4** Angle = 90°

Enlargement (pp. 76–77)

1 scale factor = 2 scale factor = 3
scale factor = 4
2 scale factor = 3 scale factor = 2
scale factor = 4
3 scale factor = 4 scale factor = 2
scale factor = 3

Mixing it up (pp. 78–79)

1 Reflected **2** Enlarged
3 Translated **4** Rotated
5 Enlarged **6** Reflected
7 Rotated **8** Translated
9 Rotated **10** Reflected

Challenge 4 (p. 80)

Check with your teacher if you have different answers.

1 M
Reflection

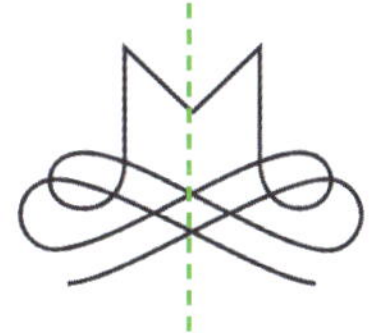

2 A
Reflection

3 K
Reflection

4 N
Translation

5 A, T
Reflection

6 M, A
Reflection

7 B
Reflection

8 K
No transformation

ISBN: 9780170451970

9 H, X
No transformation

10 CC
Reflection and translation

Revision 1 (pp. 81–83)

1 quadrilateral isosceles polygon

2 **a** Polygon **b** Trapezium
c Isosceles triangle

3 **a** ∠ADC or ∠CDA
b Acute

4 **a** $a = 30°$ **b** $b = 152°$
c $c = 40°$ **d** $d = 27°$

5 Vertices 6
Edges 12
Faces 6

6 **a**

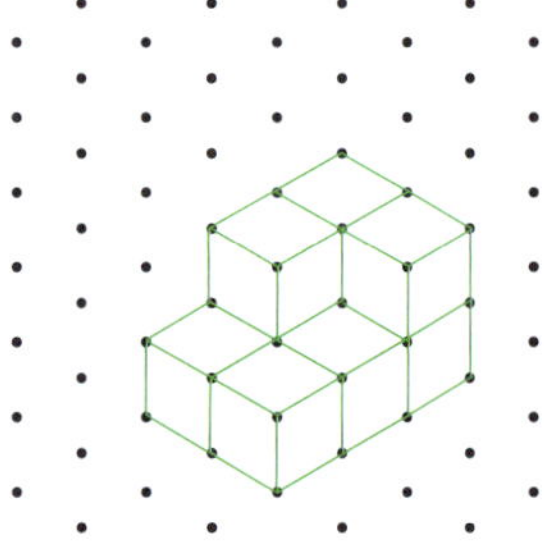

b

1	2	2
1	1	2

c

Top Left Front

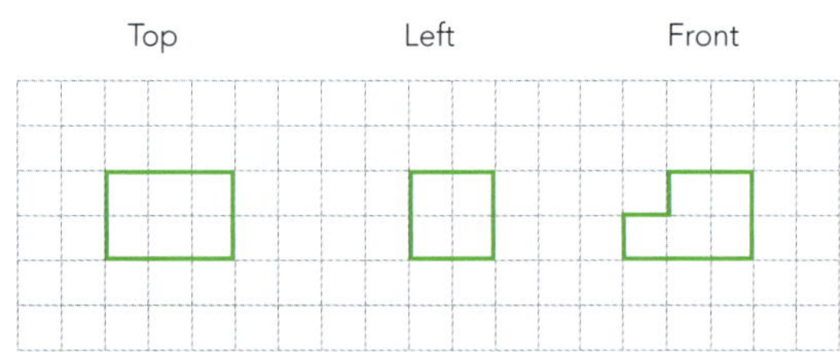

7 **a** Merry-go-round **b** R8
c SW **d** Bumper cars
e Balloons, Ferris wheel, stage.

8 **a** It moved to the right 8 squares and up 2 squares.
b Rotated 90°.

Revision 2 (pp. 84–86)

1 isosceles polygon

2 **a** Arrowhead **b** Hexagon
c Scalene triangle

3 **a** ∠BCD or ∠DCB
b Obtuse

4 **a** $a = 42°$ **b** $b = 42°$
c $c = 38°$ **d** $d = 40°$

5 Vertices 8
Edges 12
Faces 6

6 **a**

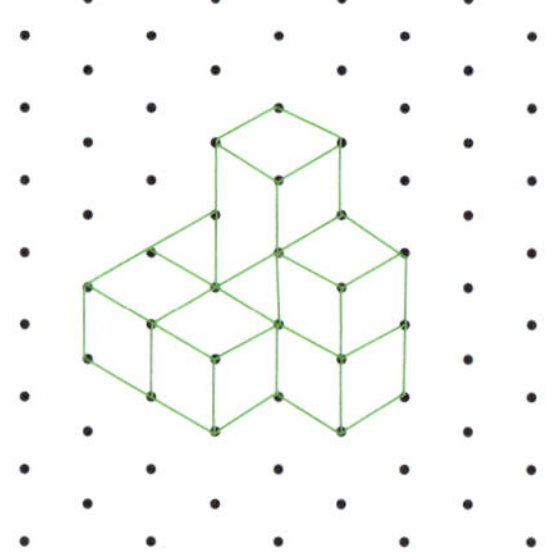

b

1	3	2
1	1	0

c

Top Left Front

7 **a** Bumper cars **b** O5
c NW **d** Ice creams
e Bumper cars, pendulum ride, rollercoaster, train, ice creams.

8 **a**

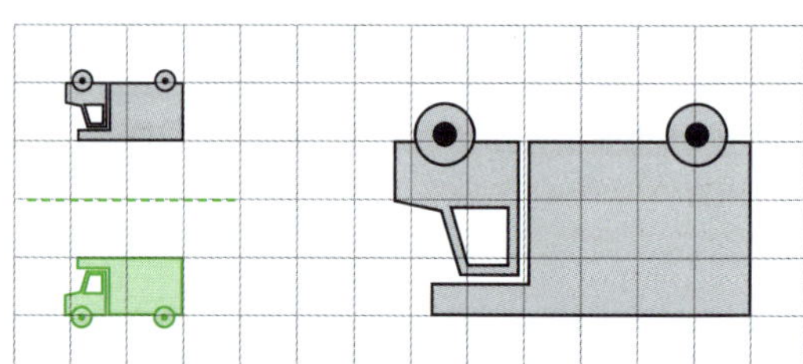

b Scale factor = 3

ISBN: 9780170451970